BELIEVING IN JESUS

BELIEVING IN
JESUS

A Popular Overview of the
Catholic Faith

sixth revised edition

LEONARD FOLEY, O.F.M.

Franciscan
MEDIA
Cincinnati, Ohio

Nihil Obstat: Hilarion Kistner, O.F.M.
Imprimi Potest: Jeff Scheeler, O.F.M. Provincial

RESCRIPT

In accord with the *Code of Canon Law,* I hereby grant my permission to publish *Believing in Jesus: A Popular Overview of the Catholic Faith: Sixth Revised Edition.*

Reverend Joseph R. Binzer
Vicar General
Archdiocese of Cincinnati
Cincinnati, Ohio
May 28, 2009

The permission to publish is a declaration that a book is considered to be free from doctrinal or moral error. It is not implied that those who have granted the permission to publish agree with the contents, opinions or statements expressed.

Unless otherwise indicated, Scripture texts used in this work are from *The New American Bible With Revised New Testament and Revised Psalms,* copyright ©1991, 1986, 1970 by the Confraternity of Christian Doctrine (CCD), Washington, D.C., and are used with permission. All rights reserved. No part of *The New American Bible* may be reproduced in any form without permission in writing from the copyright owner.

Cover and interior design by Mark Sullivan
Cover photo: istockphoto.com/LordRunar

LIBRARY OF CONGRESS CATALOGING-IN-PUBLICATION DATA
Foley, Leonard, 1913-
Believing in Jesus : a popular overview of the Catholic faith / Leonard Foley. — 6th ed. rev.
p. cm.
Includes bibliographical references and index.
ISBN 978-0-86716-939-3 (pbk. : alk. paper) 1. Jesus Christ—Person and offices. 2. Catholic Church—Doctrines. I. Title.
BT203.F65 2009
230'.2—dc22
2009019356

ISBN 978-0-86716-939-3

Copyright ©1981, 1985, 1994, 2000, 2005, 2009 by St. Anthony Messenger Press.
All rights reserved.

Published by Franciscan Media
28 W. Liberty St.
Cincinnati, Ohio 45202
www.FranciscanMedia.org

Printed in the United States of America

Printed on acid-free paper.

16 17 18 19 20 8 7 6 5 4

.| CONTENTS |.

. | FOREWORD TO THE SIXTH EDITION | .

FATHER LEONARD FOLEY'S *BELIEVING IN JESUS* HAS STOOD THE TEST OF TIME, being widely used in RCIA programs, in schools and by individuals wanting a comprehensive presentation of the Catholic faith. He was preparing its third edition when he died in 1994. To keep current with church documents and events, Pat McCloskey, O.F.M., (editor, *St. Anthony Messenger* magazine), Lisa Biedenbach (editorial director, books, St. Anthony Messenger Press) and Jeremy Harrington, O.F.M. (former publisher, St. Anthony Messenger Press) prepared the fourth edition in 2000. One major change was to place the Discussion/Reflection Starters within the text and to expand Appendix B (print, video and audio resources useful in conjunction with *Believing in Jesus*). Pat has prepared the fifth and sixth editions, mostly updating the recommended resources.

May all who read this book come to know, love and follow Jesus as deeply, intensely and generously as Leonard Foley did.

Daniel Kroger, O.F.M.
Publisher, St. Anthony Messenger Press

. | FOREWORD TO THE THIRD EDITION | .

FATHER LEONARD FOLEY, O.F.M., DIED EASTER SUNDAY MORNING, 1994, IN HIS sixty-second year as a Franciscan and his fifty-fourth as a priest. He was very conscious of his sharing in the suffering, death and resurrection of Jesus, the paschal mystery.

The previous October he had spent his eightieth birthday in the hospital recovering from surgery to remove a tumor from his spine. Before and after that hospitalization, one of his main projects was revising *Believing in Jesus*. He wanted it to be completely consistent with the new *Catechism of the Catholic Church*. He wanted to study the new *Catechism* personally and revise *Believing in Jesus* accordingly. When I brought him an early English translation of the *Catechism*, he was as excited as if I had given him a new car.

The passion of Leonard's life was telling people about God, Jesus, the church, God's love for them. He was distressed by the misshapen images some people had of God and their false ideas of what God expected of them. From years of preaching parish missions, hearing confessions and doing spiritual direction, he knew the faulty ideas, unfounded guilt, fears and scruples that tortured people. "Poor people!" was one of Leonard's frequent exclamations.

The driving desire of his life was to communicate the gospel to "ordinary people," "real people," like his Aunt Mamie. Especially after Vatican II, he frequently spoke at adult education programs and enjoyed the give and take with people. As editor of *St. Anthony Messenger* he gave new direction to the magazine. He was the founding editor of *Homily Helps* and *Weekday Homily Helps*. He wrote, edited or contributed to fifteen books for St. Anthony Messenger Press, and wrote many articles and homilies. The many *Catholic Updates* and *Youth Updates* he wrote sold literally millions of copies.

He wrote *Believing in Jesus* in 1981 and revised it in 1985, as he put it, to help "born Catholics" come to a "deeper understanding of the beliefs and practices they have held all their lives" and to help "those who approach the Catholic Church for the first time." He added, "I hope this book will help some scared and scarred people and challenge some others."

In 1993 we asked an expert involved in reviewing the various drafts of the new *Catechism,* and who had studied the final edition in French, to critique *Believing in Jesus* to see if anything should be changed. He found no inconsistencies; *Believing in Jesus* was true to the new *Catechism.* He noted that the order of presenting the material was different, but that the universal catechism does not dictate that local catechisms follow the same structure.

The new *Catechism* starts with the Creed, then treats the Sacraments, Commandments and Prayer. *Believing in Jesus* begins with the Bible Jesus knew, the Old Testament, and then moves to the Gospels and New Testament. As the chapter titles indicate, all the teaching is related to Jesus. Jesus tells us about the Father and the Spirit (the Trinity). The church and the sacraments continue the ministry of Jesus. By his example and word Jesus teaches us how to pray and how to live. He explains the Ten Commandments and his way of life. Jesus is our way to the future.

In his last months Leonard completed his study of the new *Catechism,* added material to *Believing in Jesus* and many cross-references to the *Catechism.* After Leonard's death Carol Luebering, who understands his mind and methods from editing his earlier works, took all of his notes and prepared this final version. In the Foreword to the earlier editions, Leonard wrote: "I must extend immense gratitude to Carol Luebering and Karen Hurley of St. Anthony Messenger Press, who patiently deciphered, organized, streamlined, sanitized and biblicized the hieroglyphics that came from my typewriter. May their eyesight be restored." I add my personal thanks to Carol for her work on this edition.

Leonard read extensively the best and deepest theologians and Scripture scholars. After Vatican II he did graduate study in theology at the University of Detroit. He knew *about* Jesus. But more, as a man of faith and prayer, he *knew* Jesus. In his last days he spoke of greater realization of his utter dependence on Jesus and his complete trust.

We catch a glimpse of Leonard's personal relationship with Jesus in an article he was working on a few weeks before his death. He speaks of Jesus emptying himself and coming to us with "no threats, no show of power." He has Jesus saying to the reader (and surely to himself): "You have your cross. It's with you every day. Let me help you carry it. And above all, believe that I'm leading you to where I am. All your life is a period of preparation and testing, purification and growth. Some day your cross will be set aside and I will lead you through the veil of death to happiness that even I cannot describe to you."

Leonard wants that happiness for each of his readers. In this revised book, he shares his knowledge and his faith with you.

Jeremy Harrington, O.F.M.
Publisher, St. Anthony Messenger Press
(1975–1981 and 1991–2007)

PART ONE

GETTING TO KNOW THE BIBLE

. | CHAPTER 1 | .

JESUS' BIBLE: THE OLD TESTAMENT

IF YOU CAN GET THROUGH THIS FIRST CHAPTER, THE REST OF THE BOOK MAY BE comparatively easygoing. If we are to understand as much as possible about Jesus, we have to be acquainted with his roots in Jewish history and with the only Bible he had—the "Old" Testament.

We may be tempted to say, "Why bother with all that ancient history? Is it really important for today—Moses and the Red Sea, Jonah and the whale, Adam and Eve and the snake? We have the Ten Commandments, and that's enough."

Well, suppose you wanted to understand the life of Abraham Lincoln. Could you ignore everything before 1809, the year he was born? Could you know what his aims and values and sorrows were without some knowledge of slave ships from Africa and the development of a "North" and a "South"? Shouldn't you also know about the precarious new world of thirteen colonies, the cold and fear of Valley Forge, the long debate over the Constitution?

In a somewhat parallel way, we cannot begin to know Jesus as he really is unless we have at least a glimmering of what was in his consciousness as he heard the story of his people read in the synagogue all his life, or took the scrolls into his own hands for study. He pondered the love of his Father, the glory of his people and their sin. He heard the fierce denunciations of the prophets and their consoling assurances that someone would come to free his people from misery. He must have seen himself, and his future, in each column of the unrolling parchment and accepted his vocation.

The life of the chosen people was a journey toward Jesus. We will try to enter into that life. In many respects, perhaps more than we realize, their story is our story even now. It is not really an "old" testament; it is the perennial story of humanity with and without God, and the story of the determination of that loving God to save us in spite of ourselves.

The Bible is not merely a record of events, but it is also an interpretation of those events. It is the sad-wise account of the ups and downs of the chosen people's relationship with God and of the meaning of God's acts in their history.

The chosen people gradually built up a collection of narratives, songs, prayers, meditations, prophetic utterances and "underground" writings—all centering around their God, Yahweh. Much of this tradition was transmitted by word of mouth from generation to generation. It was sung around campfires and commemorated in liturgical feasts like Passover. Finally, over a period of centuries beginning about the year 1000 B.C.E. (Before Common Era), this tradition was written down.

For a people not allowed to have carved images of God, the chosen people had a daring way of describing Yahweh. God has a face, eyes and ears and nostrils, a strong arm. He speaks and laughs, whistles and hisses; he is delighted and disgusted; he loves and hates with a passion; he regrets; he pities. He is alive.

Israel is his child, even his spouse. God holds his people like an infant to his cheek, while Israel vacillates between being a tender lover, a spoiled child and an adulteress. God gives and demands total surrender, but is faithful and endlessly forgiving.

The Bible cannot, therefore, be read as merely a list of dusty dates and long-ago battles. It must be experienced by someone who has outgrown the childhood fallacy that the world started when he or she was born, and who now puts an adult meaning to the question, "Where do I come from?" This question found a thrilling answer in the consciousness of Jesus, and we can all share his experience by making the story of the Bible our own story.

In this chapter we try to combine a basic consideration of the main events of Israel's history in chronological order with the books in which these events (and their meaning) are recorded.

The contents page of your Bible will reveal that there are three kinds of books in the Old Testament: historical books tracing God's relationship with a people; prophetic books recording the prophets' warnings in the face of the people's sin, as well as their consoling assurances; and the wisdom books, prayerful meditations on human life.

Many kinds of writing—literary genres—fill these books: narrative, poetry, prophecy, fiction and a strange thing called apocalyptic (more about that later). In order to understand what the writers are trying to tell us, we will have to take that into account. We also must consider what's going on in their time and culture, and how they express themselves (see the *Catechism of the Catholic Church*, #110).

Why? Well, imagine trying to explain a "Big Mac attack" to an Israelite facing Assyrian spears or "Lions devour Patriots, 55–0" to a first-century Roman Christian.

HISTORICAL BOOKS

The first five books of the Bible are called the Pentateuch ("five books") or the Torah ("the Law"), which Tevye in *Fiddler on the Roof* longed to contemplate in retirement. The first of these, Genesis, deals with the origin of the human race and, more importantly, of the chosen people.

GENESIS. For our present purpose, let us summarize the first eleven chapters of Genesis as follows: God creates man and woman and gives them divine friendship along with a world in which to enjoy it. But Adam and Eve choose to be little gods themselves; they abandon God's friendship and their innocence and their honesty.

Made to be like God, humans decided to play at being God, thumbing their noses at the Creator and refusing to be who they are—creatures. The "tree of the knowledge of good and evil" symbolizes the limits of creaturehood (see *Catechism*, #311, 398).

Untruth and unlove seep through the world like poison, until people are so absorbed in their own selfishness that no one can understand or communicate with others. Everyone seems to speak his or her own "foreign" language. Humanity plunges from Paradise to Babel.

This is not merely an earthly setback or tragedy; it is the total collapse of life itself—physical and spiritual. "[T]he moment you eat from it [the forbidden tree] you are surely doomed to die" (Genesis 2:17b). Humankind embraced sin and begot death.

Abraham, Our Father in Faith. Now God intervenes in a special way. About nineteen hundred years before Christ, God chooses a man, Abraham, who lived in what is now Iraq, to be the father of a new people. Through this man and his household, God enters human history in a new way and begins a special self-revelation. Abraham is the seed of the Savior to come, as God begins to unveil, in Paul's words, "the mystery hidden from ages and from generations past" (Colossians 1:26a).

It may sound odd to us that God "intervenes" in our history by his special relationship with Abraham and his people, Israel. After all, God "has the whole world in his hands" and is "here" already, supporting every atom and spirit in existence. Nevertheless, it is true to say that God now begins to unfold an eternal plan that will be fulfilled by definite historical events beginning with Abraham and "ending" with Jesus.

God's purpose is to prepare (and at the same time save from sin) an "acceptable" people. God must free human beings without forcing them to love—which, ultimately God does by a free act of love in Jesus' death.

God's basic purpose is liberation. We are by inheritance and by choice enslaved to our own pride and passion. God must continually throw light on both real beauty and real ugliness, let us suffer the logic of sin (called punishment) and bring us, painfully, to what should be a commonsense decision—to choose to live.

Israel, symbol of humankind, has a monotonous history of being loved, of responding with sin, of being punished, of repenting, of being forgiven, of being unfaithful again, on and on. God has a refreshing history of being God: one who loves faithfully.

EXODUS. The Book of Exodus ("a way out") is the story of Israel's liberation from physical and spiritual slavery in Egypt—the model of our ultimate liberation in Jesus. We join his "exodus" through death to life.

God strikes the Egyptians but passes over the homes of the Israelites, who have put the blood of a lamb on the doorposts of their homes and partaken of a meal of its flesh. Now, under the leadership of Moses (foreshadowing Jesus), they go (perhaps as a straggling mass of refugees) through the water of the Red Sea to freedom.

The Exodus, together with the covenant that followed at Sinai, is the central event of Israel's history.

We cannot exaggerate the importance of these events for the Jews and, ultimately, for us. What the death and resurrection of Jesus is to us, the Exodus-covenant was to the chosen people. It foreshadows our own exodus, in Jesus, from slavery to freedom, from death to life, again in the blood of the Lamb. It foretells the family meal of the Eucharist and the "drowning" and "rising" in the water of baptism.

The Exodus is not a simple affair. The Israelites wander in the Sinai desert for forty years—sometimes faithful, sometimes grumbling. Yahweh gives them signs of divine presence and protection. As always, Yahweh was a hidden God who could be seen only by faith.

In the desert, Israel was alone with God. There was no place to run and hide. The desert is the symbol of death and of human loneliness. There we must each decide either to die or to survive in the only way possible: by total surrender to God.

The Ten Commandments. At the mountain of Sinai, God makes a covenant with the Israelites. Through Moses, God says,

> You have seen for yourselves how I treated the Egyptians and how I bore you up on eagle wings and brought you here to myself. Therefore, if you hearken to my voice and keep my covenant, you shall be my special possession, dearer to me than all other people.... You shall be to me a kingdom of priests, a holy nation.... (Exodus 19:4b–5a, 6a)

The people all answered together, "We will do everything that the Lord has told us" (Exodus 24:3b).

The Covenant. God gave his people the Ten Commandments not as a burden but as a way of keeping the Sinai Covenant. They were, when not unfaithful, happy to have this guide on how to be God's people. In the Book of Exodus, the list of the commandments is followed by several chapters of guidance and specific details on observing God's way.

The Blood. It is important to realize what blood meant to the Israelites: Blood was life. So, at the dramatic liturgy ratifying the covenant, Moses took the blood of an animal and poured half of it on the stone altar—

representing God—and threw the other half on the assembled people, saying the words Jesus would fulfill: "This is the blood of the covenant which the Lord has made with you" (Exodus 24:8b).

It is *one blood* on the altar and on the people. God and the people are united. The blood of the covenant is the symbol of the marriage of God and the chosen, of their union, their oneness. "I will be your God, and you will be my people" (Leviticus 26:12b).

Covenant Love. In the generations after Moses, the covenant remained a focus of Israel's life. Beneath all the customs and ceremonies that gradually developed and in spite of continuing unfaithfulness, the Israelites, like spoiled children, could always be sure of one thing: They might sin and wander, but God is faithful. They used a special word for this love: *hesed.* It is a love that cannot be worn down, the love of kinship that is simply faithful (see *Catechism,* #214).

This love goes beyond all expectation, all just dues. It pours itself out in generosity. Best of all, it is unstoppable, unquenchable. The more God's children sin, the more God pursues them with mercy. Yahweh is faithful to the spouse who is continually adulterous.

Passover. It is extremely important to understand three things Jesus did: He lived the covenant perfectly, he celebrated the Passover and he transformed the "old" covenant into a new and eternal one. His death and resurrection were his own passover-exodus, and they became the exodus for all humankind.

Why did Jesus celebrate the Passover? First, because he was an observant Jew. The Jews had always said, down the centuries, that God's covenant is remade with each new generation. With their usual children-of-the-house boldness, they said, "[N]ot with our fathers did he make this covenant, but with us, all of us who are alive here this day" (Deuteronomy 5:3b).

Every year at Passover each household procured a lamb, one year old and without blemish. They ate it with loins girt, sandals on their feet and staff in hand—like those who are in flight (see Exodus 12:11).

Our Passover is Jesus, in whose blood the new and eternal covenant is made. His blood is "upon us" and in us, symbolizing a true union between God and us. We eat his flesh as those who are in flight from slavery. We drink his blood, sealing the covenant.

The Law: Powerless to Save. The Torah—the Law—cannot save. As Saint Paul keeps on saying, it is merely our teacher (see Galatians 3:24). It is powerless, except to reveal all the obstacles of sin between us and God.

Our reverence for the Ten Commandments should never deceive us into thinking that we can save ourselves by observing them. Saint Paul spent most of his Christian life insisting on this. We have the Law, but we cannot observe it by ourselves. We are not self-righteous (though that is the word we use for people who think they are). God leads us, chosen people, through glory and misery, sin and faith, to a growing consciousness that we need God absolutely.

LEVITICUS. The third book of the Bible gets its name from Levi, head of the priestly tribe. The book gives many directives for sacrifice and ritual. The central theme is this: "Be holy, for I, the Lord, your God, am holy" (Leviticus 19:2b; see also 11:44; 20:26).

NUMBERS. The Book of Numbers (so called because it records two censuses of the Hebrew people) continues the story of the journey begun in Exodus. It describes the life of the Israelites for thirty-eight years in the desert, from their coming to Sinai to their arrival at the border of the promised land.

For their murmuring, God prolongs the people's stay in the desert while simultaneously deepening the covenant relationship and preparing them to be a missionary nation.

DEUTERONOMY. The name means "Second Law." It is not really a new Law, but a repeating and completing of the Law given on Mount Sinai. Moses, in a series of discourses (similar to those of Jesus in Matthew's Gospel), presents the theme of covenant renewal, of living religion. He exhorts and threatens his people, reminding them of the special claim the Lord has on them.

The events described in this book took place between the end of the desert journey and the crossing of the Jordan into the promised land under Joshua. The book was written after the Israelites had lived in the promised land for centuries and is presented as a kind of testament of Moses.

JOSHUA. This book shows God's faithfulness in giving the Israelites the inheritance of land he had promised. God acts through Joshua, and the chosen people cross the Jordan and begin the gradual capture of the promised land. At this point Israel renews the covenant with Yahweh.

The history of the conquest of Canaan is a foretelling of the spiritual conquest of the world under the leadership of Jesus (*Joshua* is an earlier form of the name *Jesus*). Under Jesus, the New Moses, there will be a new covenant, a new Mount Sinai, a new Passover, a new Passover Lamb, a new commandment.

The book of Joshua may be summed up by these words,

> In the future, when the children among you ask their fathers what these stones mean [twelve stones from the Jordan], you shall inform them, 'Israel crossed the Jordan here on dry ground.' For the Lord, your God, dried up the waters of the Jordan in front of you until you crossed over, just as the Lord, your God, had done at the Red Sea...; in order that all the peoples of the earth may learn that the hand of the Lord is mighty, and that you may fear the Lord, your God, forever. (Joshua 4:21b–23b, 24)

JUDGES. This book takes its name from the "judges," twelve military heroes sent by God to lead the people in the interval between the death of Joshua and the institution of the monarchy. The book shows that Israel's fortunes go up and down according to whether or not they obey God's Law. When they rebel, they are overcome by pagan nations; when they repent, God raises up new leaders to liberate them.

It is the same cycle again: from faithfulness to unfaithfulness, to punishment, to repentance, to forgiveness and deliverance.

Kingship—Under or Instead of God? Eventually Israel decides it wants earthly kings instead of being a theocracy, a people ruled directly by God. Three pairs of books (each one a single scroll) describe the period: 1 and 2 Samuel; 1 and 2 Kings; 1 and 2 Chronicles.

1 AND 2 SAMUEL. The books of Samuel span the history of a century (about 1100–1000 B.C.E.) and relate a series of episodes centering around the persons of Samuel, Saul and David. Central to our interest is the oracle of

Nathan (2 Samuel 7) which promises David an eternal dynasty. This is the basis for the development of the idea of an earthly Messiah.

1 AND 2 KINGS. The two books of Kings cover similar ground, but also extend to the most tragic happening in Israel's history: the exile in 587 B.C.E., about which more will follow in a moment.

A central figure of the Old Testament is King David, who foreshadows the King to come. He succeeds in forming the confederation of twelve tribes into a united kingdom and setting up a new capital, Jerusalem. God renews his eternal covenant with this king. (David sins, as movies have emphatically pointed out, but does penance with equal vigor.)

The kings were, as was to be expected, a poor substitute for the rule of God. Consequently, the prophets (about whom more will follow) spend a large part of their careers denouncing both moral and religious aberrations. A later biblical writer looks back over history and says sadly of the kings, "Except for David, Hezekiah and Josiah, / they all were wicked" (Sirach 49:4).

In 930 B.C.E. David's united kingdom is split into two: in the north, the ten tribes of Israel; in the south, Judah (whose people come to be called "Jews"), consisting of the two tribes of Judah and Benjamin—the tiny remnant that will eventually fulfill God's promises.

In 721 B.C.E. Assyrian invaders conquered the northern kingdom of Israel, deporting its citizens and recolonizing the land with foreigners. The descendants of these Israelite-pagan marriages were the Samaritans of Jesus' day. Thus the expression: "the lost tribes of Israel." It is important to note that the sacred writer says, "The king of Assyria then deported the Israelites.... This came about because they had not heeded the warning of the Lord, their God, but violated his covenant, not heeding and not fulfilling the commandments of Moses, the servant of the Lord" (2 Kings 18:11a, 12).

The terrors of exile also came to the southern kingdom (587 B.C.E.) under the armies of Babylon. Again the sacred writer sees the meaning:

Early and often did the Lord, the God of their fathers, send his messengers to them, for he had compassion on his people and his dwelling place. But they mocked the messengers of God, despised his warnings, and scoffed at his prophets, until the anger of the Lord against his people was so inflamed that there was no remedy. Then he brought up against them the king of the Chaldeans, who slew their young men in their own sanctuary building.... They burnt the house of God, tore down the walls of Jerusalem, set all its palaces afire.... Those who escaped the sword he carried captive to Babylon.... All this was to fulfill the word of the Lord.... (2 Chronicles 36:15–17a, 19a, 20a, 21a)

1 AND 2 CHRONICLES. The two books of Chronicles treat the same period as the two pairs of books just described, but from a different viewpoint. They cover the period from Samuel to the return from exile in 538 B.C.E.

Solomon is presented as an ideal king, second only to David. His great achievement is building the temple and promoting a magnificent liturgy of sacrifice, prayer and praise. The ideal of one people united in the worship of the true God in Jerusalem is achieved.

But at the end, in the return from the agony of exile (a second Exodus) the *remnant* knows the political greatness of Israel is past. They have had a national "holocaust." They will now be a people under God or they will be nothing. The past will show the way to the future: There will be emphasis on David's blessed line, on Jerusalem as the divinely established place of worship. But the way into the future is not easy. When the remnant returns they find the "people of the land"—descendants of those who had escaped being carried into exile—have mixed with foreigners and developed a new religion; hence, tension.

PROPHETIC BOOKS

The word prophet means "one who speaks for" ("in the place of" or "on behalf of"). Prophets communicate with God in prayer, visions, dreams and, by God's grace, understand the meaning of God's self-revelation and the horror of the sin that repudiates it. They stand up courageously against sin and injustice, whether in king or slave. They warn of God's punishment and, when it befalls, bring God's consolation. They demand faithfulness and promise deliverance.

They attack all violations of the covenant: sexual immorality, social injustice, human degradation. They are the conscience of Israel.

Moses may be considered a prophet, and also Elijah, the "troubler of Israel." Some prophets, like Nathan, are written about in the historical books. Other prophets, or their followers, recorded their own vision and message.

The eighteen prophetic books are the work of the so-called "classical," or writing, prophets. They cover a period from Amos's denunciation of the sins of Israel in the north around 750 B.C.E. to the hopeful book of Daniel, written in the second century before Christ.

AMOS. Let us spend a few moments with Amos, a shepherd from the southern kingdom who was sent north sometime between 780 and 740 B.C.E. The people of Israel are not even aware how deeply their conduct offends a holy God, who must therefore say,

> I hate, I spurn your feasts,
>   I take no pleasure in your solemnities;
> ...
> Away with your noisy songs! (Amos 5:21, 23a)

Like the prophets after him, Amos speaks of the "remnant" that God will save—though it will be like a shepherd rescuing from the mouth of the lion "a pair of legs or the tip of an ear of his sheep" (Amos 3:12b).

He gives a new meaning to an expression that runs throughout the Bible: "the day of the Lord." To a suffering people, it meant the day God would judge the enemies of Israel and vindicate his people. But now Amos reminds the chosen people that it will also be a day of gloom for them—not just their enemies. For those who are sinners, unfaithful, it will be a day of judgment when God destroys their pride.

HOSEA. Like Amos, Hosea thunders in the north, and at about the same time (during the later years of the reign of Jeroboam II—786–746 B.C.E.). Yet he is one of the most touching examples of God's mercy. His own marriage to the prostitute Gomer becomes a symbol of God's marriage relationship with Israel. After three children, Gomer reverts to being a prostitute. But Hosea seeks her out and takes her back—as no Jewish husband could or would do—as an example of the way God pursues and welcomes back an unfaithful people.

ISAIAH. The writings of several prophets appear in the one book we now call Isaiah. Only the first segment (Isaiah 1—39)—and not all of that—is the work of the actual person Isaiah, who prophesied between the years 742 and 687 B.C.E. Isaiah 40—55, sometimes called Second Isaiah, is generally attributed to an anonymous poet at the end of the Babylonian exile (around 538 B.C.E.). Isaiah 56—66 was written at a still later period by followers of the prophet.

Excerpts from the book of Isaiah are read fifty-seven times in the three-year cycle of Sunday readings—an indication of the importance these prophets still hold for us. They are used extensively in Advent and Lent.

First Isaiah. Isaiah is the greatest of the prophets. He lives at a crucial time in salvation history, his career covering the years 742–687 B.C.E. After the north is destroyed, Judah in the south has its turn on center stage. It is to Judah that Isaiah preaches.

His great vision is of the holiness of God—and the horror of human sinfulness in contrast. The frightful abyss between God's holiness and human sin overwhelms Isaiah. He denounces both north and south for seeking security in military alliances; he summons Judah to faith in God as its only hope.

But again, in the tradition of Amos, Isaiah foresees that only a remnant will be saved to see the desert bloom and God's splendor:

> Here is your God,
>   he comes with vindication;
> With divine recompense
>   he comes to save you. (Isaiah 35:4b)

Second Isaiah. Isaiah 40—55 is called "The Book of Consolation" and was written toward the end of the Babylonian exile. The anonymous author sees that the chosen people will be liberated; the captives will return. The prophet rebuilds their shattered morale and paints a vision of a glorious future:

> It is I, I, who wipe out,
>   for my own sake, your offenses;
> your sins I remember no more. (Isaiah 43:25)

Can a mother forget her infant,
  be without tenderness for the child of her womb?
Even should she forget,
  I will never forget you. (Isaiah 49:15)

Very prominent in Second Isaiah is the promise to the remnant. There will be a small number of humble and faithful people who will be God's new Israel, with whom God will make a new covenant. They are purified by the sorrows of exile. They are the "poor" and the "poor in spirit" whom Jesus praised. From our perspective we can see Mary, the flower of Israel's faith, standing at their head.

The four "Songs of the Suffering Servant" are an important feature of Second Isaiah (42:1–4; 49:1–7; 50:4–11; 52:13—53:12). The Servant is, first, the motley remnant of the poor who listen faithfully to the prophet's words; and, second, he is also an individual figure who will save the people from their sins. Isaiah 53 reads like a description of the passion of Jesus.

Still, when the return from exile is complete, the ideal Israel is not fully restored, God must still create a new heaven and a new earth. Someone will come who will be the true Servant.

THE MESSIAH. Much of the teaching of Isaiah, as well as the other prophets, converges on the Messiah who is to come. The figure takes form slowly, very slowly, over the centuries.

The word *Messiah* means "anointed," that is, commissioned like a king, priest or prophet. The Messiah will fulfill Israel's destiny, save his people, protect them. He will lead his people to delight in the fear of the Lord. He will judge—that is, vindicate—the poor and "with the breath of his lips he shall slay the wicked" (Isaiah 11:4c).

Coming in the line of King David, he will create a holy nation, which will be "a royal priesthood, a holy nation" (see Exodus 19:6; also 1 Peter 2:9). The inner core of his work is to eliminate sin and restore humankind to intimacy with God. Isaiah sees his work as centered in the temple. All nations will come there, as to the center of the earth. He heartens his fellow Jews with a vision:

The people who walked in darkness
  have seen a great light. (Isaiah 9:1a)
For a child is born to us
  ...
His dominion is vast
  and forever peaceful. (Isaiah 9:5a, 6)

JEREMIAH. Jeremiah was called to be God's prophet about 627 B.C.E. For forty years—through the reigns of Judah's last five kings—he warned of coming disaster and begged king and people to turn back to God. He was ignored, abused, arrested and publicly disgraced. In 587 B.C.E. the Babylonian army destroyed Jerusalem and took the most influential people into exile. Many people fled to nearby countries. Jeremiah stayed behind with the remnant in Judah, but later was forced into exile in Egypt and according to one tradition was murdered there.

Speaking for the Lord, Jeremiah says,

Two evils have my people done:
  they have forsaken me, the source of living waters;
They have dug for themselves cisterns,
  broken cisterns, that hold no water. (Jeremiah 2:13)

But Jeremiah has words of hope of the eventual victory of God: "The days are coming, says the LORD, when I will make a new covenant with the house of Israel and the house of Judah.... I will place my law within them, and write it upon their hearts; I will be their God, and they shall be my people" (Jeremiah 31:31, 33b).

Jeremiah's influence was greater after his death than before. The exiles read and meditated on his lessons, and his influence can be seen in Ezekiel and Second Isaiah.

EZEKIEL. Ezekiel becomes a prophet while he suffers among the deportees in Babylon (c. 587 B.C.E.). He is often called the "prophet of the exile." He helps the exiles accept the destruction of Jerusalem, pointing out, like his fellow prophets, that the people's past and present sins are wreaking their necessary fulfillment. Perhaps the saddest words in the Bible are those of Ezekiel 10:18: "Then the glory of the Lord left the threshold of the temple...."

But, finally, Ezekiel offers a sure hope. He begins to announce God's promise of a new covenant and describes a new and ideal Israel rising from the graveyard of Babylon (the dry bones come together in Ezekiel 37). But salvation will be the work of God, not man. God will create a new heart and a new spirit in the people (see Ezekiel 36:26). The temple will be purified, and God will be present among the people (see Ezekiel 43:1–7).

After the Exile Until the Time of Christ. Just as the people had been liberated from Egypt in the Exodus, so eventually the small remnant is delivered from captivity in Babylon in 538 B.C.E. They are a chastened people. They discover the Torah anew and become more convinced than ever that they are God's chosen ones.

The exile has made them a people with an unshakable faith in the one God. They no longer have earthly kings, only God, whose representative is the high priest.

The Jews are never again a nation of power. But after the exile they are benevolently treated by Cyrus the Persian. A very modest new temple is built by 515 B.C.E.

The Persians retain control until the time of Alexander the Great. With him begins a "Greek period" whose influence continues into New Testament times, even though the land was under the Ptolemies of Egypt in the third century B.C.E. and the Seleucids of Syria until the time of the Maccabees one hundred years later.

JONAH. This much debated book was written some time between 400 and 200 B.C.E. It is not historical narrative, but didactic fiction, a story designed to teach a lesson. The lesson is this: God loves all people, not just the Jews. When Jonah is sent to prophesy to the pagan Ninevites, they turn to God; but the chosen people sometimes refuse. It is a parable of mercy aimed against narrowness and self-righteousness.

EZRA AND NEHEMIAH. The transformation of the Jewish people after the exile is important for our understanding of Jesus. This is the period of the Restoration. The two men most responsible for this reorganization of Jewish life are Ezra and Nehemiah. (The books attributed to these men fall into the category of historical books, but are treated here for the sake of chronology.)

Ezra provides spiritual unity. Without his firmness, Judaism has no chance of resisting absorption by Greek culture. He sets the tone for a postexilic community characterized by fidelity to the Torah.

Nehemiah, like Ezra, helps Judaism maintain its identity during difficult days in the postexilic restoration.

DANIEL. This book represents a special kind of biblical writing called "apocalyptic." It looks to a direct intervention of God as the only way the world will be transformed. The writing abounds in symbols, often difficult to understand—parts of the body, animals, colors, numbers. Apocalyptic writers foresee a cataclysm: The heavens will open and the future will crash into the present.

In the New Testament the book of Revelation (the Apocalypse) is written in this style. Jesus uses this form in his description of the Day of the Lord (see Mark 13).

The book of Daniel was born during the persecution of the Jews in the second century before Jesus. It firmly asserts that God is the Lord of history. Deliverance and glory are coming; God's people should stay strong amid temptation and suffering.

In the seventh chapter the author speaks of

One like a son of man coming,
   on the clouds of heaven;
...
His dominion is an everlasting dominion
   that shall not be taken away,
his kingship shall not be destroyed. (Daniel 7:13a, 14b)

1 AND 2 MACCABEES. Again, for the sake of chronology, we insert a book classified as part of the historical writings.

Judas Maccabee (and later his brothers) led a Jewish revolt against the Seleucid kings, who were persecuting the Jews. It was a courageous reaction to the attempt to suppress Judaism in Palestine in the second century before Christ. For a time the Jews again have religious and political independence. Again it is hoped that the salvation of the Jews will involve the creation of a Jewish state with political autonomy from foreign conquerors.

The Roman power enters Palestine in 63 B.C.E. Herod the Great, a Jew favored by the Romans, is declared "King of Judea," reigning from 37 to 4 B.C.E. Herod's son Herod Antipas rules Galilee until 39 C.E., but Roman governors, called procurators, hold the real power.

One of them is named Pontius Pilate.

WISDOM BOOKS

A third type of literature in the Old Testament is the wisdom books. These are meditations on human experience and the problems of life: good and evil, death and life, happiness and suffering. They are concerned with moral information—that is, how to live in God's presence. There are seven of them, comprising about one-fourth of the Old Testament.

PSALMS. The psalms are the prayers of Israel and continue to be the prayers of the Catholic Church today. They are a collection of 150 religious poems, about half of them attributed to King David. Some were undoubtedly written during the exile or even later, until about 300 B.C.E.

These are the prayers Jesus said with all his family and friends. They are an intimate part of the church's prayer today and should receive our special attention.

PROVERBS. This is an anthology of didactic poetry aimed at helping the young and inexperienced along the road to wisdom; consideration is also given those who desire advanced training. Solomon is the author of at least part of the collection.

JOB. The book of Job, written between the seventh and fifth centuries B.C.E., is a drama in poetic form that treats the problem of the suffering of the innocent.

Why do the good suffer? There is no answer, if one wants to know why God did not create a world free of suffering. God wants instead humble and trustful acceptance of divine providence and deep faith in God's steadfast covenant love.

THE SONG OF SONGS. Written after the exile, this is a portrayal of ideal love between man and woman. This love is a symbol of the love between the Lord and the chosen people.

ECCLESIASTES. The author, writing about 300 B.C.E., considers such human ambitions and aspirations as the pursuit of wealth, pleasure, luxury, knowledge, wisdom, bravery. Are they good or bad? He concludes: "[V]anity of vanities! All things are vanity!" (Ecclesiastes 1:2b). The meaning: These values are not deserving of a wise person's full time and energy because the human spirit cannot be fulfilled by any earthly values—human, social or material.

SIRACH. This catechism of good conduct, cast in the traditional categories of sin and virtue, was written about 200–175 B.C.E. How can one be wise for God? The author treats humility, giving alms, filial piety, sincerity, friendship, pride and presumption, prudence and temperance.

WISDOM. This exhortation, addressed to Jews scattered in lands far away from Palestine, urges them to be faithful and warns them not to be taken in by the pagan immorality of their surroundings. It is the Old Testament book written last (about 100 B.C.E.).

SUMMING UP

Over a period of two thousand years, God forms a people. God chooses a missionary group, liberates them from slavery in the great Exodus from Egypt and makes a covenant with them at Sinai. They waver between faithfulness and sin, between majestic worship in the temple and adulterous running after idols.

They go through the cycle of friendship, rebellion, punishment and reconciliation over and over again—a paradigm of the life of the church. They—or at least a faithful remnant—are purified in the fires of oppression and exile. Reduced to human helplessness, they long for the Messianic Age. Some look for a new time of prosperity, others for the great king who will rival the glory and power of David and lead them to freedom, reestablishing the kingdom.

Among the poor of God who wait is a girl of Nazareth, the virgin womb of Israel, prepared for by prophet, priest and king. She, the flower of the "poor of Yahweh," the remnant, sums up all her people's longings and the love of those who have kept faith. She learns of the Passover lamb, the covenant, the promise.

And we can imagine her praying these words of Isaiah, not knowing the full depth of the words which had come down to her:

> I rejoice heartily in the LORD,
>   in my God is the joy of my soul;
> For he has clothed me with a robe of salvation,
>   and wrapped me in a mantle of justice,
> Like a bridegroom adorned with a diadem,
>   like a bride bedecked with her jewels.
> As the earth brings forth its plants,
>   and a garden makes its growth spring up,
> So will the Lord GOD make justice and praise
>   spring up before all the nations. (Isaiah 61:10–11)

REFLECTION/DISCUSSION STARTERS

1) What does it mean to say the Bible is not simply a record of events but also an interpretation of these events?
2) Reflect on the ways the God of the chosen people is described by Old Testament writers. How is this God similar to or different from the God of your experience?
3) The Exodus—Israel's liberation from physical and spiritual slavery in Egypt—is a model for our ultimate liberation in Jesus. Discuss how the Passover-Exodus parallels and foreshadows the death-resurrection of Jesus.
4) What is the covenant relationship God makes with the Israelites? Discuss the love God offers in this relationship and the response of the people. Do you see your own relationship to God as one of covenant?
5) What, in general, was the role of the prophets for the chosen people? Does any one prophet speak particularly to you? Why?
6) What are the concerns of the wisdom books? Are your prayers as candid as those found in the book of Psalms?
7) Discuss the recurring theme of oppression and exile in the life of the chosen people. Have you ever felt oppressed or in exile in your own life? What freed you?

SCRIPTURE READINGS

In covering the entire Old Testament, this chapter can provide only a brief view of its contents. You may wish to examine more closely some of the books discussed. Four short passages that are significant as both a reference to a faithful remnant of the people and a foreshadowing of a savior are the "Songs of the Suffering Servant": Isaiah 42:1–4; 49:1–7; 50:4–11; 52:13—53:12.

SUPPLEMENTARY MATERIAL*

Catholic Updates: "The Bible and Prayer: Themes from the Synod" by Michael Guinan, O.F.M.; "Choosing and Using a Bible: What Catholics Should Know," by Ronald Witherup, S.S.; "A Popular Guide to Reading the Bible," by Macrina Scott, O.S.F.; "How to Understand the Bible: Examining the Tools of Today's Scripture Scholars," by Norman Langenbrunner; "The Whole Bible at a Glance: Its 'Golden Thread' of Meaning" and "Finding Your Way Through the Old Testament," both by Virginia Smith.

Scripture From Scratch: "The Bible From Square One," written by Elizabeth McNamer; "Interpreting the Bible: The Right and the Responsibility," by Sandra Schneiders, I.H.M.; "The Use and Abuse of the Bible," by Ronald D. Witherup, S.S; "Mapping the Biblical Journey" and "Exodus and Exile: Shaping God's People," both by Virginia Smith; "From Mount Sinai to the Sermon on the Mount: The Laws of Moses and Jesus," by Alfred McBride, O. PRAEM.; "From Spirit to Holy Spirit in the Old Testament," by Leonard Doohan; "The Dead Sea Scrolls," by Elizabeth McNamer.

CD: New Great Themes of Scripture, by Richard Rohr, O.F.M.

Books: The Great Themes of Scripture: Old Testament, by Richard Rohr, O.F.M., and Joseph Martos; *The Bible Made Easy: A Book-by-Book Introduction,* by Timothy Schehr; *When God Speaks: Reflections on the First Readings of the Sunday Lectionary,* by Daniel E. Pilarczyk.

---

* In the Supplementary Material sections throughout this book, *Updates* refers to issues of *Catholic Update*, published by St. Anthony Messenger Press. *Scripture From Scratch,* is a St. Anthony Messenger Press newsletter. Books, CDs and DVDs listed are available from St. Anthony Messenger Press. Study guides can be downloaded from http://catalog.AmericanCatholic.org/guide.

CHAPTER 2

JESUS IN INSPIRED HUMAN WORDS: THE NEW TESTAMENT

DROP A STONE INTO WATER, AND THE RIPPLES RUN IN CIRCLES TO THE EDGE OF the pond. Explode the resurrection of Jesus at the center of human history, and its power ripples to the very edges of time—past and future— and is merged in the mystery of eternity.

What began in the darkness of a Jewish "Monday morning" became a light and fire ignited first in the hearts and minds of a few men and women, and then in concentric circles of Christians down the centuries.

Twelve men, transformed by a vision, went out to proclaim boldly the simple, unbelievable fact: Jesus is *alive*! He has conquered the evil that strangles the world and has risen to a mysterious, new, vibrant life in accordance with what all the Jewish Scriptures had promised. All that Israel had believed and hoped for in its blessed/tragic history is now fulfilled—though still awaiting full completion when Jesus "comes again." He is not "somebody back there," but one present among us, in us and with us.

The apostles did not "preach"; they "proclaimed"—that is, gladly declared, as a fact, the Good News of Jesus (see *Catechism*, #571). They were heralds, hurrying into cities and towns to announce the fact that the slaves are freed. The Good News may be summarized like this:

The prophecies are fulfilled; the new age has dawned. The Messiah, of the House of David, has come. He is Jesus of Nazareth, who was baptized by John, did mighty works by the power of God, suffered and died for us, rose from the dead, was exalted at God's right hand, will come again in judgment. Repent and be baptized for the forgiveness of sin. (Summary by Patrick Fannon in *The Four Gospels;* see examples of the apostolic proclamation in Acts 2:22–24, 32–33; 3:12–26; 10:36–43.)

NEW TESTAMENT WRITINGS

The twenty-seven books of the New Testament include:

Four Gospels: Matthew, Mark, Luke, John
The Acts of the Apostles
Thirteen Letters of Saint Paul
Seven "Catholic" Letters of John, Peter, James, Jude
The Letter to the Hebrews
The book of Revelation, or Apocalypse

As in the Old Testament, we have here a "library" of diverse styles and purposes: the clear simplicity of the synoptics (Matthew, Mark and Luke); the mystical depth of John; the ardent personal witness of Paul; the excitement of a growing church in Acts; the practicality of apostles' advice given in letters; the quiet contemplation of Christ our Priest; the serenity of a people faithful in persecution.

THE GOSPELS. Like the books of the Old Testament, the New Testament writings are equally concerned with facts and faith. The Gospels are not cold, impartial history (supposing there is such a thing), but the announcement of salvation through Jesus. The writers make no bones about stressing the importance of Jesus. And they are more concerned about the meaning of his life than with a tape-recorded account.

They want to inform us, but they are more concerned to inspire us. They want to shout out their own faith and arouse it in us. It doesn't really matter to them whether "scientific" history, archaeology or whatever gives us evidence that Jesus actually had a home in Nazareth or was crucified on a hill outside the walls of Jerusalem or left the imprint of his body on a shroud. Faith does not ultimately rest on any "proofs."

We may compare the Gospels to a memoir. Suppose you and your brothers and sisters want a special remembrance of your mother. One of you has the gift of writing, and you tell that person to "put Mother on paper." This writer now combines events with meaning: blending, for instance, many glowing family dinners into one typical one, making up a song or poem that expresses your mother's endless cheerfulness with words gathered from a hundred or a thousand days; expressing the writer's own feelings through hers at the time of your father's death; making a scenario of their courtship through the letters left behind.

This would not be a dull list of things she did and said, but a record of her spirit, her soul, her meaning. And you would all say, "That's Mom."

So the New Testament writers let faith color all their narratives. Their concern is to show the working of God in history. They are not concerned with "proving" anything to outsiders; they are writing for the family.

The Gospel According to Mark (65–70 C.E.). The earliest Gospel was put together by John Mark. He is called "the interpreter of Peter" by one of the earliest church writers and is described in Acts as working with both Peter and Paul. We may presume that this Gospel gives at least the flavor of Peter's preaching.

Mark never lets us forget that Jesus is a suffering, crucified Savior, but one who proclaims both penance and Good News. In Mark, Jesus' "teaching" is the gradual unfolding—mostly in action—of the mystery of Jesus as embodying and revealing the kingdom. Sadly running through the Gospel is the strain of the disciples' obtuseness and lack of understanding.

The Gospel According to Matthew (70–85 C.E.). Matthew is thoroughly Jewish, exploring the Hebrew Scriptures for the messianic signs now fulfilled. Jesus is the new Moses, giving us a new covenant on a new Mount Sinai. He is the son of David the king, the Messiah the Jews could recognize. Jesus brings the Law to perfect fulfillment and is superior to it. He is Lord over it, but he does not annul it any more than adulthood annuls childhood. The Law can now be reduced to one commandment: love.

Matthew is a gold mine for quotations from Jesus, who is never so much the "Teacher" as here. Matthew records five "sermons" of Jesus: on the Mount (5:1—7:29), about his missionaries (9:35—11:1), the kingdom (13:1–52), the church (18:1–35) and the last things (24:1—25:46).

A central theme in Matthew is the kingdom, the rule of God in human hearts and minds. This kingdom comes in Jesus, whom Matthew shows to be the Messiah—not the king Messiah ruling over a Jewish world empire, but a humble suffering Messiah who offers the kingdom to those who will submit freely to the will of God.

The Gospel According to Luke (70–85 C.E.). Luke wrote a two-volume work, a Gospel and the Acts of the Apostles. Some identify him with Luke the physician, friend of Saint Paul. He was a Gentile—hence he always feels the need to explain Jewish customs to his readers. As a Gentile, he understandably stresses the universal nature of salvation. He shows Jesus as friend to sinners, outcasts, the suffering and, particularly, women, then in a despised social condition.

Luke has a sensitive and cultured mind. Some of the optimism and joy of the early church breaks through his writing. The church is beginning to realize that the "day of the Lord" is not necessarily imminent; the coming of the Holy Spirit, for whatever length of time, is the all-important "substitute."

The Jesus of Saint Luke is very human, sympathetic, merciful, but Luke is perhaps sterner than the others in presenting the demand to carry one's cross every day.

The rich variety of the Gospel can be seen in the various titles it has been given: "The Gospel of the Great Pardons," "The Gospel of Universal Salvation," "The Gospel of the Poor," "The Gospel of Absolute Renouncement" and "The Gospel of Prayer and the Holy Spirit."

Luke's Acts of the Apostles (80–85 C.E.). This book concentrates on the "acts" (that is, the work) of primarily two apostles, Peter and Paul, from the events of the Ascension and Pentecost to Paul's captivity in Rome (63 C.E.), when the gospel has been preached to the ends of the known world. Luke's purpose is to show how the Christian community grew under the guidance and control of the Holy Spirit. In the pages of Acts, Christians start to separate from Judaism, welcome Gentiles and spread the Good News to the world.

The Gospel According to John (90–100 C.E.). We immediately recognize this as a different kind of Gospel. It is written "from scratch," as it were, rather than being a combination of polished beads on a string, as the other Gospels are.

John has the deepest theology as well as the longest and most dramatic accounts. His is the most symbolic of the Gospels, moving through the familiar, mysterious world of water, wine, blood, bread, life and light. His emphasis is on the "already now" rather than the "not yet" in the history of Jesus' saving work.

More forcefully than in the other Gospels, the mature faith of the church in the divine Jesus shines through. In John, Jesus speaks with the majesty and assurance of one already raised to the right hand of the Father, from the beginning of his public life. The world does not pursue and crush him; he is in command. The world is on trial, not he.

"More symbolism is found in John than in the other Gospels," points out Raymond Brown in *The Jerome Biblical Commentary*. "More attention is called to the spiritual significance of apparently routine happenings and to the fuller meaning of words and events. The 'beloved disciple,' the man born blind, Lazarus represent at times not only historical personages but all Christians.

"Mary, the Mother of Jesus, is the church itself. Such symbolism is extended to other events and persons and makes it necessary for us to read John with close attention lest his full meaning escape us."

THE LETTERS OF SAINT PAUL (50–64 C.E.). We will be devoting a later chapter to a short course on Saint Paul (chapter nine). Suffice it to say here that thirteen letters are attributed to him (though he may not personally have written the Pastorals—1 and 2 Timothy, Titus—or even Ephesians and Colossians). The letters are written over a period extending from about the year 50 (at least twenty years after the Resurrection) to the year of his death in 64 C.E. These are the earliest writings of the New Testament, predating all the Gospels.

Paul usually wrote to deal with a particular problem or occasion in one of the churches, but his fiery spirit always rises above that situation to shout the Good News of Jesus. Jesus is central, the beginning and the end. There is no salvation in human effort; the initiative is God's. The Jews are privileged, but they are not the whole of God's people; God's love in Jesus is seen eagerly reaching out for every human being on earth, Jew and Gentile alike.

THE SEVEN "CATHOLIC" LETTERS. These letters are so-called because their authors (James, Peter, John and Jude) address the universal church rather than believers in a particular city.

James, a salty, practical man, writes in the spirit of Old Testament wisdom literature. This letter is famous for having been rejected by Luther ("a straw epistle") because of its insistence on the need for good works.

The two Letters of Peter are addressed to Gentile Christians, the new People of God. Some scholars think that First Peter is taken substantially from an early Christian baptismal liturgy because of the many references to that sacrament.

The most important of the three Letters of John is the first, written to certain Christian communities where some members were advocating false doctrines. As in his Gospel, John's emphasis is on the great commandment of love.

THE LETTER TO THE HEBREWS (80–90 C.E.). This letter, of a high literary style, is often attributed to Saint Paul, but it was not written by him. It is notable for its treatment of the priesthood of Jesus. He is the great high priest who expiated our sin in loving faithfulness to his Father. His is an everlasting priesthood which fulfills the promise of the Old Testament and its sacrifices. We have a high priest with God, one who understands our life, praying for us.

THE BOOK OF REVELATION OR THE APOCALYPSE (81–96 C.E.). This most difficult of the New Testament books was written in a time of crisis to assure Christians that Jesus is always with his people. It is "resistance" literature, sustaining those who suffer persecution. It stresses the fact that, although ultimate salvation and victory will take place only when Jesus appears in glory, the victory has already been won. It is a prophetic book, reminding the church that she is being purified in suffering for her wedding with "the Lamb that has been slain" (see Revelation 5:6).

The difficulty arises from the literary style, called "apocalyptic" (see chapter one). One must realize the symbolic meaning of numbers, animals, colors, clothing and such. Without the help of biblical scholars, the reader may be led into fanciful conclusions.

THE FORMATION OF THE NEW TESTAMENT

The New Testament grew over a period of time. The original basic proclamation was enlarged to include first a detailed account of the passion and death of Jesus, then a gathering of many little units of narrative and teaching. These had been passed around orally and become well-worn and polished over the years by constant repetition. Unimportant details fell away and the result was a collection of "beads" which the writers could then "string" as they chose.

In 1964 the Pontifical Biblical Commission approved the conclusion of scholars concerning three stages of tradition by which the life and teaching of Jesus have come down to us in the Gospels.

1) First, there is what Jesus actually did and taught. In his words Jesus followed the ways of reasoning and explaining that were in vogue at the time.

2) As the apostles proclaimed the death and resurrection of Jesus and the whole meaning of his coming, they took into consideration the circumstances of their listeners. As the church prayed about and lived the Christ-life, its understanding deepened. The apostles "interpreted his [Jesus'] words and deeds according to the needs of their listeners. They used catechesis, stories, testimonies, hymns, doxologies, prayers and other literary forms" (Biblical Commission, 1964).

3) When the actual Gospel writers took up their task, each one used "a method suited to the peculiar purpose which each author set for himself. They selected the things which were suited to the situation of the faithful and adapted their narrative to that same situation." They explained the words and deeds of our Savior now in one context and now in another, depending on their usefulness to the readers.

Pope Pius XII wrote in 1943 that the interpreter of Scripture must examine the particular literary genre (style, form) used by the writer to see how this contributes to a true and genuine interpretation.

The book of Revelation, for example, is a literary form quite different from the straightforward narrative of Mark. Paul's Letter to the Romans is really addressed to the whole church in Rome, whereas the Letter to Philemon is very personal. Matthew's is a "teaching" Gospel; John's, written after the other three, shows a greatly advanced stage of theological reflection in the church.

Different but equally authentic interpretations of the parables are offered. In Mark, for instance, a time of persecution is in the background of the parable of the seed: "[T]ribulation or persecution comes because of the word" (Mark 4:17). Luke applies the parable to the trials of everyday life: "[T]hey believe only for a time but fall away in time of trial"

(Luke 8:13b).

Content and emphasis are determined by purpose. As the church's faith fastened on Jesus, there were two choices. One was to concentrate on the earthly life of Jesus, his words and actions up to his ascension. This is the way of the Synoptic Gospels.

The other way was to concentrate on the risen Jesus, established in power and glory, lifted to the right hand of the Father and present with and in his friends on earth. This is the emphasis of Saint Paul and, in a way, Saint John.

KEY CONCEPTS FOR UNDERSTANDING THE BIBLE

We conclude with a brief discussion of three key terms that recur in connection with the writing and reading of the Bible.

INSPIRATION. The Bible is a unique book. It is, literally, God's Word in human words. To say that the Bible is inspired is to say that God had more to do with this book than with any other writing in history, even the most lofty flights of mysticism or the most ardent outpourings of the saints. Somehow, God is behind this book. God chose the authors; their writing fulfilled God's intention (see *Catechism*, #106).

This does not mean that God "dictated" words or thoughts to the minds of the writers. They remain themselves—with their own literary style, their particular purpose, their opinions, their temperament and background—and it all comes through.

What does it mean to say, then, that God is the "principal author"? It means, first, that God comes to people through many avenues of revelation: through the events of God's relationship with them from Abraham through the life, death and resurrection of Jesus through all the experiences of the church. The people of God are aware of the divine presence, but they can't put all the facts and ideas and feelings into words very well. Among them and of them is the poet/prophet, one of those who in any culture speaks what the heart knows. This speaker-for-God comes to a more explicit understanding of the meaning of all God is doing and saying, especially in Jesus. Under the guidance of the Spirit and the whole believing community, this prophet finally gets the truth into words.

The words have such power that the meaning keeps on unfolding for generation after generation. Gradually, such writings were recognized as wonderfully fitting expressions of what the faith was all about. Eventually they were "canonized" by the church as inspired. They are not inspired because the church says they are; they are called inspired because the church's faith recognizes in them its faith in Jesus.

There were many spiritually uplifting documents current in the early church, even other "Gospels." Why did the church not include them in the sacred list? In some of them the instinct of faith saw error or a false direction; others made no claim to being part of the original proclamation. It may be a surprise to some to know that the "canon," or official list of books of the Bible, was not explicitly defined by the church until the sixteenth century, though there was a clear listing as early as the fourth century.

REVELATION. As was said above, revelation is not concerned only with truth, but with God's personal self-giving. God gives a message, indeed, but more importantly gives the divine self to the people. We have a knowledge of God's acts and purposes, but we also have this very God given to us out of infinite love. The raw material of revelation is the everyday life of chosen people, beginning with the first human beings and developing in the children of Abraham. The biblical authors understood God's actions and helped us realize and accept not just a meaning but also a person.

Finally, God communicated perfectly in Jesus. He is the full revelation of God-truth, indeed, but also eternal life within us.

TRADITION. Catholic faith, however, is not just a biblical religion. It depends not just on ancient words but also on the living Word, Jesus, who continues to open our hearts to understanding. This ongoing communication we call Tradition (see *Catechism,* #78, 108).

In *Fiddler on the Roof,* Tevye's song should be written with a small *t* : tradition. Small-t traditions are customs that may be a century old, even more, but are transitory. There is a tradition of jostling jollity in Times Square on New Year's Eve, but this is hardly something essential to the spirit of the United States. But the celebration of the Fourth of July is something we will never cease doing. It is imbedded in our history.

In the church there are many traditions. To mention a noncontroversial few: It is small-t tradition to have pews in church, for bishops to wear special headgear called *miters*, to use white smoke to indicate that a pope has been elected or to make the Sign of the Cross.

It is big-*T* Tradition, on the other hand, that Jesus is truly God and man, that his passion, death and resurrection are made present to us in the Eucharist, that he gathered a visible people around him and appointed Peter and the other apostles to guide and sanctify them. Sacraments, prayer, mission—the list is long.

Tradition literally means "handing on"; it also refers to what is handed on. After the last of the apostles died, their successors—right down to today's pope and bishops—handed on the Good News of Jesus (see *Catechism*, #77).

Tradition is expressed in (and grows from) the church's creeds, the records of the church's liturgy, the writings of the great teachers, the decrees of popes and councils, the prayer and faith of the people.

In the polemics of the Reformation, now softening, Protestants rejected what they thought was an undue Catholic emphasis on Tradition and relied on Scripture alone. Catholics asserted all the more firmly that, although Tradition is under the judgment of the inspired word, it nevertheless existed before the New Testament, the words and acts of Jesus were not mechanically transmitted by tape recorder and movie camera. Tradition is the way the *essentials* of Christianity are lived by the church throughout the centuries.

Tradition develops in the sense that the church probes more deeply into the meaning of all that has been handed on. The Holy Spirit guides its growth and explanation. Each age must express the age-old Tradition of the church in the forms of its day. The essentials remain; the application and form may change.

The church is a living organism; in each generation it must respond to God through the language, culture, problems and opportunities of its own day. The *church remembers its experience and listens to the living word of Jesus in the Bible* and is thus led by the Spirit to show Christ to the world.

REFLECTION/DISCUSSION STARTERS

1) The New Testament writers were writing for believers and not simply to

offer historical facts. Discuss how this approach colored their writing.

2) What distinguishes each of the four Gospels? Examine their major themes and individual approaches.

3) The letters of Saint Paul and others were written out of different situations and for different purposes. What are some of the themes with which they deal?

4) Discuss the formation of the New Testament—how scholars believe it developed out of Jesus' life and teachings into the form we know today.

5) What does it mean to say the Bible is "inspired"?

6) Discuss how the interpretation of Scripture must be guided by considering the style, form and purpose used by the individual writers.

7) The author speaks of two kinds of tradition. What are they two types and what role does Tradition play in the beliefs of the church?

SCRIPTURE READINGS

It would be helpful to read at least one of the Gospels all the way through. In addition, you may wish to sample other books of the New Testament. Specific passages to examine include examples of the apostolic proclamation: Acts 2:22–24, 32–33; 3:12–26; 10:36–43.

SUPPLEMENTARY MATERIAL

Catholic Updates: "How the Gospels Were Written," by Leonard Foley, O.F.M.; "Jesus Christ: Why the Word Became Flesh," by Stephen Doyle, O.F.M.; "What Is 'The Kingdom of God'?" by Richard P. McBrien.

Scripture From Scratch: "Inspiration: God's Word in Human Hands," by George Martin; "Exploring the Synoptic Gospels: Mark and His Careful Readers," by Steve Mueller; "Acts of the Apostles: Luke's Dramatic Sequel," by Elizabeth McNamer; "From Jesus of Nazareth to Lord of All," by Eugene LaVerdiere, S.S.S.; "Who Do People Say That I Am? (Jesus in the Gospels)," by Arthur E. Zannoni; "Gnosticism and the Creation of the Canon," by Elizabeth McNamer; "The Challenge of Fundamentalism," by Eugene LaVerdiere, S.S.S.

Books: Bible Stories Revisited: Discover Your Story in the Gospel of Luke and Acts of the Apostles, by Macrina Scott, O.S.F.; *A Father Who Keeps His Promises: God's*

Covenant Love in Scripture, by Scott Hahn; *Finding Your Bible: A Catholic's Guide,* by Timothy Schehr; *Following Jesus: A Disciple's Guide to Luke and Acts,* revised and updated by William Kurz, S.J.; *Jesus: A Historical Portrait,* by Daniel Harrington, S.J.; *Journeys Into Matthew, Journeys Into Mark* and *Journeys Into Luke,* all by Raymond Apicella; *Journeys Into John,* by Carolyn Thomas, S.C.N.; *Meeting Jesus in the Gospels,* by George Martin. *Things Hidden: Scripture as Spirituality,* by Richard Rohr, O.F.M.

CD: *New Great Themes of Scripture* and *Sermon on the Mount,* both by Richard Rohr, O.F.M.

DVD: *Seeking Jesus in His Own Land: Scriptural Pilgrimages with Father Stephen Doyle, O.F.M.* (one disc); *Terra Sancta: A Pilgrim's Guide to the Holy Land* (one disc).

PART TWO

JESUS' JOURNEY TO DEATH AND LIFE

. | CHAPTER 3 | .

THE MISSIONARY JESUS:
"HE WENT ABOUT DOING GOOD"

IMAGINE JESUS, AFTER HIS LONG SLOW TRIP DOWN THE JORDAN VALLEY FROM Galilee, as he stands watching the prologue of his life's drama. A spiritual revival is taking place on the banks of the Jordan, just above the Dead Sea. Every day people are flocking to hear the rugged desert prophet, John the Baptist. He is announcing tremendous news: The Messiah is finally coming, and he will baptize his people with the fire of the Spirit. In preparation, John baptizes them in the waters of the Jordan as a sign of their repentance.

Jesus sees the new people of God being formed, and he loves them. He walks into the water to be one with them. John at first refuses to baptize him, apparently because of long acquaintance with his cousin's holiness. But Jesus insists. He is an observant Jew eager to share all the practices of good Jewish life.

As Jesus comes up out of the water, he sees the sky "rent in two" in fulfillment of Isaiah's prayer that God rend the heavens and come down (see Isaiah 63:19—64:3). Jesus sees the Spirit, in the form of a dove, come and rest on him. The dove, which referred to the Israel of old, is the sign of the new Israel, the new people of God coming up out of the water in a new Exodus as they once came through the Red Sea to freedom.

A voice from heaven thunders the fulfillment of the prophecy of Isaiah about the Suffering Servant to come: "You are my beloved Son; with you I am well pleased" (see Mark 1:9–11). God had said, in Isaiah:

Here is my servant whom I uphold,

   my chosen one with whom I am pleased,

Upon whom I have put my spirit;

   he shall bring forth justice to the nations. (Isaiah 42:1)

Then the Spirit *drives* (see Mark 1:12) Jesus into the hot and barren Judean desert. Alone with the wild beasts, he faces the devil. What kind of Messiah will he be? Why not a powerful one, Satan urges. Just a practical little beginning would do—like, say, turning stone into bread to still his hunger.

Not that? Well, Scripture says that the Messiah shall not even so much as stumble on a stone. What is to prevent a spectacular leap off the pinnacle of the temple? *That* would bring followers!

The final practical way to go, of course, is political. The devil offers Jesus the world, his kingdom, for a simple price: a Faust-like selling of his soul.

Unlike the old Israel that was often unfaithful in its forty-year sojourn in the desert, Jesus stands unmoved. He is totally given to his Father (see *Catechism*, #535–540).

THE GOOD NEWS. Now one career ends and another begins. John the Baptist is suddenly silenced in prison by a vengeful Herod and will soon be put to death. Jesus now steps into the public eye, knowing he faces the same dangers as John. Mark says, very simply, "Jesus came to Galilee proclaiming the gospel [good news] of God" (1:14b).

What was—and is—the Good News? It was that God was making the long promised "move." Now God would decisively defeat the powers of evil in the world and *definitely*, once and for all, establish the Kingdom.

This may sound very warlike and political. It took Jesus a long time to convince people (relatively few people) that victory would come through defeat and life through death, and that the Kingdom was not a place or even a people, but exclusively God's powerful saving and loving action— God's *reign*.

Jesus therefore says, in so many words, "This is it. The time God set is here. All promises will be fulfilled. God will rule! My Father will destroy evil and fill you with his life, his love and his power. Believe this Good News! Change your whole way of thinking and acting!" (see *Catechism*, #543).

Remember that Mark, like all the Gospel writers, is looking backward from the time after the Resurrection of Jesus. By then it had become obvious that *Jesus himself was the Good News.* He was God fulfilling an eternal plan. He was the Promise fulfilled, the Gift of God. He was God.

JESUS' TWO GREAT ACTIVITIES: HEALING AND PROCLAIMING THE GOOD NEWS. The simplest way to describe Jesus' life is to use Saint Peter's words: "He went about doing good works and healing all those oppressed by the devil..." (Acts 10:38b). There is danger that in trying to summarize Jesus' teaching, miracles and proved mastery over the devil (see *Catechism,* #548–549), we may end with another "butterfly on a pin," a list of events as dead as a newspaper index. But let us try.

The picture of Jesus in Mark's Gospel is that of a man *totally available,* totally generous, almost always in the middle of a pressing crowd. Almost the first thing told of him is that he went out into the street to help people in need. Mark spends little space on what Jesus said. He is concerned to show Jesus immediately curing a man possessed, healing Peter's mother-in-law and welcoming "...all who were ill or possessed by demons" (Mark 1:32b).

He is doing much more than being sorry for people. But Mark will never let us forget that he was sorry for them, pitied them, suffered with them. Jesus is moved at the sight of a leper and cures him (1:41). Then the fuller secret begins to appear when he heals both soul and body of a paralyzed man (2:1–12).

Then a new element (3:1–5): Dare he cure on the sabbath? No question. A good deed does not violate the sabbath.

He goes over into pagan territory and releases a wild man from the devil's power—a graphic short story (5:1–20); he comes back across the Sea of Galilee and raises a little girl back to life, adding the touching instruction that they take care to give her something to eat.

A trembling woman is cured just by touching his garment, and he gives her his peace. He looks around at the crowd following him and pities them, "for they were like sheep without a shepherd" (Mark 6:34b). Mark begins to be overwhelmed by his task, so he simply says, "Whatever villages or towns or countryside he entered, they laid the sick in the marketplaces and begged him that they might touch only the tassel of his cloak; and as many as touched it were healed" (6:56).

And always the great crowds—from Galilee in the north to Judea in the south.

Except for one chapter of parables, there is hardly a line of teaching in the first half of Mark's Gospel. That section ends with the climactic declaration of Peter that Jesus is the Messiah (Mark 8:29). The first explicit teaching, which immediately follows, is the doctrine of the cross (8:34–38).

This is not to say that the teaching of Jesus is unimportant, but to emphasize that Jesus put first things first: He first showed his love, unmistakably, in concrete actions, and then taught people its source: the infinite love of his Father.

His greatest act was to restore peace to hearts miserable in sin—the paralytic, Levi, Peter—but he was also concerned about empty stomachs and sightless eyes, leprous sores and crippled legs.

THE MEANING OF JESUS' "SIGNS." Jesus once reproached some people for "seeking signs and wonders." Yet he himself performed many "signs." He told those who wanted a razzle-dazzle Messiah that they would not believe even if someone were to rise from the dead. Yet he rose from the dead as the greatest "sign" of our hope.

Evidently, then, there are signs and there are signs. The danger seems to be that we expect *extraordinary* signs, miracles "coming through" from God, and we sometimes forget that love alone can see the real miracles.

Science has enriched our lives, no doubt. But it has taken away our childlike excitement at everyday wonders. We know the chemical composition of violets and how a sunset looks on radar. Jack Frost depends on isobars and sunspots, and we can write "music" with computers.

Not so boringly overinformed was the biblical person. If it rained, God sent the rain; thank God. If we lost the war, we were being punished. God told the sun, every morning, to get up and do it again.

So the "miracles" of the Bible are not much more marvelous to the Hebrew than sunrise over the desert or the birth of a deer. It would never have occurred to a contemporary of Jesus to worry about whether he should call a cure "natural" or "supernatural," or if the man possessed merely had epilepsy.

God's greatest "sign" is Jesus. Not just certain things Jesus did, but simply Jesus—whatever he did or said or was—then and now.

Jesus is, above all, *the* "sign" or "sacrament" of God. As Jesus himself said, "Whoever has seen me has seen the Father" (John 14:9b).

He is the Word made flesh. He is, in fact, God's last word. In Jesus God expressed and continues to express divinity as perfectly as possible in human form, word and action. So Jesus' "signs"—whether the extraordinary ones we call miracles or the "ordinary" ones like putting the infinite love of God into a simple "good morning"—are the openings through which human love sees God and receives divine life.

Many people saw Jesus' signs—raising a widow's son from the dead and asking a Samaritan woman for a drink of water—but the signs did not register. I don't know why. Maybe they were looking for entertainment. Maybe they wanted God to prove something. Maybe they wanted someone who could smash the Roman army.

But those who let God create a disposition to receive, to be healed, to be liberated—they read the signs.

They saw Jesus' Father assuring them of his love, and definitively breaking the power of evil, sin, suffering, death and the devil. They saw signs of love and signs of power. They accepted the reality behind the signs—God's own life and love—and they were saved.

JESUS' POWER OVER THE DEVIL AND ALL EVIL SPIRITS. In the Bible evil and good spirits are simply taken for granted. In the New Testament the devils form a kingdom opposed to the Kingdom of God and manifested in the enslavement of human beings. The church teaches that God created Satan and other devils to be good by nature, but that they chose evil by their own free will. The Bible sees these evil spirits as *personal.*

If we are to be moved to faith by Jesus' power over the devil, we had better ask whether we really believe there is such a thing. Some, after seeing "cute" devils on Halloween and being persuaded to buy lighter fluid by red-suited creatures with "devilishly" attractive mustaches, have relegated the devil to a sideshow in Disneyland. This temptation not to take the devil seriously is a phenomenon explored with deadly perception by C.S. Lewis in *The Screwtape Letters.*

Saint Paul reminds us that our warfare is against "principalities and powers" (see Ephesians 6:12). *The Good News Bible* translates this passage: "We are not fighting against human beings but against the wicked spiritual forces in the heavenly world, the rulers, authorities and cosmic powers of this dark age." These, according to the *Theological Dictionary,* have been "vanquished in the cross and resurrection of Jesus Christ, but their impotence has not yet been laid bare; they still saturate the atmosphere of 'this world,' so that it exposes Christians to temptation and leads to their persecution."

One of the clearest "signs" of the devil I have seen is the picture of grinning soldiers driving little sticks into Vietnamese children's eardrums. I believe it was the same group who shipped severed human ears back to their families.

Some references to "possession" in the Bible may refer to human illness such as epilepsy. This is probably the case, for instance, in Mark 9:14. But the New Testament writers often attribute disorders to the devil. This comes from seeing the devil, sin, death, suffering and all human ills as the miserable inheritance of sin. Jesus is God's final, definitive destruction of all evil, and those who let Jesus possess them will be liberated from all evil.

The synoptics place Jesus' head-on confrontation with the devil at the very beginning of his public life, immediately after his baptism. Mark almost immediately relates an incident which shows Jesus' power over the devils. In the synagogue at Capernaum "was a man with an unclean spirit; he cried out, 'What have you to do with us, Jesus of Nazareth? Have you come to destroy us? I know who you are—the Holy One of God!' Jesus rebuked him and said, 'Quiet! Come out of him!' The unclean spirit convulsed him and with a loud cry came out of him. All were amazed and asked one another, 'What is this? A new teaching with authority. He commands even the unclean spirits and they obey him'" (Mark 1:23–27). In Mark's "typical day's ministry" in Capernaum (1:21—3:5), Jesus' expelling demons is referred to twice in the first thirteen verses (see *Catechism,* #550).

In Luke's Gospel the seventy-two disciples Jesus sent to cure the sick and proclaim the Kingdom exclaimed upon their return, "Lord, even the demons are subject to us because of your name!" Jesus replied, "I have observed Satan fall like lightning from the sky" (10:17b, 18b).

When Mark's Jesus sends forth the Twelve into the whole world after the Resurrection, he says that one of the signs that will accompany *those who have professed their faith* is that "in my name they will drive out demons" (Mark 16:17b).

An essential part of Jesus' saving work in Matthew is the conquering of "the devil and his angels" for whom an everlasting fire is prepared (see Matthew 25:41). All who give Jesus their lives are safe. No evil can touch them, even though they die on crosses, as he did, or suffer the humiliation of hatred and misunderstanding.

But nothing is automatic. If a person's new cleanliness is merely external, if one does not let the power and love of God possess the soul as totally as any devil ever possessed the human heart, then the unclean spirit "goes and brings back with itself seven other spirits more evil than itself, and they move in and dwell there; and the last condition of that person is worse than the first" (Matthew 12:45).

It is the height of irony—and of the diabolical—that Jesus himself is accused of being in league with the devil. After Jesus frees a mute, some Pharisees say, "He drives out demons by the prince of demons" (Matthew 9:34b); and, later, "This man drives out demons only by the power of Beelzebul, the prince of demons" (Matthew 12:24b).

THE LAST ENEMY: DEATH. We will reflect, in the next chapter, on the central tragedy of humanity—physical and moral death—and how God liberated us from its enslavement. The Gospels relate three incidents of Jesus raising persons from the dead, but these events are not particularly emphasized by the synoptics. The conclusion of the story of Jesus' raising Jairus's daughter from the dead (Mark 5:21–24, 35–43) is delayed to insert an account of his healing of the woman with a hemorrhage (Mark 5:25–34). Only Luke has the touching story of Jesus raising the widow's son (7:11–17). Death, disease, devils, the forces of nature—all are equally subject to the liberating power within Jesus. To the loving heart, one sign is as good as another.

John's Gospel, however, places climactic emphasis on the raising of Lazarus. It is the last and the greatest of Jesus' special "signs." To quote *The Jerome Biblical Commentary*: "In the narration of this miracle John gives at one and the same time a supreme proof of the Lord's life-giving power and a visualization of the doctrine contained in the conversations of vv. 23–27."

That conversation goes like this:

Jesus said to her [Martha], "Your brother will rise." Martha said to him,

"I know he will rise, in the resurrection on the last day." Jesus told her, "I am the resurrection and the life; whoever believes in me, even if he dies, will live, and everyone who lives and believes in me will never die." (John 11:23–26a)

The miracle is "a sign, therefore, both of the final resurrection and of the rising from sin that takes place in the soul of the believer" (*The Jerome Biblical Commentary*).

All the "signs" of Jesus' life lead to the central event of his life and ours: his saving death and resurrection.

REFLECTION/DISCUSSION STARTERS

1) Mark writes that Jesus proclaimed "the good news of God." Discuss what the "Good News" might have meant for those hearing it at the time. What does the Good News mean to you today?

2) What is your concept of the devil? Discuss the ways the Gospels treat the devil or satanic forces.

3) Discuss some of the "signs" Jesus worked. What was the mind-set of the people toward "miracles"? Do you believe miracles take place today?

4) Reflect on the author's statement that Jesus' signs—both "extraordinary" and "ordinary"—"are the openings through which human love sees God and receives divine life." What signs in your life have become openings to God for you?

SCRIPTURE READINGS

Isaiah 63:19—64:3; the Gospel of Mark.

SUPPLEMENTARY MATERIAL

Scripture From Scratch: "Mark's Urgent Message," by Sean Freyne; "Exploring the Synoptic Gospels: Mark and His Careful Readers," by Steve Mueller.

Books: Jesus' Plan for a New World: The Sermon on the Mount, by Richard Rohr, O.F.M., with John Feister; *Jesus: A Historical Portrait,* by Daniel Harrington, S.J.; *John the Baptist: Prophet and Disciple,* by Alexander J. Burke, Jr.; *Journeys Into Mark,* by Raymond Apicella; *Things Hidden: Scripture as Spirituality,* by Richard Rohr, O.F.M.

. | CHAPTER 4 | .

JESUS' TEACHING STORIES: THE PARABLES

JESUS' WHOLE LIFE, EVERY WORD AND ACTION, WAS HIS TEACHING. BUT A SPECIAL part of his teaching was done in the form of parables. In these fictitious stories people could recognize situations of everyday life: housekeeping, fishing and farming; wedding celebrations, midnight visits and happy meals; crooked judges, beggars and playing children; planting seed, baking bread and making wine. Sometimes, no doubt, Jesus' story referred to a recent happening—a burglary, a discovery of treasure, a rich man's downfall.

The parable has something in common with all stories: We want to know how it comes out. But Jesus' parables often carry us along, conceding the truth of one step after another, until we find that we have been trapped by the truth. What we have so readily admitted forces us to a conclusion which surprises and challenges us.

The best example of this technique occurs in the "story" Nathan told King David after the latter had stolen Uriah's wife and then arranged to have him killed in battle. Once, Nathan said, there was a rich man and a poor man. The poor man had only one little ewe lamb, which grew up with him and his children, sharing his food, sleeping in his bosom. The rich man had huge flocks. Now the rich man, to entertain a visitor, stole the ewe lamb to make a meal. David was furious and interrupted Nathan to say, "The man who has done this merits death!"

Then Nathan said to David, "You are the man!" David was thus brought to an unsuspected judgment on himself (see 2 Samuel 12:1–13).

Many of Jesus' parables do this. They tease us; they lead us to suspect there is more here than meets the eye, something which applies to our own life and which we ought to face.

In the parable of the Prodigal Son (see Luke 15:11–32), with whom do we identify? The erring son, the elder brother, the father? Am I a Pharisee bragging in the front of the temple or the contrite publican in the back (see Luke 18:9–19)? Am I the priest or the Levite passing by the needy, or am I—surprise ending—being loved most by those whom I most despise—the "Samaritans" of my life (see Luke 10:29–37)?

Many parables explicitly refer to the Kingdom—"the kingdom of heaven/the reign of God is like...." They reveal not so much what the Kingdom actually is, but the kind of dispositions one must have to enter it. We are drawn into a realization of the divineness that lies within what seems to be merely the "natural" in life.

The parables were no leisurely and patient explanation of a religious system by a famous rabbi. Rather, as events were quickly to prove, they were related to crisis—with Jesus in the center. They did not speak of some comfortably distant, terrible/beautiful "Day of the Lord." Rather, the time is now. You are the one. Jesus' whole public life is pressured by a crisis situation: This is God's last word; we must decide now (see *Catechism*, #546).

One of Mark's verses regarding the parables must be clarified. Jesus says to the Twelve:

> The mystery of the kingdom of God has been granted to you. But to those outside everything comes in parables, so that
>> they may look and see but not perceive,
>> and hear and listen but not understand,
>> in order that they may not be converted and be forgiven. (4:11–12)

This harsh quotation is from Isaiah 6:9 and can only reflect the Hebrew mind which saw God as doing *everything*. If a man killed himself with drink, God did it. If wheat sprouted or the rainbow filled the sky, they did not think of the laws of physics and botany; God did it. So when some people heard Jesus' message but did not understand, they saw this, too, as part of the divine plan. The results of humanity's own free decisions are said to be caused by God, because nothing happens outside God's power.

We are not used to thinking this way, of course, and we must simply say: Jesus spoke his parables to everyone. It is true, however, that he did explain the parables to his disciples, not to the unbelievers.

Scholars have shown that some of Jesus' parables acquired new applications as the church grew older. For example, the parable about the workers who got full pay for the last hour's work was first directed against those who murmured at the Good News of God's mercy. Later it was also seen as exemplifying an insistence that no "work" earns salvation; it is purely God's gift.

The great German scholar Joachim Jeremias has summarized the meaning of the parables in this way:

1) Salvation is here.
2) God is merciful.
3) God will certainly deliver you from the coming tribulation.
4) Catastrophe is imminent; the nation is rushing to its destruction.
5) It may be too late; take resolute action now.
6) The way will be the way of the cross.

Here is a most unpoetic capsule summary of what the parables tell us about the Kingdom (see *Catechism*, #541–542).

WHAT JESUS SAYS ABOUT THE KINGDOM. The Kingdom comes in Jesus, and this is as evident as the coming of spring in the green leaves (Matthew 24:32–35). It starts very small, like a tiny seed, but it will grow into a large tree (Mark 4:30–32) because, in spite of all difficulties, God makes it grow (Mark 4:26–29). It will grow to an unbelievable harvest: thirty, sixty, even a hundred times the planting (Matthew 13:1–9). The Kingdom of God's power will work irresistibly through all humankind, like yeast through dough (Matthew 13:33).

God calls everyone to the Kingdom, everyone on the highways and byways of life, even people we may consider unlikely (Luke 14:15–24). All are invited to the banquet (Matthew 22:1–14). God gives the Kingdom for nothing: It is totally free; it is not merited or earned. God is like the vineyard owner who pays wages out of all proportion to the work done (Matthew 20:1–16). So, even though it may seem that we work very hard for God and are deserving of great reward, we are really only servants. We are receivers, not givers. We do nothing for God; we only receive and respond to God's power and love (Luke 17:7–10).

The Kingdom of God is the forgiveness of huge unpayable debts of sin out of God's mercy. Since this is so, obviously we must pay the comparatively small debts of forgiveness we owe others (Matthew 18:23–35). God is like a merciful father who welcomes back his son to the table even though the son has deserted him and wasted his inheritance in sin. Other members of the Kingdom dare not resent this mercy of the Father (Luke 15:11–32).

God is happy over the return of a sinner, the way a woman cries with joy when she has found a precious coin that was lost (Luke 15:8–10). God is the Good Shepherd who leaves the flock of ninety-nine to seek the one sheep that is lost and carries it home on his shoulders (Luke 15:3–7). Even if we do not bear fruit at first, God will be merciful; but ultimately our tree will be cut down and thrown into the fire if we bear no fruit (Luke 13:6–9).

Some will reject the Kingdom, like tenants in a vineyard who will not give even some of the fruits to the rightful owner (Matthew 21:33–46). They will be destroyed. Rejecters of the Kingdom are hypocrites: They complain both about too much strictness and too much leniency (Luke 7:29–35).

So the Kingdom will have good and bad in it, like a net that gathers all kinds of fish (Matthew 13:47–50) or like a field where both wheat and weeds grow. But they will be separated forever at the end (Matthew 13:24–30).

The end will come suddenly. Watchfulness—that is, living constantly in God's love—is all-important. Then we are ready in gladness, not fear, for whenever God comes, even if suddenly (Luke 12:35–40).

The Owner of the Kingdom may come to claim it at any time, like a man who has left his home in charge of servants (Mark 13:32–37). We are servants ready for God's coming at any time (Matthew 24:45–51). We are ready for the marriage feast, even if the Bridegroom, Jesus, comes at midnight (Matthew 25:1–10).

The Kingdom is important beyond anything else. It is like a treasure that a man finds, or a pearl. He gives up everything else as secondary in order to have the treasure, the pearl (Matthew 13:45–46). Accepting the Kingdom is the greatest common sense, or prudence, such as worldly people use in business or war (Luke 14:25–35).

In the Kingdom it is those who turn to God and remain faithful to the end who will be saved (Matthew 21:28–32). For, having received God's generosity, we must respond to his love and accept the invitation to the Kingdom feast (Matthew 22:1–10). But having entered, we must wear the garment of grace God gives us (Matthew 22:11–14). For if Jesus does not replace the devil who is thrown out, the devil will return and it will be worse than before (Matthew 12:43–45).

If we want to be forgiven members of the Kingdom, we must humbly ask God's pardon like the sinful tax collector, not brag before him like the Pharisee (Luke 18:9–14). We should settle our accounts while we are on our way, not wait until we are brought into court (Matthew 5:25–26).

In the Kingdom God wants us to pray to him unceasingly in order to realize our dependence on him, like people desperately knocking on a friend's door asking for bread at midnight (Luke 11:5–8); we should be so persistent that it seems God answers us just to get rid of us, like an unjust judge finally giving in to a widow (Luke 18:1–8).

In the Kingdom everyone is our neighbor, not just those we like. It doesn't exclude those, like Samaritans, who are not "our own." Sometimes people we despise (Samaritans) are the real neighbors (Luke 10:29–37). Many sins are forgiven to those who love; and those who have been forgiven much love God very much (Luke 7:36–50).

The Kingdom is lost to those who put all their trust in the things of this world, like a rich man with full barns (Luke 12:13–21). We must use earthly things and money as a means to heaven, not obstacles (Luke 16:1–12).

Everyone in the Kingdom has a different gift. God expects us to do what we can with the gifts given to us (Matthew 25:14–30).

Members of the Kingdom may seem to have a terribly painful life—like that of a beggar in the street—but they will be with God, while those who seem to be having a happy life may find themselves outside at the judgment (Luke 16:19–31). At the judgment it will be revealed that though many people talked a good game, Jesus did not know them, nor they Jesus (Luke 13:22–30).

Most important of all, at the final judgment Jesus will reveal that what we did to others—or did not do—was done or refused to him (Matthew 25:31–46).

REFLECTION/DISCUSSION STARTERS

1) What are some common characteristics and themes of the parables Jesus told?
2) What is meant by the Kingdom of God? Discuss what the parables say about the Kingdom.
3) Which parable speaks the most to you? Why?
4) How do you experience the Kingdom in your life? Could you create your own parable to convey your experience of the Kingdom?

SCRIPTURE READINGS

(In a group, the parable readings given below can be divided among individuals or smaller groups, with persons or small groups discussing the specific passages assigned to them.)

In Matthew: 5:25–26; 12:43–45; 13:1–9, 24–30, 33, 47–50; 18:23–35; 20:1–16; 21:28–32, 33–46; 22:1–14; 24:32–35, 45–51; 25:1–13, 14–30, 31–46.

In Mark: 4:26–29, 30–32; 13:32–37.

In Luke: 7:29–35, 36–50; 10:25–37; 11:5–8; 12:13–21, 35–40; 13:6–9, 22–30; 14:15–24, 25–35; 15:3–7, 8–10, 11–32; 16:1–12, 19–31; 17:7–10; 18:1–8, 9–14.

SUPPLEMENTARY MATERIAL

Catholic Update: "What Is 'The Kingdom of God'?" by Richard P. McBrien.

Scripture From Scratch: "The Tantalizing Parables Jesus Told," by Virginia Smith.

CHAPTER 5

JESUS, A DANGER TO
CHURCH AND STATE

VERY FEW ISRAELITES EXPECTED A MESSIAH LIKE JESUS. EVEN HIS FAMILY thought he was a bit mad. Except for the few who saw in him the shadow of the Suffering Servant in the Old Testament, people felt that he simply turned human values upside down—which in fact he did—and were not prepared for such an anticlimax of history.

At the final showdown almost nobody was for him, and the might of both the religious and the secular establishment was against him. Like sunlight showing things exactly as they are, he first frightened and then enraged the leaders of these two worlds who, with hands piously folded or swords hanging discreetly ready, had arranged a world with which God presumably agreed. In their world, external correctness was essential. Salvation was gained by mighty personal effort. Conformity to the letter of the Law, rather than a free growth in responsibility, was of the essence. And "Roman peace" hung over all.

The little people heard Jesus gladly. He taught in the synagogue and "the people were astonished at his teaching, for he taught them as one having authority and not as the scribes" (Mark 1:22). Matthew uses the same word, astonished, after the Sermon on the Mount.

After the curing of the paralyzed man, Mark records that "they were all astounded and glorified God, saying, 'We have never seen anything like this'" (Mark 2:12). He uses the word *astounded* to describe their reaction to the healing of both the Gerasene demoniac and the deaf-mute (5:20; 7:37).

In Mark, Jesus seems always surrounded by crowds, so that at times he could not even find time to eat (see Mark 3:20). After the multiplication of the loaves, they wanted to "carry him off to make him king" (John 6:15b).

And at the climax, when he knew that death would soon remove any danger of an earthly enthronement, Jesus allowed the full adulation of the crowd. As he entered Jerusalem the week before Calvary,

> The very large crowd spread their cloaks on the road, while others cut branches from the trees and strewed them on the road. The crowds preceding him and those following kept crying out and saying:
>
> "Hosanna to the Son of David;
> blessed is he who comes in the name of the Lord;
> hosanna in the highest."
>
> And when he entered Jerusalem the whole city was shaken.... (Matthew 21:8–10a)

But, in a sad commentary, John says, "While he was in Jerusalem for the feast of Passover, many began to believe in his name when they saw the signs he was doing. But Jesus would not trust himself to them because he knew them all, and did not need anyone to testify about human nature. He himself understood it well" (John 2:23–25).

And Jesus was forced to say to those who followed him after the multiplication of the loaves:

> ...[Y]ou are looking for me not because you saw signs but because you ate the loaves and were filled. Do not work for food that perishes but for the food that endures for eternal life, which the Son of Man will give you. (John 6:26b–27a)

Something had to happen before all the signs would merge into the one great sign of the cross. Enthusiasm, admiration, inspiration kindled by courageous and pure leadership—none of these was enough. The Kingdom could come only through the foolishness of the cross and the mystery of resurrection.

His enemies would make him victorious.

JESUS; CORELIGIONISTS. If ever there was a people whose religion influenced every facet of life, it was the chosen people. They were the "people of the Book." The Torah—plus the endless commentaries made on it—regulated life down to the smallest detail. Several times a day the practicing Jew (like Muslims around the world) stopped to pray. The sabbath was an absolutely holy day set apart for God. Great feasts brought multitudes to Jerusalem; others were observed in the family and local community. Each village had its synagogue for prayer and meetings. And at the center of all was the magnificent temple in Jerusalem (rebuilt by Herod the Great), undoubtedly one of the most majestic pieces of architecture to be seen at the time.

The Jews were a theocracy—that is, a nation ruled by God. God's representatives were the high priest and the Sanhedrin, a kind of senate and supreme tribunal made up of members of the priestly class, the scribes and doctors of the Law and the elders, outstanding laymen from the chief families.

An aristocracy of intellect and piety molded the thought of the nation. These were the "doctors" (that is, teachers) of the Law. To the Western mind, the way in which they scrutinized the Bible was opposed to logic. Searching the minutest details, they found metaphorical meanings that went far beyond the writer's intended meaning. Their interpretations guided the people's life. Their purpose was to keep the people specifically Jewish—that is, real followers of Moses.

Like the doctors of the Law, the scribes were scholars and intellectuals who had *the* knowledge of the Law, the sum of wisdom, the only true learning. Though not necessarily of any sect or party, they were often Pharisees.

PHARISEES AND SADDUCEES. All the people, from the highest to the lowest, thought of themselves as men and women of God; but there were two great divisions, corresponding to two reactions to paganism. One group held that there could be no dealing whatever with pagans. The good Jew must cast aside everything that was not purely Judaic. The true believer was to remain separate from paganism and all that smacked of it. This group became known as "the separated," in Hebrew the *perushim*, from which comes our word Pharisees.

On the other side, the Sadducees believed in preserving the People of God by intelligence and diplomacy. The majority were truly religious, though most had no problem accommodating to the pagans. The Sadducees drew their numbers chiefly from the well-to-do classes: higher officials, merchants, property owners, priests.

A second disagreement between the two had to do with the Law. The Sadducees held only to the written Law of Moses and its 613 great principles. Where the Law was mute, they let reason decide. But the Pharisees insisted that the laws of religion must permeate the whole of human life. So the written Law had to be completed with the tradition or oral laws that the scribes (theologians) had been formulating since the return from exile. Most of the doctors of the Law were Pharisees.

In Jesus' time the Pharisees could be compared to a powerful political party in modern terms. The real party members (the truly "separated") numbered between five and ten thousand. But a large part of the Jewish people, especially the poorer classes, were sympathetic.

The Pharisees also felt they had a monopoly on the truth and many had a profound contempt for those outside the Law. They no doubt had a deep and rigorous faith. They taught and practiced true charity. Paradoxically, they saw the oral tradition as constantly developing—under their interpretation. But once developed, their tradition became as sacred and rigorous as the Law itself.

Jesus sometimes accused the Pharisees of *hypocrisy, pride and externalism,* thereby neglecting "the weightier things of the law: judgment and mercy and fidelity" (Matthew 23:23c). His words become almost vitriolic. Some think this tone is sharpened in the Gospels because of later disputes between Jewish Christians and Jewish synagogue leaders. It may come as a surprise to some how much of the Gospels is taken up with this controversy. But the result is no surprise at all.

CONFLICT OVER SABBATH RIGORISM. A typical example of Pharisaic rigorism, if not hypocrisy, is found in the following incident. On their way to the synagogue on the sabbath, Jesus' disciples pluck ears of wheat and rub the grains in their hands to make a rough meal. When the Pharisees complain, Jesus gives both a rabbinical answer to show precedent in the Bible and then offers a humanitarian view of the Law: It is to be interpreted according to human needs and possibilities. "The sabbath was made for man, not man for the sabbath" (Mark 2:27b).

On another occasion Jesus cured a man with a withered hand on the sabbath. "The scribes and the Pharisees watched him closely," Luke notes, "to see if he would cure on the sabbath so that they might discover a reason to accuse him" (Luke 6:7). Jesus does not quibble. He simply says, "I ask you, is it lawful to do good on the sabbath rather than to do evil, to save life rather than to destroy it?" (6:9b). At this, Luke says, "they became enraged" (6:11), and Mark adds, "The Pharisees went out and immediately took counsel with the Herodians [strange bedfellows] against him to put him to death" (3:6).

On another occasion Jesus made mud paste and used it to cure a blind man. Some of the Pharisees said, "This man is not from God, because he does not keep the sabbath" (John 9:16b). One of the thirty-nine works forbidden on the sabbath (others included tying knots and walking more than three thousand feet) was kneading, and Jesus had kneaded the clay with his spittle to make mud.

Later conflicts with Jewish leaders probably led the evangelists (especially Matthew) to make Pharisaic opposition to Jesus sound more ominous.

RIGORISM BECOMES HYPOCRISY. The words Jesus used most often of the Pharisees were *hypocrites* or *frauds.* These words are used seven times in seventeen verses of that terrible chapter, Matthew 23. Jesus says, "How well you have set aside the commandment of God in order to uphold your tradition!" (Mark 7:9b). He gives as an example their not being "able" to support their parents because their money has been dedicated to God!

The charge of seeing the speck in another's eye and not the plank in one's own was aimed at the judgmentalism of the Pharisees. The teachings on prayer, fasting and alms in the Sermon on the Mount are put in the form of a contrast between the ostentatious piety of the Pharisees and the genuine piety which tries to conceal itself (see Matthew 6:1–18).

Jesus tells the people to follow the teaching of the Pharisees but not their practice, because their actions do not match their words. They interpret the Law severely, not humanely. Their religious garb is used to show off; they are greedy for public honors. They evade truthfulness by tricky formulas in taking oaths. They lay great stress on trivia and neglect the great commandments of justice, mercy and faithfulness.

In their fanaticism for externals they are "...like whitewashed tombs, which appear beautiful on the outside, but inside are full of dead men's bones and every kind of filth" (Matthew 23:27b). They are the true heirs of their ancestors who killed the prophets—and they will kill the one who is now continuing to speak with prophetic, fearless truthfulness.

Therefore, Jesus says, the people are to "beware of the leaven—that is, the hypocrisy—of the Pharisees" (Luke 12:1b). Many Pharisees were, however, truly religious people. Jesus told one of them, "You are not far from the kingdom of God" (Mark 12:34).

THE "SCANDAL" OF JESUS. In the eyes of the Pharisees, Jesus compounded the error of his ways by associating with disreputable people: tax collectors (the hated quislings who "farmed" taxes for the Romans) and "those known as sinners"—that is, nonobservant Jews. When the Pharisees asked why he ate with tax collectors and sinners, Jesus' answer was framed in double-meaning words that were well understood: "Those who are well do not need a physician, but the sick do. I did not come to call the righteous but sinners" (Mark 2:17).

Some Pharisees followed Jesus; for instance, Nicodemus, who came to see Jesus under cover of darkness. But for the great majority the cost was too great. It would have required as shattering a change of heart as occurred to that strictest of Pharisees, Saul of Tarsus. Many Pharisees were truly religious people. They had the greatest influence in redefining Judaism after the Jerusalem Temple was destroyed by the Romans in 70 C.E. It is not to the credit of Christians that they have turned the word "pharisaic" into a synonym for "hypocritical."

And this "free" man should be the Messiah? It was an insult to God that such a one should presume to reveal and mediate God's glory to Israel!

And so some of the Jewish religious and political leaders came to the conclusion that Jesus had to be destroyed. Some trick was needed to arrest and kill him. But, "Not during the festival, that there may not be a riot among the people" (Matthew 26:5b).

Standing by were the Romans. Let there be found, then, some "Roman" reason to dispatch this dangerous man.

REFLECTION/DISCUSSION STARTERS

1) There were several points of contention between Jesus and some of the Pharisees. Which practices of these Pharisees did Jesus speak against? Do you see the qualities that Jesus criticized in these Pharisees present in people today? In society? In your own life?

2) Which of Jesus' actions and teachings disturbed some Pharisees the most? If Jesus were acting and teaching among us today, do you think some people would see him as the "scandal" that those Pharisees did?

SCRIPTURE READINGS

Matthew 23; 6:1–18

SUPPLEMENTARY MATERIAL

Scripture From Scratch: "King of the Jews: The Herod Dynasty," by Elizabeth McNamer.

. | CHAPTER 6 | .

THE DYING AND RISING OF JESUS: THE HEART OF CHRISTIAN LIFE

MANY GOOD MEN AND WOMEN I'VE KNOWN DON'T THINK OF THEMSELVES AS "holy." There's nothing neurotic about it; they don't hate themselves. They just feel they could be more deeply "into" their religion than they are.

This used to bother me and I tried to tell them that Saint Paul calls ordinary people *saints*, that it is God who makes us holy, not our own efforts.

But now I see there is something deeper here: *Ordinary Christians sense the depth of the mystery of Jesus and are humble before it.* They realize that the life, death and resurrection of Jesus have a depth that is divine.

We can only feebly express or even experience what it means that God loves us so much. In love God bound a human body and soul to divinity, lived our life in all its joy and pain, and entered freely into a degrading and apparently hopeless human death. Then, in a totally unexpected (though promised) and bewildering turnabout, Jesus is raised up newly alive—different, real and yet mysterious. He is seen only by those who believe. He is glorious and victorious, offering life, freedom, liberation, eternal happiness.

It is too much to grasp. It is frightening because it offers more than we want to receive; yet it fulfills our deepest yearnings. It is also frightening because the price is absolutely high: We must do what Jesus did—die and rise. The dying is not just a one-time occurrence, but a daily happening. Deep down, we know that this is what it means to be a follower of Jesus: to die and to rise every hour. Or better, to let the power of Jesus put to death in us all selfishness and replace it with his Spirit.

We are reluctant to accept the offer. It is true, but it is too good. We know that in dealing with God it can only be a matter of one hundred percent—not in terms of effort, but receiving, trusting, loving. And we—not instinctively, as the phrase goes, but in world-taught caution—hold back. Could it possibly be enough, we hope, to love God almost totally?

And so we say we are not "holy"—meaning, I think, that we are not ready to let God give us all God wants to give.

The dying and rising of Jesus stands at the center of all history. Not merely in the center of time, as if there are to be as many years after as before, but in the center of today. Whether anyone knows it or not, accepts it or not, the dying and rising of Jesus is the central reality in every home, every factory, every school, every hospital, every theater, every prison, every supermarket.

With this feeble attempt to set the stage, we try now to understand two things: (1) what happened, from a human viewpoint; (2) why it happened, from God's viewpoint.

THE EVENTS OF HOLY WEEK

Luke arranges his Gospel in a journey narrative. Jesus, at a certain point, begins his free and deliberate journey toward Jerusalem from his native Galilee, fully aware that he will be put to death. The apostles realized what the trip meant. Thomas says bluntly and bravely that the rest of them might as well go along and be put to death, too.

It is a literal "going up"—from below sea level in Galilee and from the depths of the Dead Sea up to the mountain of Jerusalem. John will continue the "lifting up" theme: Jesus is lifted up on the cross by human agents, lifted up out of death by his Father and lifted up in glory to the throne of God from which he came.

On Palm Sunday Jesus finally allowed people to celebrate him as Messiah. There were only a few days left, hardly time for a revolution to form. He rode down from the Mount of Olives on a donkey, and then up through the Golden Gate, while people spread palm branches and even their clothing in his path, crying out:

Hosanna to the Son of David;
blessed is he who comes in the name of the Lord;
hosanna in the highest. (Matthew 21:9)

"The whole city was shaken," Matthew adds (21:10), but one group was stirred by a special passion. The four Gospel writers variously identify them as chief priests, elders, scribes or Sadducees. They began to look for some way to "dispose" of him, Luke says.

Then Satan entered into Judas, the one surnamed Iscariot, who was counted among the Twelve, and he went to the chief priests and temple guards to discuss a plan for handing him over to them. They were pleased and agreed to pay him money. He accepted their offer and sought a favorable opportunity to hand him over to them in the absence of a crowd (Luke 22:3–6, see the note on pages 73 and 74 for more on this topic.)

The night before he was crucified, Jesus gathered his Jewish "family" of followers for a Passover meal. They did not realize it, but this was the fulfillment of all the Passovers since Moses and the beginning of a transformed Passover. His dying and rising a few days hence was "caught," real, living and all-powerful, in the Eucharist that began that night. In spite of all the human agony that would follow, he was ready. He was resolved to give himself for his friends. His victory, his liberating new life, were already present. His whole sacrificial love was embodied in this simple giving of Passover loaves and wine. They became himself, as the sign of his total self-giving and of the life-giving nourishment he would be for all who wished to live (see *Catechism*, #610–611). (We will consider this more fully in chapter fifteen.)

After the supper, down in Gethsemane in the deep valley below the Mount of Olives, Jesus felt the full human terror of death (see *Catechism*, #612). Because his vision was so pure and his life so fully human, he realized, more than any of us can, the horror of human life being choked off. Perhaps the greatest consolation any suffering or dying person can have is to experience this Jesus in his naked, helpless humanness, so transfixed with fear that "his sweat became like drops of blood..." (Luke 22:44b).

His enemies came with their power and he did not defend himself.

THE CHARGES. It is difficult to interrelate the trial scenes in the four Gospels, probably because the Gospel writers, as usual, were writing not mere history but a record of faith. A generation or two later when the Gospels were written, the church could see what was really happening, and it did not matter whether there was a trial or a pretrial hearing, whether it took place during the night or in the morning or both.

The real reason why Jesus was condemned to death by the Sanhedrin was that he claimed to be their king/Messiah and the prophet Daniel's mysterious "Son of Man."

After rejecting the title of Messiah all his public life, Jesus speaks clearly (in Mark) in answer to the high priest's question: "'Are you the Messiah, the son of the Blessed One?' Then Jesus answered: 'I am'" (14:61b–62a).

In the light of the Resurrection, Christians down the centuries would hear echoes of Yahweh's only self-description: "I AM" (see Exodus 3:14).

By the term "Son of the Blessed One" the Sanhedrin meant no more than the phrase signified in the Old Testament—the specially chosen one, especially the great Davidic king through whom God promises that the nation will reach fulfillment (see 2 Samuel 7:14). The *Jerome Biblical Commentary* explains: "In the Sanhedrin's eyes, that Jesus should claim such a privilege insulted God: for this humiliated, rejected man to presume to reveal and mediate the Lord's glory to Israel was a supreme irreverence to God." And so they accused him of blasphemy.

They said he had threatened to destroy the temple, choosing to take his words literally. What he actually said was, "Destroy this temple and in three days I will raise it up." John adds, "But he was speaking about the temple of his body" (John 2:19b, 21). False witnesses chose to take his words literally (see Mark 14:58). Besides referring to the resurrection of his own body, Jesus no doubt often criticized the temple and the cult for which it stood. The prophets had done that before him, most scorchingly Jeremiah, who stood at the entrance and said to the people entering: "Put not your trust in the deceitful words: 'This is the temple of the Lord! The temple of the Lord! The temple of the Lord!' Only if you thoroughly reform your ways and your deeds…will I remain with you in this place…" (Jeremiah 7:4–5, 7).

Even the false witnesses did not agree, but the Sanhedrin's mind was made up. "He deserves to die!" (Matthew 26:66c).

There can be little doubt that Jesus did have some bitter conflicts with some of the religious leaders. He was a prophet (and more than a prophet). Like the prophets of old, he would have flung some dire threats against those who refused to do God's will. Also, like the prophets, it was because he loved even his enemies that he tried to wake them up out of their selfish ways. Still, it may be true that the evangelists colored and even sharpened their accounts because of later conflicts between Jews who rejected Jesus and those who accepted him.

Again, remembering the prophets, we should not be surprised if some of the Jewish leaders plotted to get Jesus executed. This did not mean, however, that all Jews were guilty historically of having Jesus crucified. The impression from the Gospels is that some of the chief priests, priests, elders and scribes were instrumental in handing Jesus over to the Romans. (See the footnote on pages 73 and 74.)

One further observation: When we as Christians read about Jesus' enemies and how they opposed him, we should not waste time and energy in condemning them. Christians should look to themselves and see how their own attitudes and behavior might mirror the attitudes and behavior of some of Jesus' coreligionists. (See 2 Timothy 3:16: "All scripture is inspired by God and is useful…for correction….")

THE DEATH SENTENCE. Putting people to death was beyond the power of the Sanhedrin (see John 18:31), so the enemies of Jesus had to suffer the humiliation of approaching the hated Romans, the occupying power in a police state.

The Romans were totally uninterested in what they would have called the "religious squabbles" of their subjects. But they were wary of political activities. So now the charge becomes: "We found this man misleading our people; he opposes the payment of taxes to Caesar and maintains that he is the Messiah, a king" (Luke 23:2b).

Jesus assures Pilate that his Kingdom is not "of this world"—a statement, one authority has noted, that cannot be imagined in the mouth of the kind of Messiah popularly expected. The Jews expected a Messiah with a this-worldly kingdom—even if he were the more spiritual type of Messiah portrayed in the psalms.

In three of the Gospels Pilate finally gives in simply because the mob keeps shouting, "Crucify him!" It is merely a cowardly act of political expediency. In John's Gospel a deeper reason is clearly stated: Pilate wanted to release him, but the Jews insisted, "If you release him, you are not a Friend of Caesar. Everyone who makes himself a king opposes Caesar" (John 19:12). This was the ultimate weapon: the threat of denouncing him to the emperor for having favored the emperor's enemies.

According to the Gospel of Matthew, Pilate washes his hands, a pitiful charade of non-responsibility, and gives them their way. But he will have the last, cynical word: He orders an inscription placed on the cross which reads, *"Jesus the Nazorean, the King of the Jews"* (John 19:19c).

THE CRUCIFIXION. Jesus is scourged and made sport of by brutal Roman soldiers throughout the long night. Then the heavy crossbeam is placed on his shoulders and he is driven through the twisting, narrow streets of Jerusalem. Perhaps the hucksters did not even pay attention as he passed—just another poor wretch who had fallen afoul of the Romans.

They took him to a place of degradation outside the city walls and crucified him on a little hill that looked like a skull. It was the most humiliating of capital punishments.

As the *New Catholic Encyclopedia* explains,

The Romans considered crucifixion so shameful a penalty that it could not be inflicted on Roman citizens. Roman crucifixion was always preceded by a scourging of the victim at the place of judgment. Then the criminal, still naked after the scourging, was made to carry his own cross (that is, the crossbeam) to the place of execution, where he was exposed to public ridicule and death. On top of the upright stake was fastened a placard with the culprit's name and a statement of the crime for which he was being put to death. The full weight of a body hanging by the arms would prevent the correct functioning of the lungs and so cause death by asphyxiation after not too long a time. Therefore, to prolong the agony of the victim, support was given to his body by a kind of seat block and by binding or nailing his feet to the cross. Death could later be hastened by breaking the victim's legs, so that shock and asphyxiation soon ended his life. Sometimes, however, the side and heart would be pierced by a spear to cause immediate death. After death the body was left to rot on the cross as an additional sign of disgrace, and as a warning to the passers-by.

The Jews objected to a man's going about naked in public, so the Romans in Palestine allowed the condemned criminal to put his clothes on again after being scourged. When Jesus arrived at the place of execution, he was offered a drink of spiced wine to numb the pain, but he refused it. He was stripped of his garments and nailed to the cross, at least by his hands, probably also with ropes around his wrists.

JESUS' LAST WORDS. Jesus spoke seven statements, or "words," on the cross. Three are recorded by Luke, three by John and one by both Matthew and Mark.

1) *"Father, forgive them, they know not what they do"* (Luke 23:34b). The form of the verb Luke uses indicates that Jesus kept saying this over and over again. This is the great summation of his life: He came to bring God's forgiveness to all the world—indeed, to all sinners. It was only consistent that he show this boundless mercy of God at the moment of sinners' greatest cruelty to him.

2) *"Amen, I say to you, today you will be with me in Paradise"* (Luke 23:43b). The words are spoken to the "good thief" who confesses his guilt and repeatedly begs to be remembered when Jesus enters into his royal glory. Jesus assures him that he will be with him today in his Kingdom. In contrast to those who should have known better, the criminal sees the truth and welcomes it.

3) *"Woman, behold, your son. . . . Behold, your mother"* (John 19:26c, 27b). This is the loving concern of a son for his mother, but it is more than that. Mary is also the "woman" of Genesis 3:15, where God says to the serpent: "I will put enmity between you and the woman, / and between your offspring and hers." Jesus' words show Mary as the new Eve, the true "mother of all the living" (see Genesis 3:20) through the death and resurrection of Jesus. She is the spiritual mother of the church—that is, all Jesus' disciples as represented by John as well as a symbol of the "mother" church itself.

4) *"My God, my God, why have you forsaken me?"* (Matthew 27:46d; Mark 16:34d). Jesus is praying the opening words of Psalm 22. Jesus was in pain,

in emotional fear and agony. In the core of his being, he never was without the loving presence of his Father, but the prayer surely fit his human emotions. The psalm is almost a description of the passion of Jesus, and its latter words should be noted. Jesus could have prayed them, too, as he remembered the psalm:

> Then I will proclaim your name to the assembly;
>   in the community I will praise you.... (Psalm 22:23)

5) *"I thirst" (John 19:28c)*. Again, John intends more than one level of meaning. He sees the fulfillment of the messianic Psalm 69:

> I looked for compassion, but there was none,
>   for comforters, but found none.
> Instead they put gall in my food,
>   for my thirst they gave me vinegar. (Psalm 69:21b–22)

Father Raymond Brown in *The Gospel According to John* comments:

> Perhaps the most plausible symbolism is to connect the episode with John 18:11: "Am I not to drink the cup the Father has given me?" The cup was one of suffering and death; and now having finished his work, Jesus thirsts to drink that cup to the last drop, for only when he has tasted the bitter wine of death will his Father's will be fulfilled.

6) *"It is finished"* (John 19:30b). Jesus has done what he came to do: the will of his Father, which was to save all his wandering, sinful children. Jesus utters a cry of victory, of accomplishment. He has succeeded in a most unlikely way: by being defeated by the very sin he came to destroy. As always in John, it is Jesus who is in command. He has willingly been "lifted up," and the Father and he have achieved their purpose of salvation.

John adds, "And bowing his head, he handed over the spirit" (19:30). Jesus was handed over by traitors, but now he hands himself over gladly to the Father.

7) *"Father, into your hands I commend my spirit"* (Luke 23:46b). In Luke the last words of Jesus are from Psalm 31:6, to which Luke adds the word Father. The words sum up Jesus' perfect disposition: Everything is in his Father's hands, and now he sums up his whole life by placing himself,

body and soul, into those loving hands. He totally trusts his Father as he deliberately steps into the darkness of death. Humanly, it is a fearful moment: The darkness is the same as for anyone. But Jesus is the absolutely trusting child, the totally dependent creature, and his act replaces all the self-sufficiency and independence that have characterized human history. Jesus makes death the greatest act of love in his life.

Now the human actors must quickly finish their work. The Law must be observed scrupulously: A dead body could not be left hanging on the cross on the sabbath. A lance is thrust into Jesus—assuring all that he is really dead—and blood and water pour out. The body is taken down and bound up "with burial cloths along with the spices" (John 19:40b). It is placed in a friend's new tomb nearby. A huge stone is rolled over the opening. It is officially sealed, and guards stand by.

The apostles sit numbed with fear and sadness behind locked doors. It is indeed "finished." As two disciples would say two days later, walking with Jesus and not knowing him, "But we were hoping that he would be the one to redeem Israel..." (Luke 24:21a).

The women who had followed the body of Jesus to the tomb "rested on the sabbath according to the commandment" (Luke 23:56b). They did not know there was a new Law.

DYING AND RISING—FROM GOD'S VIEWPOINT

We have considered the reasons why Jesus' enemies wanted to kill him—fear, envy, resentment. And it is easy to understand why he grated on some consciences. He contradicted the world in the name of simple, total love, of truthfulness and humility before God. He suffered the fate of the pure person who, without uttering a word of condemnation, exposes the falsity and selfishness of others.

But these are human reasons, even if true. What did God have in mind, in what Saint Paul calls the mystery hidden from all eternity (see Colossians 1:26)? What is the Father trying to do for us today in the dying and rising of Jesus?

We believe, first of all, that God let the world do its worst, and put his plan within the hateful actions that led to Jesus' death. He planted a seed amid hostile forces much as a farmer sows grain amid the benign forces of earth and water, sun and wind. God intervened through Jesus, but assumed powerlessness before ignorance and hatred.

Why did Jesus die? Why did he consistently say, especially in the record of Saint Luke, that he must die?

Let us obliterate as completely as possible one totally false reason: that God "punished" Jesus for the sins of humankind. The idea of a "punishment of Christ" in place of sinners, says theologian Father Karl Rahner, is rightly rejected.

Jesus bore no guilt; he never sinned. But out of love, he took on our guilt, the distance we put between ourselves and God, so that he could cry our anguish from the cross, "My God, My God, why have you forsaken me?" (see *Catechism*, #603).

The fact is, God desired with infinite love to find a way to save the world from sin without destroying the gift of freedom. It was almost as if the Trinity had a meeting and decided it was best for the Son to enter the sinful world as a real man. Saint Paul is clear on this: "...God was reconciling the world to himself in Christ..." (2 Corinthians 5:19).

What was it, then, that the God-man Jesus could do to reunite God's sinful children with his Father?

First, Jesus himself is perfectly united to God. He is truly human, and therefore humankind, at least in one human being, is united forever to God. Even should all the world rebel, God and humanity are now inseparable.

In this one man there is perfect human love and loyalty, trust and obedience. He is the perfect opposite of sin, which is an attempt to be independent, to be self-sufficient, self-willed, self-powered. Jesus, the most mature human being who ever lived, was the perfect child before his Father (see *Catechism*, #613–616).

The life and death of Jesus was not an "act," some "nice" gesture, but a reflection of reality. Reality is our total dependence on God's love and power and creation at every second of our lives. This does not involve any "putting down" of us by God; it is simply the way things are. Only God is God; all else is creation, dependent creation. "Even our desire to please you is itself your gift" (*Sacramentary*, Preface #40).

We must not inflict a mechanical holiness on Jesus. As a living, breathing, feeling human being, he allowed himself to be taken over completely by the love of God. He was simply wide open to all the goodness his Father wanted to give him, all the good that was to be done. He not only emptied himself, as Saint Paul says, of the external glory due him as God; he also was empty and virginal as far as any self-will was concerned.

Again, let us remind ourselves: Jesus was not putting on an act or doing something extra. He was merely acting as a creature should act. He was simply open to the ever-present gift of his Father's love. He let it enter and empower his every thought, feeling, word and action. It was what kept him alive: "My food is to do the will of the one who sent me" (John 4:34b).

But if Jesus is already the perfect loving child of his Father, why does he *have* to die?

Because giving up one's life is the *total* gift. Anything else would be less than perfect. There is nothing greater to give than life.

So Jesus had to give up his life because there was no greater way he could show his love for his Father. He had to give up his life because anything else would have been a lesser gift, and he wanted to do the perfect human thing.

But there is another reason why Jesus had to die. He came to a world lost in sin. How could he save that world? By showing it how God acts in the face of hatred. God refuses to be vindictive. God wants only to forgive, to heal, to reconcile.

So Jesus enters into the world and all its misery, except that of sin. He is soaked through, as it were, with the misery of the human condition. And he maintains his perfect, never-swerving devotion to his Father.

In other words, he chose to be the totally loyal son. He would let his Father's love fill his life. If that aroused the hatred of evil—and it inevitably would—so be it. There was nothing the world could do to him that could deflect his childlike love one degree. He walked defenseless into an evil world.

It is sublime irony, as John points out, that because men "lifted up" Jesus on the cross, his Father was able to "lift him up" to new life and eternal glory. The verse, "His blood be upon us and upon our children" (Matthew 27:25b), has been so distorted by some Christians that the Catholic Church at Vatican II felt it necessary to address this issue (see note on pages 73–74).

Jesus had to reeducate his people as to the meaning of the Messiah. They would have to go back and read Isaiah 52. And at the moment when Peter makes his magnificent act of faith ("You are the Messiah"), Jesus must immediately set him straight: "He began to teach them that the Son of Man must suffer greatly and be rejected by the elders, the chief priests, and the scribes, and be killed, and rise after three days" (see Mark 8:31).

Jesus was speaking of himself—not just of his followers—when he said that one must die to live, one must lose in order to win (see Mark 8:34–38).

This was the real Exodus. As the new chosen people, Jesus would walk out of the imprisonment of humanity through the water of death, through the desert of perfect faith, to a new covenant on a new Mount Sinai.

From God's viewpoint, to use a heartless word, it was merely logical. To use the words of lovers, Jesus "had" to die because his love demanded that he give the greatest gift.

No wonder we shy away from the cross. Our problem is not that it is painful, but that it is too great a sign of love. We do not love that way, and we are embarrassed when God does.

Our life of faith, it would seem, is a gradual coming to accept the unbelievable tenderness of God. To be a member of Christ is to die every day, and rise every day.

Jesus' everyday dying was not like ours. He did not have to turn away from private deposits of self-will. But he did know the pain that total absorption with his Father can cost. We, on the other hand, must every day let the power of God's healing cut all the tendrils and vines and chains that want to tie us down in our own selfishness. That is our daily cross— and our greatest blessing.

For as we die, we rise. Salvation is letting Jesus bind us to himself. He is "safe," and so we are safe. He is God and with God; he is human and with us. If the power of his cross is in us, we are, with him, lifted to new life (see *Catechism*, #628).

REFLECTION/DISCUSSION STARTERS

1) What does it mean to you to say that Jesus is the Messiah? How did this claim lead to Jesus' death?

2) Reflect on Jesus' last words and the ways they express themes within his life and message. Which speak to you most strongly for your own life?

3) Three of Jesus' last statements echo the psalms. Read the corresponding psalm (Psalms 22, 29, 31) and discuss the way(s) its words are fulfilled in Jesus.

4) Why was Jesus' life and death, as the author says, not simply "some 'nice' gesture, but a reflection of reality"? What does Jesus' death mean to you?

5) The mystery of the cross is that "one must die to live, one must lose in order to win." Do you see that mystery present in your life? Have you or have others you know ever had to lose in order to win, to die in small ways in order to live?

SCRIPTURE READINGS

Mark 8:27–33, 34–38; the Passion Narratives: Matthew 26—27; Mark 14—15; Luke 22—23; John 18—19.

SUPPLEMENTARY MATERIAL

Catholic Update: "Who Is Jesus?" by Leonard Foley, O.F.M.; Agony in the Garden: Understanding the Passion of Jesus," by Ronald Rolheiser, O.M.I.

Scripture From Scratch: "Who Killed Jesus?" by Daniel J. Harrington, S.J.; "The Passion Narratives: The Cross Takes Center Stage," by Carol Luebering; "The Cross Makes a Christian," by Jerome Murphy-O'Connor, O.P.

Note: It is as unjust for Christians or others to blame "the" Jews for Jesus' death as it would be to say that "the" Americans killed Lincoln or that "the" Arabs murdered a schoolhouse full of children in Israel. Nor is it correct to say that Pilate and the other Romans represented us, "the" Gentiles (see *Catechism*, #597–598).

On the other hand, the killing of Jesus is indeed the act of "the" human race, as we hope to understand in this chapter. If some Jews and some Romans were cold-heartedly responsible for the death of Jesus, they are no more guilty than any human being who destroyed the life of God in his or her own heart by cold-blooded sinfulness. The Christian church has deep roots in Judaism.

Vatican II's *Declaration on the Relation of the Church to Non-Christian Religions* (*Nostra Aetate*, 4) says:

> Even though the Jewish authorities and those who followed their lead pressed for the death of Christ (see John 19:6), neither all Jews indiscriminately at that time, nor Jews today, can be charged with the crime committed during his passion. It is true that the church is the new people of God, yet the Jews should not be spoken of as rejected or accursed as if this followed from the holy scripture. Consequently, all must take care, lest in catechizing or in preaching the word of God, they teach anything which is not in accord with the truth of the Gospel message or the spirit of Christ.

During a Jubilee Day of Pardon (March 12, 2000), Pope John Paul II prayed: "God of our fathers, who chose Abraham and his descendants to bring your name to the nations. We are deeply saddened by the behavior of those who in the course of history have caused these children of yours to suffer, and asking your forgiveness, we wish to commit ourselves to genuine brotherhood with the people of the covenant."

PART THREE

THE WORLD
STARTS OVER

. | CHAPTER 7 | .

THE RISING OF JESUS FROM THE DEAD

WE COULD SAY THE WORLD STARTED OVER WHEN THE SON OF GOD WAS MADE flesh in the womb of the Virgin Mary. From that moment on, history was fundamentally changed. Or we could say the world started anew with the birth of Christ, when poor Jewish shepherds and inquiring Gentile astrologers represented the whole world before his crib.

But it is nearest the truth to say that the world started over with the death and resurrection of Jesus, for in that event God's saving plan was perfectly fulfilled (see *Catechism*, #647). In the center of time and eternity, radiating power to the universe, is the risen Jesus, glorious in new and mysterious human life, divinity shining through humanity, inviting and empowering all the children of Adam to be joined to him in his victory and glory.

We must say "death-resurrection" for it is both these events or, perhaps better, this combined event that is crucial in all history. "Was it not necessary that the Messiah should suffer these things and enter into his glory?" (Luke 24:26). With typical Jewish parallelism Paul says, Jesus was "handed over to death for our transgressions and was raised for our justification" (Romans 4:25).

As we shall see through the rest of this book, this dying-rising of Jesus is the essence of Christian life. With him and in him we die every day and, in so doing, we rise every day.

WHAT HAPPENED? The Gospel accounts of the Resurrection leave us with a feeling of mystery. Jesus is seen only by those who believe in him. He takes the initiative and comes to them, but obviously he must give them the power to recognize—to know again—him whom they had seen twisted in death on the cross. Magdalene, for instance, and the Emmaus disciples look at him without knowing who he is—until he opens the eyes of their faith.

We recall again that the Gospels are a family book—the record of the church's experiences of faith and love centered in Jesus. Therefore we cannot use the New Testament to prove to atheists that Jesus really rose from the dead, that he is truly God, or anything else. But even an atheist would admit that Easter morning got off to a bad start as far as the faith of the church was concerned. If there was a conspiracy to "make up" the story of the Resurrection, it was very unconvincingly done.

Mark says that the women who found the tomb empty fled away "seized with trembling and bewilderment. They said nothing to anyone, for they were afraid" (Mark 16:8b). The only possibility Magdalene could think of was that the body of Jesus had been taken from the tomb (see John 20:2). Peter looked into the tomb, saw the wrappings that had clothed Jesus' body, and "went home amazed at what had happened" (Luke 24:12b). To the apostles "their [the women's] story seemed like nonsense and they did not believe them" (Luke 24:11).

Jesus therefore had to *give* them vision, and the Gospel writers follow a pattern in narrating these "recognition" scenes: first, bewilderment on the part of people who are not expecting anything; then, the initiative of Jesus, enabling them to be aware of him; finally, their expression of faith.

So, for instance, Mary is weeping at the empty tomb. She sees Jesus and thinks he is the gardener. She suspects he is the one who may have taken the body (note: no concept of resurrection). Then Jesus says, "Mary!" and she "sees" who he is. She recognizes, knows again, the one who was Teacher. It is the same Jesus, now in new form (see John 20:11–18).

Another example of this is Luke's report of the experience of the two disciples on the road to Emmaus. They see Jesus as a fellow traveler and discuss with him, as with a stranger, the events of recent days. They stop to eat and invite him to join them. Then, "he took bread, said the blessing, broke it, and gave it to them. With that their eyes were opened and they recognized him, but he vanished from their sight" (Luke 24:30b–31).

A third recognition scene focuses on the doubting Thomas. He finally becomes a believer when Jesus gives him unmistakable proof of his reality —and praises the millions of Christians who would believe without seeing (see John 20:24–29).

Besides the recognition appearances, the Gospel writers also record "mission" appearances in which Jesus sends his disciples into the world to be the witnesses of his death-resurrection to all people (see *Catechism*, #571, 737). For example, Matthew's Gospel ends with these words:

> All power in heaven and on earth has been given to me. Go, there-
> fore, and make disciples of all nations, baptizing them in the name of
> the Father, and of the Son, and of the holy Spirit, teaching them to
> observe all that I have commanded you. And behold, I am with you
> always, until the end of the age. (Matthew 28:18b–20)

In John's Gospel Jesus commissions the apostles in his first appearance on Easter evening: "As the Father has sent me, so I send you." And when he had said this, he breathed on them and said to them, "Receive the holy Spirit. Whose sins you forgive are forgiven them, and whose sins you retain are retained." (John 20:21b–23)

Notice that John has Jesus breathing the Holy Spirit on the apostles in his first appearance, emphasizing the fact that in the new timeless life of Jesus everything happens at once, as it were. For John, the death of Jesus means his resurrection, which is his glorification at the right hand of the Father (that is, his ascension, which is the pouring out of his Spirit (Pentecost).

Luke's second volume (Acts), on the other hand, spreads Jesus' appearances over the forty days before his Ascension. During this time Luke records the "privileged" appearances of Jesus. There is a difference for Luke between these days and all following time. Even the appearance of Jesus to Paul (recorded four times!) Luke would put in a different category. He describes Jesus' pouring out his Spirit in the thrilling experience of Pentecost. It is now the age of faith. The special appearances of Jesus are over.

The evangelists' approaches to the Resurrection are different, but the meaning is the same. Something unbelievable has happened. The Jesus who was dead is alive in a new, mysterious life that can be seen only by faith. Despite human doubt and despair, Jesus fills the consciousness of his friends. Their reaction may be summed up in two sentences from the New Testament: The first is the reaction of the two on the road to Emmaus who say, "Were not our hearts burning [within us] while he spoke to us on the way and opened the scriptures to us?" (Luke 24:32b). The second is the comment of bystanders at the conduct of the newly bold apostles after Pentecost: "They have had too much new wine" (Acts 2:13b).

WHAT KIND OF BODY DOES JESUS HAVE? The impossibility of recognizing Jesus without faith indicates that his risen body has different qualities than it had before his death (see *Catechism,* #645–646). Obviously the resurrection of Jesus does not imply the resuscitation of a six-foot, one hundred ninety-pound man. He did not "come back" like Lazarus. Jesus' risen body is a real body—material, yet now "spiritual."

What can this mean? Paul may help us, as he speaks of the kind of bodies we will have:

> With what kind of body will they [the dead] come back?
>
> You fool! What you sow is not brought to life unless it dies. And what you sow is not the body that is to be but a bare kernel of wheat, perhaps, or of some other kind; but God gives it a body as he chooses, and to each of the seeds its own body....
>
> So also is the resurrection of the dead. It is sown corruptible; it is raised incorruptible. It is sown dishonorable; it is raised glorious. It is sown weak; it is raised powerful. It is sown a natural body; it is raised a spiritual body. (1 Corinthians 15:35b–38, 42–44a)

Jesus no longer belongs to our space and time. There is now no hourglass in his life, and his power flows to the universe. He is simply "available" to anyone and everyone, anyplace and anytime. He appears in special ways sacramentally, as we shall see.

THE INNER MEANING OF THE RESURRECTION. Lest we miss the forest for the trees, we must ask ourselves what the resurrection of Jesus means for us today.

Starting at the end, we know that it means our bodies will rise as he did, and we will share his victory and glory and joy forever. But in a once-and-for-all sense, it means that his Father, as eternally planned, responds in this faithful way to the perfect childlike trust and obedience of Jesus. He raises him up, and with him all who wish to join him. Jesus rose by his own power, and he was *raised* by the Father (see John 10:18; Romans 6:4). It is all one—the merciful plan the Father, Son and Spirit formed from eternity.

Jesus is God's "last Word." His death-resurrection-glorification-outpouring of Spirit are "all" that even the infinitely merciful God can do (see *Catechism*, #516–519). Now there is nothing left to do—whether the world lasts a day or a million years—but to draw all who wish into the saving, enlivening life of Jesus. What Jesus is, all can be: free from death, sin, suffering, evil.

The union of God and human beings is sealed now, forever. It can never be broken because Jesus, the fully human one, has made the exodus through the waters of death to new life, which he shares with all who desire it. The dead heritage of sin is wiped out. God's life replaces death in the hearts of all who turn to Jesus. The Kingdom has indeed come: It is Jesus and all his followers, living and deceased, allowing themselves to be fully possessed by the love of the Father.

The Christian life is the transformation of human beings by the power of Jesus' death and resurrection. We have seen this amazing change in those who at first stubbornly refused to believe. They bowed down and said, "My Lord and my God!" They recognized Jesus as the "Lord," one with Yahweh of creation.

So the death-resurrection of Jesus is indeed the world starting over. Jesus is the new Adam (see *Catechism*, #411), lifted up out of the old Adam, which was human life imprisoned in sin and death. The first Adam—and all of us—forfeited our gifts. The new Adam, truly human in the person of the Son, made the perfect at-onement (atonement). He fulfilled the purpose of all sacrifice: union with God.

The rest of this book—the church, the sacraments, the Christian life— is simply about living out the death and resurrection of Jesus. We cannot have a once-and-for-all dying and rising and get it over with. We must (like the sun in biblical thought) get up every morning and do it all over again. Our baptismal dying and rising must be confirmed many times over.

The power of Jesus is with us always. It gives us the power to die—perhaps a hundred times a day—to selfishness and untruth and to rise—even though the taste of it may not be there—to a greater union with the risen Jesus.

REFLECTION/DISCUSSION STARTERS

1) Why do we speak of Jesus' "death-resurrection" as "a combined event"? In what way is Jesus' death-resurrection the world starting over? Have you ever known a starting over in your life? Does your experience of Jesus' death-resurrection provide a starting over for you?

2) What does Jesus' Resurrection say about the relationship between God and human beings?

3) Reflect on the ways you experience dying and rising as a part of your daily life.

4) After the Resurrection, Jesus had to give the disciples the power to recognize him, to know him again. Does this process of recognizing Jesus go on today? Has this happened in your own life?

SCRIPTURE READINGS

The Resurrection accounts: Matthew 28; Mark 16; Luke 24; John 20—21; 1 Corinthians 15:35–38, 42–44.

SUPPLEMENTARY MATERIAL

Catholic Updates: "The Resurrection: How We Know It's True," by William H. Shannon; "St. Mary Magdalene: Redeeming Her Gospel Reputation," by Carol Ann Morrow; "We Believe in the Resurrection," by Thomas Groome; "Who Is Jesus?" by Leonard Foley, O.F.M.

Scripture From Scratch: "Acts of the Apostles: Luke's Dramatic Sequel," by Elizabeth McNamer; "Resurrection Stories: Catching the Light of God's Love," by Hilarion Kistner, O.F.M.

Book: Following Jesus: A Disciple's Guide to Luke and Acts, revised and updated by William Kurz, S.J.

. | CHAPTER 8 | .

JESUS, THE SON OF GOD:
THIS MAN

WHEN WE SPEAK OF THE "MYSTERY" OF JESUS IN SAINT PAUL'S SENSE, WE ARE thinking of him as a sacrament—a "sign" that reveals as well as hides. He is the self-revealing of God through the sign of a human body.

He is a mystery in another way also, in that there is something beyond understanding in his makeup.

He is truly God. He is truly human. He is one person (see *Catechism*, #464).

Jesus is not two persons cooperating in harmony. He is not God with a human facade, and he is not merely a human being with a very close relationship with God.

As a true human being, Jesus is psychologically a "person" in the way we understand that word today. But the doctrine of the church sees only one Person in Jesus, that of the Son of God. After centuries of wrestling with the problem, the church officially adopted the following way of talking about Jesus in the Council of Chalcedon (451 C.E.):

> We unanimously teach that the Son, our Lord Jesus Christ, is one and the same, the same perfect in divinity, the same perfect in humanity, true God and true man, consisting of a rational soul and body, consubstantial with the Father in divinity and consubstantial with us in humanity...in two natures unconfused, unchangeable, undivided and inseparable. The difference of natures will never be abolished by their being united, but rather the properties of each remain unimpaired, both coming together in one person and substance, not parted or divided among two persons, but in one and the same only begotten Son, the Divine Word, the Lord Jesus Christ.

We have to be a little philosophical for a moment.

1) *Two Natures in Christ.* "Nature" in this sense is the basic constitution of anyone or anything. When we ask, "What is that?" we are asking about its nature. "What is a pencil?" means "What makes a pencil a pencil and not something else?" "What is a human being?" means "What makes a certain class of being human?" We answer that to be human is to have a spiritual-physical way of being. We are neither angels nor animals but "embodied spirits" or "spiritualized bodies." When we say, "What makes Jesus Jesus?" we answer that he is a being who has the nature of being human and the nature of being divine, but is only one Person. He is unique.

2) *One Person in Christ.* When we say, "Who is that?" we are no longer asking what makes something to be what it is. Rather, we are now in the area of persons. We want to know the particular identity—the name—of some particular being. We can imagine ourselves saying, as we barely discern something lying in a field, "What is that?" But when we come closer and find that "it" is an unconscious human being, we say, "I wonder who this is?" We look for a name, an identity.

Now here is the mystery of Jesus. Every individual human nature we know of is a person. Joe Smith is a person, with a human nature. But Jesus is not two people more or less intimately tied together, God and human; he is one Person with a divine nature, who has assumed a human nature into his one Person. There is only one who in Jesus, but two *whats.* What he does is truly divine; it is also entirely human.

There is no "mixing" of natures, however. He is the wisdom and power of God, the eternal and infinite love of God; and he is this man with fully human emotions, making human decisions the way all his brothers and sisters make them, suffering the pains of human limitation and the joys of a full human life. How do we put these two things together? We must simply say we don't know. We let the truths exist side by side, and we believe the mystery.

JESUS, TRUE MAN. In the course of history just about every possible heresy has been advanced by somebody. Regarding Jesus, a heresy called *Docetism* (from the word for "seem") held that Christ only seemed human (see *Catechism*, #465).

Sometimes, in our determination to preserve the divinity of Jesus, we verge toward Docetism. We downplay Jesus' humanity, as if it were somehow absorbed into his divinity. But it is just as incorrect to deny Jesus' full humanity as it is to deny his divinity.

As a four-year-old boy, Jesus did not have all future scientific and theological knowledge in his head. Like all human beings, he had to develop his body, his mind, his emotions, his character. Saint Luke tells us, "Jesus advanced [in] wisdom and age and favor before God and man" (2:52).

If Jesus were not truly man, the Bible could not say: "For we do not have a high priest who is unable to sympathize with our weaknesses, but one who has similarly been tested in every way, yet without sin" (Hebrews 4:15).

We can identify with Jesus because he is one of us. He knew what it was to be hungry and thirsty, to be worn out physically with work or travel, to suffer the pain of heat or cold, of a splinter in his finger or the bite of an insect. The Gospels show him with all the human emotions: He enjoyed the company of friends, the innocence of children and the support of his followers. He could be fully angry, troubled, frustrated. He could be so humanly afraid and terrorized that "his sweat became like drops of blood" (Luke 22:44b).

He had a human mind unspoiled by narrowness or selfishness, one that was simply open to all reality, especially to his Father's self-giving. He had a free human will to decide and strive and give. He loved as no one has ever loved, yet as everyone was made to love.

What was different about Jesus, of course, was that he had no sin, nor any of the heritage or "momentum" of sin that we have. He was not only a true human but also a pure human. His humanity was not cramped or bent, but had only the normal limitations of space and time and finiteness.

Therefore he could enjoy the song of a bird or the brilliance of a sunset or the face of a human being more deeply than we who are distracted by our own selves. The truth was more thrilling to him. To love was more intense and wholehearted.

JESUS' HUMAN KNOWLEDGE. There are people who are shocked by some theologians' treatment of Jesus' human knowledge. They hold that since Jesus was God he knew everything.

The answer does not seem to be quite that simple. If Jesus was truly a human being, his mind had to work like a human mind. It had to grow from ignorance to knowledge, from known to unknown, from depth to greater depth of understanding. Because he was human he had to grow and learn from experience—just as we do (see *Catechism*, #472).

Jesus was one person, but his divine consciousness was not his human consciousness. His divinity and humanity were not mixed together, like wine and water.

But why didn't his divine knowledge simply flood his human mind with all possible information? We must answer that he would not then have been truly human. To be human is to face reality, seek truth, choose what is good. This means looking for the facts, considering alternatives, weighing consequences and then making decisions. That is how a human being takes responsibility for his or her life.

Jesus came among us to be fully human in every way except sin. He could not be characterized as human if as a four-year-old boy he was already aware of the intricacies of nuclear fission and the potency of penicillin.

The noted biblical scholar Father Raymond Brown, treating the knowledge of Jesus in an excellent book, *Jesus, God and Man*, spoke to the common objection raised to the view that Jesus had limited, human knowledge:

> But when all is said and done, the great objection that will be hurled again against any exegete (or theologian) who finds evidence that Jesus' knowledge was limited is the objection that in Jesus Christ there is only one person, a divine person. And so, even though the divine person acted through a completely human nature, any theory that Jesus had limited knowledge seems to imply a limitation of the divine person. Perhaps the best answer to this objection is to call upon Cyril of Alexandria, that Doctor of the church to whom, more than to any other, we are indebted for the great truth of the oneness of the person of Christ. It was that ultra-orthodox archfoe of Nestorianism (two

persons or powers in Christ) who said of Christ, "We have admitted his goodness in that for love of us he has not refused to descend to such a low position as to bear all that belongs to our nature, included in which is ignorance."

Perhaps the clearest statement of the meaning of Jesus' true humanity is found in Hebrews: "Surely he did not help angels but rather the descendants of Abraham; *therefore, he had to become like his brothers in every way,* that he might be a merciful and faithful high priest before God to expiate the sins of the people. *Because he himself was tested through what he suffered,* he is able to help those who are being tested" (2:16–18, emphases added).

Jesus was not "tempted" as we are, by an itch or impulse toward evil. Yet to give his bread away meant that he was hungry, to work hard meant that he was tired, and to be faithful to his Father meant that he would be killed. It cost Jesus something to be the trusting child of his Father.

JESUS' VOCATION. So Jesus' growth in knowledge was gradual, as well as his growth in the love of God and his understanding of his own identity and mission. By prayer and meditation on the Scriptures, by the words and example of his parents, Jesus experienced the self-revealing love of his Father—similar to the revelation given to all human beings, but also unique: He is the Anointed One, the Messiah long promised.

How and when his Father revealed this to Jesus we do not know. What we must say is that Jesus accepted his vocation with full freedom and loving obedience. It was a responsible choice. He took his life and put it at the disposal of the Father. He let himself be totally possessed by the Father's love and power: "My food is to do the will of the one who sent me and to finish his work" (John 4:34b). He is the new Adam, not denying his fully human response to the Father's call, but opening himself completely.

His relationship with the Father is tender, intimate. His word of address is *Abba*—no doubt an imitation of the earliest sounds made by a baby to its parents. It is the word little Jewish children used for their father; on adult tongues it expressed warm affection. Our associations with the English word *Daddy* may be hard to transfer to God, but that is the closest translation we can have for *Abba*. "Abba!" was Jesus' life.

The purpose of discussing the humanity of Jesus and all it means is to keep Jesus from being "way up there," far above the pains and pleasures and worries of ordinary mortals. We have the absolute conviction and unquestioning faith that Jesus is true God, the eternal Son of the Father. But it is equally true that he is a real human being, like us in *everything* but sin. "Everything" must apply to knowledge, conscience, body, emotions, memory, imagination, conversation, sleep, meals—there is no area excluded except the sinful.

It is only by keeping the human Jesus along with the divine that we can really believe that he knows from experience what our experience is. We can then join his prayer in pain or joy, in failure or success, in frustration or anger or serenity and have his empathy and sympathy—and his power to be childlike before his Father.

JESUS, TRUE GOD. Christians do not try to "prove" to anyone that Jesus is God. If Peter could not know Jesus was the Messiah unless the Father revealed it (see Matthew 16:17), the gigantic step to belief in his divinity is infinitely less possible. We believe because we have the gift of believing. And again, we must say, if that seems to the world naïve and unscientific, so much the worse for the world.

So we pray the Scriptures with joy and admiration rather than with questions and concern. And there is no better place to do this than the magnificent prologue of John's Gospel:

> In the beginning was the Word,
>   and the Word was with God,
>   and the Word was God.
> He was in the beginning with God.
> All things came to be through him,
>   and without him nothing came to be.
> What came to be through him was life,
>   and this life was the light of the human race;
>   the light shines in the darkness,
>   and the darkness has not overcome it.
>   . . .
> He was in the world,

and the world came to be through him,
but the world did not know him.

...

And the Word became flesh
and made his dwelling among us,
and we saw his glory,
the glory as of the Father's only Son.

...

No one has ever seen God. The only Son, God, who is at the Father's side, has revealed him. (John 1:1–5, 10, 14, 18)

Passages like this are like prisms of eternity. Theology will do its best to explain, but in the end these simple and infinitely profound statements are the best way to express the mystery. The crux of the mystery is that the love of God appeared in Jesus. Not just that God made the divine love known, but the love of God appeared. Jesus is the love of God, and the love of God made visible.

[It is Jesus]
who is the refulgence of [God's] glory,
    the very imprint of his being,
and who sustains all things by his mighty word. (Hebrews 1:3a)

"THE FATHER AND I ARE ONE." John's Gospel shows the church's sixty or seventy years of reflection on the mystery of Jesus and leads us to the mystery of the Trinity: Father, Son and Holy Spirit, one God. In John, Jesus' suffering humanity is not stressed as it is in Mark; his divinity shines through more clearly. He speaks as the God who has destroyed evil and saved his loved ones: "If you know me, then you will also know my Father. From now on you do know him and have seen him.... Whoever has seen me has seen the Father" (John 14:7, 9b).

Three times Jesus says, "I am in the Father, and the Father is in me. Believe me!" (see John 14:10, 11, 20).

The union of the Son and the Father is one of being—and of love. To this union of divine love Jesus brings a perfect, childlike human love: "The Father and I are one" (John 10:30).

What is the meaning and purpose behind all this? It is the final reason why God initiated his great plan of salvation. Just as there is a perfect union of the love in Father, Son and Spirit, so there is a perfect divine-human love between Jesus and his Father. *And this is the kind of love God in Jesus and the Spirit wants for us!* Jesus says, referring to his Resurrection: "On that day you will realize that I am in my Father and you are in me and I in you" (John 14:20).

We who like to think of God as stern and remote should be humbled and chastened by these overwhelming words:

> Whoever has my commandments and observes them is the one who loves me. And whoever loves me will be loved by my Father, and I will love him and reveal myself to him.... Whoever loves me will keep my word, and my Father will love him, and we will come to him and make our dwelling with him. (John 14:21, 23b)

In a later chapter we will consider the fullness of this "indwelling of God" by exploring that of the Holy Spirit, sent by Jesus to be another Paraclete (defender and consoler) for us and who will be within us (see John 14:17).

Jesus concludes his profound and touching discourse at the Last Supper with these words, addressed in prayer to his Father: "I made known to them your name and I will make it known, that the love with which you loved me may be in them and I in them" (John 17:26).

So the final purpose of Jesus' coming is not just to give us knowledge of the Father, but also to fill us with the Father's love and join us in a living union with Jesus and with the Father, through the presence of the Spirit. Jesus showed us what divinity is, and he showed us what true humanity is. He is God in a human way and human in a divine way. His human love is the embodiment of God's love for all of us to see and absorb.

REFLECTION/DISCUSSION STARTERS

1) What does it mean to say that Jesus is one Person with two natures?
2) Reflect on the humanity of Jesus. How is his humanity made evident in the Gospels?
3) Discuss how Jesus can be said to be a sacrament or sign. Consider the

author's words that Jesus is "the self-revealing of God through the sign of the human body" and "the love of God made visible." What does this mean to you?

4) Who is Jesus for you? Do you experience Jesus as God? As human? What difference does Jesus make in your life?

SUPPLEMENTARY MATERIAL

Scripture From Scratch: "From Jesus of Nazareth to Lord of All," by Eugene LaVerdiere, s.s.s.; "The Holy Spirit as Paraclete: The Gift of John's Gospel," by Raymond E. Brown, s.s.; "Jesus: The Man From Nazareth," by Elizabeth McNamer.

Book: The Passion of the Lamb: The Self-Giving Love of Jesus, by Thomas Acklin, o.s.b.

CHAPTER 9

JESUS IS LORD: A SHORT COURSE IN SAINT PAUL

ABOUT ONE-FOURTH OF THE NEW TESTAMENT IS MADE UP OF THE THIRTEEN letters of Saint Paul. They offer a powerful and unique vision of the mystery of Christ. Reading them, one senses a personality and approach quite different both from the writers of the first three Gospels and from another unique writer, Saint John.

Paul's letters usually deal with concrete situations in the early church, hence are independent of each other and not systematic. But Paul always manages to rise above the personal and the particular to thrill his readers with the outlines of the faith and to bring them to the practice of a more intense Christian life.

Intense seems a good word to describe Paul. He was a human dynamo, always a hundred percent—whether as zealous Pharisee or lover of Christ. His constant emphasis was on the intimate connection between our salvation and the passion, death and resurrection of Jesus. Through these events Jesus has become a power producing a new life in us, beginning with dying and rising in baptism and ending with our bodily resurrection to eternal glory in Christ.

One is tempted to say that no other Christian writer has influenced the church as much as this "apostle to the Gentiles." Some of what he wrote is difficult to understand—even Peter had difficulty with him. But the majority of Paul's words are full of a passionate devotion to Christ that can illuminate our reading of the Gospels and be the power of deeper faith in us.

This chapter will attempt to let Paul himself speak—but in a systematic, thirteen-point way. This is the real Saint Paul: the man on fire with love of Christ, the total convert, the fearless herald of the Good News. May we catch some of his spirit!

1) ETERNALLY, GOD HAD A "FAMILY" IN MIND, WITH JESUS AT THE CENTER.
Even before the world was made, God had already chosen us to be his through our union with Christ, so that we would be holy and without fault before him. (Ephesians 1:4, *Good News Bible*)

Those whom God had already chosen he also set apart to become like his Son, so that the Son would be the first among many brothers. (Romans 8:29, *Good News Bible*)

2) JESUS IS GOD AND MAN. PAUL SIMPLY LETS THESE TWO FACTS STAND SIDE BY SIDE:
He is the image of the invisible God,
   the firstborn of all creation.
For in him were created all things in heaven and on earth....
(Colossians 1:15–16a)

3) THE SON OF GOD BECAME MAN SO WE MIGHT SHARE THE LIFE OF GOD.
...[W]hen the fullness of time had come, God sent his Son, born of a woman...so that we might receive adoption. (Galatians 4:4a, 5b)

One of the magnificent passages in Saint Paul sums up the story of Jesus:

Have among yourselves the same attitude that is also yours in Christ Jesus,
   Who, though he was in the form of God,
   did not regard equality with God something to be grasped.
   Rather, he emptied himself,
   taking the form of a slave,
   coming in human likeness;
   and found human in appearance,
   he humbled himself,
   becoming obedient to death,
     even death on a cross.

Because of this, God greatly exalted him
and bestowed on him the name
that is above every name,
that at the name of Jesus
every knee should bend,
of those in the heaven and on earth and under the earth,
and every tongue confess that
Jesus Christ is Lord,
to the glory of God the Father. (Philippians 2:5–11)

4) JESUS' SAVING DEATH AND RESURRECTION ARE AT THE HEART OF HIS GOSPEL.
Jesus becomes the new Adam fully human and experiencing the suffering
of the first Adam. In a daring statement, Paul says God made Jesus to be
sin, so that in him we might become the holiness of God. Sin and evil and
death were able to "destroy" Jesus, but were themselves destroyed in the
event by the power of God in Jesus' perfect love (see 2 Corinthians 5:21):

... [T]hrough one person sin entered the world, and through sin,
death, and thus death came to all, inasmuch as all sinned.... (Romans
5:12b)

But, Paul continues:

... [I]f by that one person's transgression the many died, how much
more did the grace of God and the gracious gift of the one person
Jesus Christ overflow for the many....

For just as through the disobedience of one person the many were
made sinners, so through the obedience of one the many will be
made righteous. (Romans 5:15b, 19)

[He] gave himself for us to deliver us from all lawlessness and to
cleanse for himself a people as his own, eager to do what is good.
(Titus 2:14)

[He] destroyed death and brought life and immortality to light
through the gospel.... (2 Timothy 1:10b)

...God was reconciling the world to himself in Christ.... (2
Corinthians 5:19a)

5) Jesus joins his brothers and sisters to himself in one body, the church.

For through faith you are all children of God in Christ Jesus. For all of you who were baptized into Christ have clothed yourselves with Christ. There is neither Jew nor Greek, there is neither slave nor free person, there is not male and female; for you are all one in Christ Jesus. (Galatians 3:26–28)

He is the head of the body, the church.

He is the beginning, the firstborn from the dead. (Colossians 1:18a–b)

By the gift of God's grace, we are united to Jesus in his death and in his new life. This is the challenge of our life, and its hope.

Or are you unaware that we who were baptized into Christ Jesus were baptized into his death? We were indeed buried with him through baptism into death, so that, just as Christ was raised from the dead by the glory of the Father, we too might live in newness of life.

For if we have grown into union with him through a death like his, we shall also be united with him in the resurrection. We know that our old self was crucified with him, so that our sinful body might be done away with, that we might no longer be in slavery to sin. (Romans 6:3–6)

6) As Jesus was raised up, so are we, and so shall we be.

This saying is trustworthy:

If we have died with him
   we shall also live with him;
if we persevere
   we shall also reign with him.
But if we deny him
   he will deny us.
If we are unfaithful
   he remains faithful,
     for he cannot deny himself. (2 Timothy 2:11–13)

He will change our lowly body to conform with his glorified body.... (Philippians 3:21a)

But if Christ is preached as raised from the dead, how can some among you say there is no resurrection of the dead? …For if the dead are not raised, neither has Christ been raised, and if Christ has not been raised, your faith is vain; you are still in your sins. Then those who have fallen asleep in Christ have perished. If for this life only we have hoped in Christ, we are the most pitiable people of all.

But now Christ has been raised from the dead, the firstfruits of those who have fallen asleep. (1 Corinthians 15:12, 16–20)

7) THE BODY OF CHRIST IS THE CHURCH. It is one living organism filled with the Spirit of Jesus. That essential unity of life and love must be maintained at all costs. But within that unity there is a wonderful and beautiful variety.

[Strive] to preserve the unity of the spirit through the bond of peace: one body and one Spirit, as you were also called to the one hope of your call; one Lord, one faith, one baptism; one God and Father of all, who is over all and through all and in all. (Ephesians 4:3–6)

As a body is one though it has many parts, and all the parts of the body, though many, are one body, so also Christ. For in one Spirit we were all baptized into one body, whether Jews or Greeks, slaves or free persons, and we were all given to drink of one Spirit.

Now the body is not a single part, but many. If a foot should say, "Because I am not a hand I do not belong to the body," it does not for this reason belong any less to the body. Or if an ear should say, "Because I am not an eye I do not belong to the body," it does not for this reason belong any less to the body. If the whole body were an eye, where would the hearing be? If the whole body were hearing, where would the sense of smell be? But as it is, God placed the parts, each one of them, in the body as he intended. If they were all one part, where would the body be? But as it is, there are many parts, yet one body. The eye cannot say to the hand, "I do not need you," nor again the head to the feet, "I do not need you." …If [one] part suffers, all the parts suffer with it; if one part is honored, all the parts share its joy. (1 Corinthians 12:12–21, 26)

The great sin in the Body of Christ is to destroy its unity of faith and love by factions, false teaching, false standards:

Do you not know that you are the temple of God, and that the Spirit of God dwells in you? If anyone destroys God's temple, God will destroy that person; for the temple of God, which you are, is holy. (1 Corinthians 3:16–17)

8) THE HOLY SPIRIT IS THE LIFE OF THE CHURCH. This enlivening "soul" joins all together in oneness of love and faith. The Spirit is power and guidance. Because the Spirit lives in us, we have unshakable hope.

For those who are led by the Spirit of God are children of God. For you did not receive a spirit of slavery to fall back into fear, but you received a spirit of adoption, through which we cry, Abba, "Father!" The Spirit itself bears witness with our spirit that we are children of God, and if children, then heirs, heirs of God and joint heirs with Christ, if only we suffer with him so that we may also be glorified with him. (Romans 8:14–17)

[A]nd hope does not disappoint, because the love of God has been poured out into our hearts through the holy Spirit that has been given to us. (Romans 5:5)

... [You] were sealed with the promised holy Spirit, which is the first installment of our inheritance toward redemption as God's possession.... (Ephesians 1:13b–14a)

...But the one...who anointed us is God; who has also put his seal upon us and given the Spirit in our hearts as a first installment. (2 Corinthians 1:21a, c, 22)

In the same way, the Spirit too comes to the aid of our weakness; for we do not know how to pray as we ought, but the Spirit itself intercedes with inexpressible groanings. And the one who searches hearts knows what is the intention of the Spirit, because it intercedes for the holy ones according to God's will. (Romans 8:26–27)

As proof that you are children, God sent the spirit of his Son into our hearts, crying out, "Abba, Father!" (Galatians 4:6)

9) NO ONE CAN "EARN" SALVATION. It is first the gift of God. Once enlivened by God's life, we are able to cooperate with God's action in us. But, as the

Christian community prays in the *Sacramentary*, "Even our desire to please you is itself your gift." (See *Catechism*, #2007–2008.) This is one of the great emphases of Paul's teaching. Your faith rests, he says, "not on human wisdom but on the power of God" (1 Corinthians 2:5b).

Not that of ourselves we are qualified to take credit for anything as coming from us; rather, our qualification comes from God.... (2 Corinthians 3:5)

He saved us and called us to a holy life, not according to our works but according to his own design and the grace bestowed on us in Christ Jesus before time began, but now made manifest through the appearance of our savior Christ Jesus.... (2 Timothy 1:9–10a)

But God, who is rich in mercy, because of the great love he had for us, even when we were dead in our transgressions, brought us to life with Christ (by grace you have been saved), raised us up with him, and seated us with him in the heavens in Christ Jesus.... (Ephesians 2:4–6)

For by grace you have been saved through faith, and this is not from you; it is the gift of God; it is not from works, so no one may boast. For we are his handiwork, created in Christ Jesus.... (Ephesians 2:8–10a)

10) WE ARE A NEW CREATION. The world starts over in Jesus. Though we live in the midst of a sinful world and evil seems to dominate life, we are safe in eternal life. We must still experience the dying and rising of Jesus, but the victory has been won. Suffering, death, sin have no power to harm us against our will.

So whoever is in Christ is a new creation: the old things have passed away; behold, new things have come. And all this is from God, who has reconciled us to himself through Christ.... (2 Corinthians 5:17–18a)

...[Y]ou have taken off the old self with its practices and have put on the new self, which is being renewed, for knowledge, in the image of its creator. Here there is not Greek and Jew, circumcision and uncircumcision, barbarian, Scythian, slave, free; but Christ is all and in all. (Colossians 3:9b–11)

This is not just a "spiritual" re-creation. The created world itself, which we are learning to value and ceasing to abuse, is also in the redeeming love of God.

For creation awaits with eager expectation the revelation of the children of God; for creation was made subject to futility, not of its own accord but because of the one who subjected it, in hope that creation itself would be set free from slavery to corruption and share in the glorious freedom of the children of God. We know that all creation is groaning in labor pains even until now. (Romans 8:19–22)

11) SINCE WE SHARE THE DYING OF CHRIST, OUR LIFE IN HIM INVOLVES SUFFERING. Jesus suffered because evil people felt the silent reproach of his pure life. While never thinking of unfaithfulness, he nevertheless had to pay the price for being faithful. We suffer, in Christ, the pain of dying to all that is not the love of God: sin, selfishness, putting anyone or anything before the love of God. God's creation is good; but the "world" is the spirit of malice and purposelessness, says Vatican II. We are, Paul says,

always carrying about in the body the dying of Jesus, so that the life of Jesus may also be manifested in our body. For we who live are constantly being given up to death for the sake of Jesus, so that the life of Jesus may be manifested in our mortal flesh. (2 Corinthians 4:10–11)

But may I never boast except in the cross of our Lord Jesus Christ, through which the world has been crucified to me, and I to the world. For neither does circumcision mean anything, nor does uncircumcision, but only a new creation. (Galatians 6:14–15)

Now I rejoice in my sufferings for your sake, and in my flesh I am filling up what is lacking in the afflictions of Christ on behalf of his body, the church.... (Colossians 1:24)

I have been crucified with Christ; yet I live, no longer I, but Christ lives in me; insofar as I now live in the flesh, I live by faith in the Son of God who has loved me and given himself up for me. (Galatians 2:19b–20)

12) What, then, is the Christian life? It is love. As we have seen, God's love has been poured out in our hearts by the Holy Spirit. We are freely possessed by the presence of God. We are one with God in the love of Jesus. On this firm basis, we are able to love God as God loves us—and to show God's kind of loving to our neighbor (see *Catechism*, #826). Sin is a refusal to love, and a spoiling of the beautiful creation God has made.

> So whether you eat or drink, or whatever you do, do everything for the glory of God. Avoid giving offense, whether to Jews or Greeks or the church of God, just as I try to please everyone in every way, not seeking my own benefit but that of the many, that they may be saved. Be imitators of me, as I am of Christ. (1 Corinthians 10:31—11:1)

> Owe nothing to anyone, except to love one another; for the one who loves another has fulfilled the law. The commandments, "You shall not commit adultery; you shall not kill; you shall not steal; you shall not covet," and whatever other commandment there may be, are summed up in this saying, [namely], "You shall love your neighbor as yourself." Love does no evil to the neighbor; hence, love is the fulfillment of the law. (Romans 13:8–10)

> And do not grieve the holy Spirit of God, with which you were sealed for the day of redemption. All bitterness, fury, anger, shouting, and reviling must be removed from you, along with all malice. [And] be kind to one another, compassionate, forgiving one another as God has forgiven you in Christ.
>
> So be imitators of God as beloved children, and live in love, as Christ loved us and handed himself over as a sacrificial offering to God for a fragrant aroma. (Ephesians 4:30—5:1–2)

> Strive eagerly for the greatest spiritual gifts.
>
> But I shall show you a still more excellent way.
>
> If I speak in human and angelic tongues but do not have love, I am a resounding gong or a clashing cymbal. And if I have the gift of prophecy and comprehend all mysteries and all knowledge; if I have all faith so as to move mountains, but do not have love, I am nothing.

If I give everything I own, and if I hand my body over so that I may boast but do not have love, I gain nothing.

Love is patient, love is kind. It is not jealous, [love] is not pompous, it is not inflated, it is not rude, it does not seek its own interests, it is not quick-tempered, it does not brood over injury, it does not rejoice over wrongdoing but rejoices with the truth. It bears all things, hopes all things, endures all things.

Love never fails. (1 Corinthians 12:31—13:8a)

So faith, hope, love remain, these three; but the greatest of these is love. (1 Corinthians 13:13)

13) THE FINAL PURPOSE OF LIFE IS THE GLORY OF GOD. Happiness is a by-product. We are made to love, and all love is ultimately love of God. We do not underestimate the value of human beings: They are infinitely precious to God. But our worth is a sharing in the infinite beauty of God, and we find our final satisfaction—what we were made for—in turning from ourselves to give God "glory": to praise God, to honor God. Turning from ourselves, we find ourselves, and our eternal happiness.

Oh, the depths of the riches and wisdom and knowledge of God! How inscrutable are his judgments and how unsearchable his ways!

"For who has known the mind of the Lord
or who has been his counselor?
Or who has given him anything
that he may be repaid?"
For from him and through him and for him are all things.
To him be glory forever. Amen. (Romans 11:33–36)

To the king of ages, incorruptible, invisible, the only God, be honor and glory forever and ever. Amen. (1 Timothy 1:17)

No wonder that between June 29, 2008 and June 29, 2009, Catholics and other Christians observed a special year to mark the presumed two thousandth birthday of Paul. He is indeed the "Apostle to the Gentiles"!

REFLECTION/DISCUSSION STARTERS

1) Reflect on the different messages of Paul. Which seem particularly meaningful to you? Why?

2) What does Paul's declaration that Jesus Christ is Lord (Philippians 2:11) mean to you? Do you experience Jesus as Lord?

SCRIPTURE READINGS

The chapter includes many passages from Paul's letters. In addition, you may wish to read about Paul's life in Acts: 9; 12:25—13:14; 15:36–41; 16—28.

SUPPLEMENTARY MATERIAL

Catholic Updates: "Acts of the Apostles," by Ronald Witherup, s.s.; "Introducing St. Paul: His Life and Mission," by Ronald Witherup, s.s.

Scripture From Scratch: "The Letter to the Ephesians," by Ronald Witherup, s.s.; "Paul: Letters From a Traveling Theologian," by Elizabeth McNamer; "Paul's Letter to the Romans," by Raymond Collins; "Paul's First Letter to the Corinthians," by Mary Ann Getty; "Paul's Second Letter to the Corinthians," by Jerome Murphy-O'Connor, o.p.

Books: Live Letters: Reflections on the Second Readings of the Sunday Lectionary, by Archbishop Daniel E. Pilarczyk; *St. Paul, Called to Conversion: A Seven-day Retreat,* by Ronald Witherup, s.s.

CD: Great Themes of Paul: Life as Participation, by Richard Rohr, o.f.m., eleven discs, with study guide

DVD: Paul, Apostle to the Church Today, by Stephen Doyle, o.f.m., two discs

. | CHAPTER 10 | .

THE SPIRIT GIVEN THROUGH JESUS

LUKE WROTE A TWO-VOLUME WORK, AND IT IS PERHAPS UNFORTUNATE THAT THE pair became separated in the New Testament. His Gospel and the Acts of the Apostles were his presentation of the one full redeeming act of God. (I say "unfortunate" because the division may give the impression that Jesus goes back to heaven and rests in pleasant communion with the Father, while the Holy Spirit now goes to work for the first time.)

The unity of God demands this: The one God never stops offering every single human being life, love, healing and forgiveness, twenty-four hours a day, from the time God created the first people from the dust of the earth until the last persons are transformed from dust to eternal risen life. Even then, God's saving love does not stop. It supports the saved community forever.

Since we are human beings who can move only from moment to moment and space to space, God's saving action becomes concrete in certain historical events—primarily the earthly living, dying and victorious rising of Jesus. The full power of God's holiness, or Spirit, is unleashed— invisibly and visibly—by Jesus' death and resurrection. It is not as though God were somehow handcuffed until the moment of the Resurrection. Otherwise the mere accident of being born, say in 1980 B.C.E., would have excluded a person from salvation.

Like the atmosphere, God's love has surrounded every human being at every moment of time. But human beings did indeed handcuff God. They refused to "let him in." The doctrine of original sin means that the human race itself turned away from God, cutting itself off as a race from the

105

source of life, like a branch cutting itself off from the tree. The Genesis story of our first parents' fall speaks figuratively of an awful truth: Our earliest ancestors refused God's offer of life and love (see *Catechism*, #390).

So God "had" to resort to a plan that would bring about, in human time, the whole world's reconciliation.* This happened in Jesus' life, death and resurrection. Because of this visible, public, divine-human action, God's Spirit is now able to rush freely through the world.

An individual man or woman can still handcuff God, but every individual man and woman can, with absolute certainty, receive God's Spirit in Jesus. (The crucial point here is that, since Jesus is no longer visible, he forms a visible body of followers to be the sacrament of the outpouring of his Spirit. We will talk more about this Body in later chapters.)

THE SPIRIT IN THE GOSPELS. Acts has been called "The Gospel of the Holy Spirit," but the four regular Gospels also have a surprising number of references to the Spirit.

John the Baptist is filled with the Spirit in his mother's womb. So are his parents, Elizabeth and Zachary, filled with the Spirit. Mary is told that the Holy Spirit will overshadow her and, later, "she was found with child through the holy Spirit" (Matthew 1:18c).

Preparing for Jesus' coming, John promises that Jesus will baptize "with the holy Spirit and fire" (Matthew 3:11c). When Jesus was baptized he saw "the Spirit of God descending like a dove [and] coming upon him" (Matthew 3:16c). Jesus is then "driven" into the desert by the Spirit and returns after forty days "in the power of the Spirit" (Luke 4:14b).

---

* The Franciscan theologian Blessed John Duns Scotus (1266–1308) and his followers hold that the Incarnation was willed by God from all eternity independently of any foreknowledge of Adam's fall, simply as a manifestation of God's infinite love. In the opinion of Scotus, the Son would not necessarily have come as one who was to suffer and redeem. The fact that Christ "had" to come as Redeemer was secondary in the mind of God. Scotus could not admit that the greatest good, the Incarnation, was occasioned by an inferior good, the redemption of humankind. In other words, the primary purpose of the Incarnation was to show God's love for all human beings. (See *New Catholic Encyclopedia*, Vol. 4, pages 1104–1105).

Jesus was filled with joy by the Holy Spirit. It was by the power of the Spirit, he said, that he cast out devils.

Again, at the Last Supper, Jesus continues to reveal the Spirit:

And I will ask the Father, and he will give you another Advocate to be with you always.... (John 14:16)

In court, an advocate or paraclete is my counsel or lawyer. An advocate is a helper, a comforter, defender, consoler. Jesus himself is a "paraclete" for us, but he promises to send another: "the Spirit of truth" who can be recognized because "it remains with you, and will be you" (John 14:17b).

The Spirit will instruct Jesus' followers in everything and remind them of all that he has told them.

But there is a condition. Jesus must "go":

For if I do not go, the Advocate will not come to you. But if I go, I will send him to you. (John 16:7b)

Jesus must go all the way through death to resurrection, and then the floodgates are opened. Jesus will no longer be visible. The Paraclete is the presence of this apparently absent Jesus.

Finally the risen, glorious Jesus breathes upon his disciples, like God breathing life into the first human, and says, "Receive the holy Spirit" (John 20:22b). This is not merely the life-force given to every human being at conception; this is the breathing into us of God's life. The apostles, and after them all who will, are re-created as new beings, children of God.

PENTECOST. As we have seen, John has Jesus giving the Spirit on the first Easter. But Luke sets it apart as a separate event, fifty days after Easter, in the explosion of Pentecost (see *Catechism*, #1076). A miraculous transformation took place as the little church, gathered in one place, experienced the release of God's Holy Spirit through the power of the Resurrection:

And suddenly there came from the sky a noise like a strong driving wind, and it filled the entire house in which they were. Then there appeared to them tongues as of fire, which parted and came to rest on each one of them. And they were all filled with the Holy Spirit and began to speak in different tongues, as the Spirit enabled them to proclaim. (Acts 2:2–4)

When the crowd is amazed that each of the hearers, speakers of many languages, could understand the apostles, Peter tells them that this is the fulfillment of what Joel the prophet had promised:

"It will come to pass in the last days," God says,
  "that I will pour out a portion of my spirit upon all flesh.
Your sons and your daughters shall prophesy,
   your young men shall see visions,
   your old men shall dream dreams.
… [E]veryone shall be saved who calls on
   the name of the Lord."
(Acts 2:17, 21b)

The fire of Pentecost is the fire of Sinai. God has completed the final and the greatest covenant with his people. Now the Spirit of Jesus, the Spirit of the Father, the Spirit of Love, is the spirit and life—we might say, the "soul"—of the Body called church, the followers of Jesus. The Spirit keeps the church alive and keeps individual Christians alive. In the words of Saint Irenaeus, "Where the church is, there also is the Spirit of God; and where the Spirit of God is, there is the church."

"THE SPIRIT OF GOD DWELLS IN YOU." What does this "giving of the Spirit" mean to us living today? Is it a magnificent spectacle that subsided like fireworks in the sky? A gift reserved for the apostles and the early church? Or even something only for "special" people?

There has been great emphasis in recent years on certain gifts of the Holy Spirit, especially speaking in tongues, prophesying, interpretation. The charismatic movement was for a time almost identified with these things.

Now, no one tells God what to do. If the Spirit wishes to give these particular gifts to some of the faithful, the rest of us should be open to the good involved in them. These special gifts are not given for the sake of the recipients alone, but "to build up the body of Christ" (see Ephesians 4:12). Some special gifts are obviously needed for the continuance of the church: those given to apostles, evangelists, pastors and teachers. In a moving passage (1 Corinthians 12:1–11), Paul reminds us that there are many different gifts, but only one Spirit. All of us must use our unique gifts as best we can—and be happy for those who have different gifts (see *Catechism*, #799–800).

But, as Paul says, we should "Strive eagerly for the greatest spiritual gifts" (1 Corinthians 12:31), which are open to all, and not overvalue the lesser gifts. The greatest gift is love, and he extols its excellence in 1 Corinthians 13.

We remember, then, that the primary gift of the Holy Spirit is to make each one of us *holy*. We do not achieve but rather receive holiness, and it is nothing to be embarrassed or falsely humble about. Holiness is the gift of God's Spirit, who possesses us, silently and gently, at the slightest provocation.

First of all, our fundamental faith—not just the intellectual believing, but our personal self-giving and opening to God—is the Spirit's gift:

"And no one can say, 'Jesus is Lord,' except by the holy Spirit" (1 Corinthians 12:3).

Jesus described our life when he said:

"Let anyone who thirsts come to me and drink. Whoever believes in me, as scripture says:
'Rivers of living water will flow from within him.'"
He said this in reference to the Spirit that those who came to believe in him were to receive. (John 7:37b–39a)

The Spirit within us means the presence of God within us. Saint Paul says it very simply and forcefully: "…[T]he love of God has been poured out into our hearts through the holy Spirit that has been given to us" (Romans 5:5b). And the Spirit is given to us for the same reason it was given to Jesus: to make us holy.

We may be uncomfortable with being compared to Jesus. But we must always come back to the purpose of his life, death and resurrection: The Son of God emptied himself into human life so that our actual human lives may become divine. We are not called to do the same things Jesus did, but to do what we do with the same Spirit and spirit.

What happened to Jesus when he was baptized by John is the model of what must happen to us: We must let the Spirit lead us—drive us—to a life of total devotion to God. The comfort and strength Jesus received from the Spirit in prayer is exactly the kind of comfort and strength the Spirit in us wants to give.

The full force of the Spirit—the *gift* of the Spirit, as the prayer of confirmation says—is Jesus' final gift to us.

The Gifts of the Spirit. We must not try to "split up" the Spirit into various categories: the particular gifts, very special gifts for special purposes, versus general gifts to all Christians. The one God gives us divine life, presence, love, power, healing, glory. The Spirit of the one God possesses us.

Not forgetting this, we can speak of what might be called "general" gifts of the Spirit. They are not reserved for certain people—like, say, the gift of prophecy—but are open to all. Whether all are open to receive them, of course, is another matter.

Another name for these general gifts is the "seven gifts of the Holy Spirit." They are enumerated in Isaiah 11:2-3, but we should remember that the number seven in the Old Testament means completeness, fullness. This list is simply an attempt to show what the Spirit is trying to accomplish in us: wisdom, understanding, counsel, fortitude, knowledge, piety and fear of the Lord.

It is difficult to give precise definitions for these gifts: They are all expressions of the faith of our whole person, centered in our mind and will. They are "swift victory," as one book on the gifts was called, depending on the degree to which we let ourselves be "blown" by the wind of the Spirit.

All our good works are God's gift, of course, but the seven gifts might be compared to the sail of a boat. All we do is leave it hoisted; the wind does the rest. So, while even our cooperation, our "rowing," in good works is God's gift, in the case of the general gifts God simply gives us a certain ease in following the inspirations of the Spirit.

Saint Paul speaks of the *fruits* of the Holy Spirit in contrast to the bitter fruits of our sin. The Spirit produces in us "love, joy, peace, patience, kindness, generosity, faithfulness, gentleness and self-control" (see *Catechism,*

#736). But if we abandon God's help, the result can only be "immorality, impurity, licentiousness, idolatry, sorcery, hatreds, rivalry, jealousy, outbursts of fury, acts of selfishness, dissensions, factions, occasions of envy, drinking bouts, orgies and the like" (see Galatians 5:19–23).

Because we have experienced at least the impulse to the latter in ourselves and have seen at least the appearance of them in others, we can come to appreciate how great is the gift of the Spirit. Because its fruits seem so normal and natural, we may tend to forget they can only be the gifts of God.

Our "remembering" is the gift of faith. We try to let it be wide enough and deep enough to suspect, at least, the infinite mystery that surrounds our lives. "The wind blows where it wills, and you can hear the sound it makes, but you do not know where it comes from or where it goes; so it is with everyone who is born of the Spirit" (John 3:8).

Karl Rahner gives us a sense of this mystery of the Spirit:

Because God creates as God, he creates as Spirit everything in the world that is constantly new and fresh, free and alive, unexpected and mighty, at once tender and strong—the mystery of love. This is the Spirit of grace: God within us as our anointing and sealing, our pledge of heaven, our guest, comforter and advocate, the interior call, freedom and childhood, life and peace...the secret power of transformation within us that presses forward to the resurrection of the glorified body. (Karl Rahner and Herbert Vorgrimler, *Dictionary of Theology*, page 211)

REFLECTION/DISCUSSION STARTERS

1) Discuss the ways the Spirit is described in Scripture.
2) What is the Spirit for you? How do you experience the Spirit in your life?
3) Reflect on the statement, "The Spirit is given to us for the same reason it was given to Jesus: to make us holy." What does this mean to you? In the old Anglo-Saxon meaning of the word, holy meant "whole," "complete." Have you sensed in your life a need for wholeness? How have you tried to meet this need?

SCRIPTURE READINGS

Acts 2; 1 Corinthians 12:1–11; 13; Isaiah 11:2–3; Galatians 5:19–23.

SUPPLEMENTARY MATERIAL

Catholic Updates: "Conversions: Being Born Again and Again and Again," by James Dunning; "How the Spirit Guides the Church: Two Views in Matthew and John," by William H. Shannon; "The Incarnation: Why God Wanted to Become Human," by Kenneth Overberg, S.J.; "Jesus Christ: Why the Word Became Flesh," by Stephen Doyle, O.F.M.; "Who Is the Holy Spirit?" by Elizabeth A. Johnson, C.S.J.

Scripture From Scratch: "From Spirit to Holy Spirit in the Old Testament," by Leonard Doohan.

Book: Enkindled: Holy Spirit, Holy Gifts, by Albert Haase, O.F.M., and Bridget Haase, O.S.U.

CHAPTER 11

TO KNOW JESUS IS TO KNOW THE FATHER, SON AND SPIRIT: THE TRINITY

ALL SIMILES LIMP, THEY TELL US, AND THOSE WE USE FOR GOD LIMP THE MOST. God as "Father" is one of them.

The idea of fatherhood is a good one, but the reality we see on earth is sometimes quite different. Some fathers abandon their children, beat them, ridicule or ignore them, damage them psychologically for life. Even good fathers have their limits. They get tired, they must often go away, sometimes they are helpless and, finally, they die.

To some people, then, the idea of God as "Father" is barren. So, for that matter, may be the notion of "Mother." But Jesus chose *Father* as the best way he could describe God. What we have to do, obviously, is to keep in mind only the positive qualities of fatherhood and motherhood (God is not male, of course), and forget all human limitation.

God is a father/mother who wants children more eagerly than any earthly parents ever yearned to see their love made visible in a new person. All that we associate with parenthood is infinite in God: begetting, pouring out, sustaining and protecting, guiding, encouraging. God is gentleness and strength, patience and justice. He gives birth, nurses and carries, waits and explains, lets go and welcomes back, forgives and heals.

God is *creator* and *redeemer*, to use the heavy words of theology. But the best word is still Jesus' word: *Abba*, which seems to form naturally on the lips of babies.

Someone once said that if she could remember only one verse of the Bible on that mythical island of shipwreck, it should be this:

God is love, and whoever remains in love remains in God and God in him. (1 John 4:16b)

The prophets often had to warn people of God's absolute incompatibility with evil: that the consequences of their sin would overtake them and, thus, God would "punish" them. But the last word always echoed a parent's forgiveness and endless welcome. Hosea says it well:

When Israel was a child I loved him,
    out of Egypt I called my son.
The more I called them,
    the farther they went from me,
...
Yet it was I who taught Ephraim to walk,
    who took them in my arms;
I drew them with human cords,
    with bands of love;
I fostered them like one
    who raises an infant to his cheeks;
Yet, though I stooped to feed my child,
    they did not know I was their healer. (11:1–2a, 3–4)

CREATION, AN ACT OF LOVE. Science has taken all the poetry out of creation, leaving only an intricate pattern of molecules as lifeless as a clock. Genesis tells it better. The story God's inspired people composed to hold creation in poetic grace is a masterpiece. The purpose of creation, it affirms, is the sharing of God's glory with human beings—not an abstract human race, but you and me and your Uncle Bill and old Mrs. Kim.

Take the time to make a list of all the truths contained in that simple story: the goodness of God, the dignity of man and woman, the beauty of creation, the unity of marriage, the holiness of the body, the freedom of our will, the call to responsibility and obedience, the hope for the future....

Why did God create us? God is infinitely happy in the "community" of Father, Son, Spirit. One of the things we must say is that God doesn't need us, objectively. The danger in making this necessary statement is that it may seem to make us a sort of minor hobby of God, like a million people a man might let into his stadium for a "show" while he drives off to seek his own diversion in Florida.

Lest we feel this way, God does everything possible, considering human limitations, to make us feel the warmth of divine love. God sends us people who are signs and sacraments of that love: loving parents first, for many of us a wife or husband, and genuine friends (see *Catechism*, #1604).

All these people give us a glimmering of the gift-and-response God wants in our personal and family relationship with our Creator. God wants us to love the divine image in each other, but also wants us gradually to experience a personal, intimate, conscious relationship of love with the Trinity.

The Creator could not make us any other way except with a built-in orientation toward God. As a fish is made for water and the heart is made for love, we are made for God.

We are not "equals" with God as we are with our friends. But it is precisely in knowing the infinite grandeur of God that we discover how great our dignity is: This awesome Other is also the One within, closer to us than our own consciousness.

It is all God's initiative; yet, in the mystery of freedom, we must accept God's power in order to make a response. To "seek God" is to allow ourselves to be found.

WHY SUFFERING? We might as well face the age-old question: Why, then, is there suffering in the world? How can this good, loving God permit cruelty, sin, the senseless tragedy of the innocent?

We can "explain" suffering, of course. What God does, God does well. So, if I am made free, I am made *really* free. I can decide to do anything. In fact, I must decide what to do with my life, or I am not human. I am not forced to do either good or evil. I can search out truth and goodness and *choose* them. Or I can search out only what fattens my ego and flatters my body and *choose* these things.

Some people choose to be so selfish that others suffer. Now what is God to do? Wither the hand that is raised to strike? Deflect the bullet as it leaves the gun? Erase the vindictive or lustful decision?

Suppose God started to do that: There would be no stopping until every human being turned into a robot. And there is no love or joy in robots.

A good explanation? Perhaps, but don't try it on a mother holding a dead child.

God's "explanation" is the cross. Once we were made free, God could not stop evil except by letting evil people stop the heart of the Son in death. This is the ultimate gift: God shows how much human suffering hurts God by coming to share it. We do not explain suffering; we conquer it by the power of the crucified and risen Jesus, the sign of his Father's tender concern.

FAITHFUL, JUST AND MERCIFUL. To the Jews, the greatest "quality" of God was not just Yahweh's love, but Yahweh's faithful love, steadfast covenant love (see *Catechism*, #218–221). No matter what unfaithfulness—adultery in their covenant relationship—they were guilty of, what pigheaded and perverse sinfulness, God was always the tender Lover waiting to take them back. They knew God had to be just—it was their hope of relief for the injustice they themselves suffered. But they realized that divine justice was God's justness, God's holiness, which simply could not coexist with evil. Sin could only wither away before the fire of divine goodness, and the purifying fire was "punishment"—usually nothing but the logical result of their own stupidity.

But God's justness is mercy. God's all-knowing consciousness is not the suspicious eye of a detective, but a constant planning, if you will, how best to bring free children to God. God's being all-powerful is simply a definition of God—limitless. But God's power is never mere force. It is the relentless but gentle pursuit of the human heart, never intruding, but always calling.

GOD IS HOLY. The word *holy* seems to cause us difficulty. Perhaps the difficulty arises when we try to apply it to ourselves, whereas it should be used only of God. To say God is holy is to say God is God. When the old Anglo-Saxons used the word, they meant whole, well, complete. "God is holy" means God is goodness without limit, love without limit, being without limit and so on. We cannot imagine that kind of wholeness. We do not know what it is not to be created, not to have a beginning, not to be limited. God's love is infinitely intense, overflowing, endless. God's knowledge, power, forgiveness, justice, mercy are God's love are God's being are God, to imitate Gertrude Stein.

Our language about God is as feeble as our knowledge of God. But we keep trying to capture the divine reality in words (see *Catechism*, #40).

GOD IS ONE, BUT TRIUNE. The New Testament has not changed the most fundamental of Jewish beliefs: There is one God. Three gods would not be God, because one would limit the other. We all have a passion for unity because we sense that all things must go back to one source.

We come then to the same technical terms used in the case of Jesus: *nature* and *person*. God is one nature. God's nature is to be God, divine. So in answer to the question "What?" we say, "God is the one infinite being who is the source of all being, all creation, all meaning."

But when we say "Who?" we answer, *but only because of Christian revelation*, that "God is Father, Son, Spirit—three Persons in one God."

A person in this reference is obviously not an independent person such as each of us is. There are not three separate consciousnesses in God; there is only simple being, love, consciousness, life. There are not three intelligences in God.

How, then, do we explain that there is a "Trinity"—three divine Persons in the one divine nature of God?

The first answer is, we don't explain it. We *believe* it because Jesus very obviously took it for granted all over the New Testament.

The traditional teaching of the church, gradually developed, tells us that since God is one, all the creating and saving acts of God are acts of all the Persons of the Holy Trinity. God is not "split up." Yet we do say that only the Son became man.

What is different about the three Persons? The differences rest solely in relationships. The Father eternally "begets" the Son, though neither existed or acted before the other. This begetting is described as God's self-knowledge, perfect consciousness. God's perfect expression of this knowledge is the Word, the "only begotten" Son. (In a feeble comparison, we can express ourselves to ourselves. We "see" ourselves. Yet we are not two persons.)

Now, in God, everything is perfect. Therefore the perfect love that the Father has for himself as perfectly expressed in the Son causes another relationship. This love in God is a reality proceeding from the Father and Son, and it is called the Spirit. (Again, to use a feeble comparison, there can be a great welling up of love in us when we "see" ourselves for once divorced of all our sin and problems and precious in God's eyes, but this love does not become a separate person.)

But our words fail here. Best for us to simply use Jesus' way of speaking: We have a Father who loves us; he reconciles us to himself by giving us his Son made human; and he lives in us by the Spirit of his love. God is One, yet he is the mystery of three inner relationships.

Perhaps we can understand God best when we look into our own hearts and experience our inborn attraction to be with others. To love and forgive others is not an optional commandment pasted onto our lives to make them "nice." We are made like God, and God is, in a sense, a *community*. The very nature of God is to pour out love within eternal life.

Meditating on the Trinity, we can say that the very nature of God is to be "with"—to know and love. God is not a solitary, lonely God, but a community of Persons. If we want a final purpose for all human life, it is that we are called and enabled to "join the community." God above us (the Father) has become God with us (the Son, Jesus) and God in us (the Holy Spirit).

The church, then, prays *to* the Father, *in* the Holy Spirit, *through* Christ our Lord. Saint Paul expresses the mystery in a deceptively simple blessing: "The grace of the Lord Jesus Christ and the love of God and the fellowship [communion] of the holy Spirit be with all of you" (2 Corinthians 13:13).

REFLECTION/DISCUSSION STARTERS

1) God as Father and God as Mother are similes that can help us understand God's relationship to us. Do you experience God as Father? As Mother? As Parent? In what ways?
2) What are some ways we explain suffering? Why can we say that God's explanation is the cross?
3) To what communities do you belong? Are there some to which you belong by choice rather than by circumstance? Do you have a need to

belong to a community? Reflect on the concept of God as "community," the idea that "the very nature of God is to be with." What does it mean to you to say that we are called to "join the community"?

SUPPLEMENTARY MATERIAL

Catholic Updates: "The Trinity: The Mystery at the Heart of Life," by Leonard Foley, O.F.M.; "Are Our Images of God Growing?" by Pat McCloskey, O.F.M.

Scripture From Scratch: "Trinity: To Let the Symbol Sing Again," by Elizabeth A. Johnson, C.S.J., and Julia Brumbaugh; "Why Me? Suffering and Meaning," by Daniel Harrington, S.J.

. | CHAPTER 12 | .

JESUS' SPIRIT IN US RESPONDS TO THE FATHER: PRAYER

A HUSBAND AND WIFE WHO NEVER TALK TO EACH OTHER ARE NOWHERE NEAR being candidates for the "Couple of the Year" award.

Besides, it wouldn't work. Perhaps you can make people say words to each other, but you can't make them communicate. That comes only when they really want to share something with one another. Communication is another name for love.

When Jesus talked about prayer he spoke about its unsuspected depths, and about God's side of the communication.

PRAYER AS GIFT. God speaks first. Prayer is not something we do in order to "get to" God. Prayer is God's gift to us. We cannot pray unless God opens our minds and moves our hearts and draws us closer.

That's surprising at first, and a bit deflating. We usually think of prayer as our business. But it's also a great relief. We are indeed responsible adults who must "make it" through each day; yet we are God's children, with our hand in our Creator's, walking along together in total and peaceful dependence.

Saint Paul says it with his usual directness: "The Spirit too comes to the aid of our weakness, for we do not know how to pray as we ought, but the Spirit itself intercedes with inexpressible groanings. And the one who searches hearts knows what is the intention of the Spirit, because it intercedes for the holy ones according to God's will" (Romans 8:26–27).

So prayer is what the Spirit does in us, and the Father knows what the Spirit means—and what we mean.

Who did this praying best? Jesus, of course. The Spirit drove him into the desert, to deep communion with his Father, for forty days. Luke tells us that he often retired to deserted places to pray. We glimpse Jesus at prayer in some of the crucial events of his life: after being baptized, before choosing the apostles, alone on the mountain when people wanted to make him king and, above all, when he was in the agony of fear in Gethsemane.

"He said, 'Abba [the tender but strong word of a son or daughter], Father, all things are possible to you. Take this cup away from me, but not what I will but what you will'" (Mark 14:36). An angel appeared to Jesus to strengthen him—the comfort of his Father. Then, "He was in such agony and he prayed so fervently that his sweat became like drops of blood falling on the ground" (Luke 22:44). (One of the best ways we can pray is to enter into Jesus' feelings on various occasions in his life, for his human feelings are our human feelings.)

The first purpose of our prayer is to learn to pray as Jesus did. In describing the transfiguration, Saint Luke says, "While he was praying his face changed in appearance" (9:29). In Jesus' case, it was the divine glory shining through. In our case, it should be the *Spirit* of Jesus possessing our minds and hearts.

PRAYER, THE MOST PERSONAL THING WE DO. There are no two sets of fingerprints alike in the world—and, of course, no two persons alike. Nor are there any two pray-ers alike. God has a unique relationship with each of us, just as we have unique relationships with every one of our friends. It's not just that our love is deeper for some; but each relationship has a different tone and spirit, a different style.

In prayer I am alone with God. Me, as I am, nothing hidden and nothing uncared for by my loving Father. The problem is not praying, but getting ready to pray. Once I can come to this face-to-face consciousness of God's presence, the response called for is evident. Unless I have been misguided, I can be confident, calm, secure. I know my sins, but shame is not my prime emotion. I feel gratitude, assurance and true humility in the sense of total and perfectly willing dependence.

Saint Thérèse of Lisieux put it well: "For me prayer means launching out of the heart toward God; it means lifting up one's eyes, quite simply, to heaven, a cry of grateful love, from the crest of joy or the trough of despair." Or, as Saint Augustine said, "God thirsts that we might thirst for him." Our prayer is the meeting of God's thirst and our own (see *Catechism*, #2558–2560).

Prayer does not require a set of directions, any more than two friends need a script. This is not to ridicule certain suggestions made to keep our minds on the track or, rather, to keep us quiet enough to hear what God is saying. But it has been well said that once we have followed Jesus' advice and gone to our room and shut the door (see Matthew 6:6), it doesn't matter what we say. It's probably best when we don't say anything.

Jesus warned against thinking that the value of prayer depends on the quantity of words we manage to speak. "In praying, do not babble like the pagans, who think that they will be heard because of their many words. Do not be like them. Your Father knows what you need before you ask him" (Matthew 6:7–8). Then he taught his apostles the Our Father.

Prayer is best when it is simple. It is simple when it has only one purpose: "Be still and confess that I am God!" (Psalm 46:11).

THE CASE OF THE PESTERING PETITIONER. If this story were not in the Gospels, we would never dare make it up. Jesus teaches persistence in prayer with the example of a man who gets unexpected guests in the middle of the night.

With true Eastern hospitality, the man wants to set food before them. But he has no bread. Ah, a friend lives down the street. He goes to the friend's house and knocks on the door. There is a sleeping mat against the other side of the door. The whole family has been settled down, sardine-like, for hours. It would be a major operation even to get the door open. So, the friend says, "Please come back in the morning. Go home, go to sleep." But the empty-handed host, no doubt secure in this friendship, keeps pounding on the door. Finally, Jesus says, the head of the house capitulates, throws off the covers, scoops the children from in front of the door, and shoves a loaf out into the darkness (see Luke 11:5–9).

Jesus says we must pester the Father in the same way, perfectly aware that he cannot get exasperated.

But petition him for what? At what is our persistence aimed?

"Hallowed be thy name; thy kingdom come; thy will be done on earth as it is in heaven." Perhaps not exactly what we had in mind. (At least we would have put the "daily bread" first.) And what does it mean after all?

In our best moments—moments of real prayer, whether all alone or on a crowded bus—we want first things first. We do love our Father—his Spirit empowering us, Jesus giving us the example—and, like all who love, we want first of all what pleases and celebrates the beloved.

God's name is God's very self. The God who is holiness itself cannot be "hallowed," really. We want God to be *seen* as holy, *honored* as holy, *accepted* as holy, by all people. We want God to be holy in all of them.

And we want the kingdom to come—divine love gently possessing the minds and hearts and bodies of all. We want God's will done, that is, our Creator's endless attempt to heal and forgive, to liberate and re-create, to make happy.

Jesus said, "... [W]hatever you ask in my name I will do, so that the Father may be glorified in the Son" (John 14:13). But at the same time, "[A]sk and you will receive, so that *your* joy may be complete" (John 16:24; emphasis added).

"ASK AND YOU SHALL RECEIVE." Should we feel ashamed to ask for such things as a job, a home, a cure or a spouse? Not so. But the standard of our asking is always that which we use with those we most deeply love. At least when we are unselfish (and how can we deeply love if we are selfish?), we want their good first.

Our prayers of petition are not attempts to persuade God to do something; still less to inform God of our need. They are our persistent attempt to be wholly aware of our dependence. The more we think we need something—health, reconciliation, employment, protection—the more we realize that we are ultimately helpless.

That is not a disgrace, just the fact of being a creature. We have a Father who wants to share infinite riches with us. Persistent, humble prayer is the way God can give us the best he wants to give. Sincere, open prayer gives us the mind and heart of Jesus. Our only concern then is to be perfectly attuned to our Father's way.

PRAYER AND PRAYING. Our prayer is our life. If our lives are faith-filled, they are prayer. If our prayer is genuine, our life is faith-filled. This communion is the way of life for all who love.

Just to be working in the house together is a source of satisfaction and pleasure to many husbands and wives. But this is not enough. Precisely because they love each other, friends and lovers want to reserve certain times when they do nothing *but* communicate with each other. They simply want to *be with* each other.

So with prayer. Much as we may do our work in the peaceful awareness of God's presence, we are easily absorbed by that work. We do not see God as we see our friends. Our love needs to be nourished and stimulated— kept alive, we might as well admit—by times when we do nothing *but* communicate with God.

Anne Morrow Lindbergh once wrote that if her friends called to invite her to a party and she told them that she had an appointment with the hairdresser, it would be a perfectly valid reason for not going. But if she said she needed time for prayer, people would be puzzled. Yet without those "reserved" minutes each day, we can easily become undernourished, a little less convinced, a little less ardent.

The way we pray is much less important than the fact that we do it.

KINDS OF PRAYER

1) *Vocal prayer* is prayer which has a set form, such as the Our Father, the Hail Mary. It may be said aloud or silently. It gives a concrete form to expressions of faith and love. We do not have to worry about "making up" what we want to say. Especially when we are in physical or emotional pain or find it hard to concentrate, familiar set prayers are our guide and sustenance.

2) *Mental prayer*—not a very apt name—is simply prayer which has no set form. It is not exactly the opposite of vocal prayer, however. It does not necessarily consist of "making up" words; it may be nothing but silence in the presence of God. It is informal and spontaneous, though it may follow some pattern. It is as hard to systematize as a conversation between friends.

This prayer may need a focus, something to fasten our thoughts on. Hence prayerful reading, especially from the Scriptures, may be a good way to begin. Not reading for information, or because we find an interesting subject; this is not a time of study. This reading is listening to the voice of God telling us about God's own self, so that we can respond.

Prayer is the response—in adoration, praise, thanks. It may be sorrow for sin. It may be petition, hopefully for the highest good, for God first; it may be thanks or petition concerned with other people.

It may be anything, as long as it comes from the heart. A better name than mental prayer, indeed, would be "prayer of the heart."

3) *The Jesus Prayer.* In recent years one form of prayer has been reemphasized under the influence of Eastern spirituality: the so-called "Jesus prayer." One simply says, "Lord Jesus Christ, Son of God, have mercy on me, a sinner." This prayer is repeated—without hurry, from the heart, often rhythmically.

Other short prayers of this kind, of course, are at everyone's disposal, especially in Scripture: "Lord, I believe, help my unbelief." "Come, Lord Jesus!" "Be it done to me according to your word." Above all, the traditional "doxology," the liturgical hymn of praise: "Glory to the Father, and to the Son, and to the Holy Spirit, as it was in the beginning, is now, and ever shall be!"

"WASTING" TIME. Anyone who has tried to pray knows that more often than not it is just plain hard work. Like the writer who must first sharpen the pencil, then empty the wastebasket, then rearrange the books on the shelf, then do anything but write—so we avoid prayer. We not only find a hundred things to do before beginning to pray, but we also seem to have a thousand things we would rather do when we finally begin. In this difficulty, we are at least in good company. Even great saints sometimes found it hard to pray—or rather, they did not find it easy to pray.

God is silent and mysterious. God wants us to be closest friends, but that involves truth, and the truth is that we are totally *creatures*, totally dependent. It is only when we admit our nothingness that our real "somethingness" in grace comes into being. This means total trust in God—often in silence, in lack of the supposedly necessary "enjoyment" of prayer, in trust.

Our prayer may get down to this: simply being in the presence of God. There may be no satisfaction in it for us, but we may in this way be led by a surprising route to a sense of what it means to depend on God.

Prayer, says Thomas Merton, cannot be measured in terms of *usefulness*. That is, we may not "get something out of it" or manage a neatly arranged series of emotional spasms or come to clear conclusions. Prayer, he says, can only be understood as a complete surrender, a "waste" of time.

By "waste" Merton means being willing to give the time to God absolutely, because we owe our absolute Lord everything. This is not self-hatred but a sincere statement of the deepest reality. God is all, I am nothing. I have been made precious in God's sight—I know that deep down—but all honor and praise belong to God.

Prayer, Merton continues, has fruitful effects, but usefulness is not its purpose. In this, prayer is like friendship, which offers many "useful" benefits. But if these are the sole purpose for cultivating a friendship, there is really no friendship at all, only a business relationship.

Merton has some reassuring words for us when we find prayer very dry and tedious. Especially in meditation, he says, we have to learn patience in the weary path that takes us through the dry places in prayer. This dryness grows more and more frequent, more and more difficult as time goes on. In a certain sense, aridity can almost be taken as a sign of progress in prayer, provided it is accompanied by serious efforts and self-discipline.

So prayer may sometimes have to be—or finally attain the privilege of being—just "wasting" time with God; that is, remaining in God's presence without being concerned about any personal benefit, but simply saying, "You are God. You are all. I adore you. I love you."

REFLECTION/DISCUSSION STARTERS

1) Do you experience prayer as a one- or two-way communication? Who initiates the communication—you or God?

2) Reflect on how Jesus prayed. How does Scripture present Jesus at prayer?

3) Do you find that words are necessary in your prayer? Or are they a hindrance?

4) How much of your prayer involves petitions? What did Jesus say about petitionary prayer?

5) Reflect on the statement that "our life is our prayer." If this is so, is it still necessary to take particular moments to pray?

6) Which different ways of praying do you use? Do you use different ways at different times or for different reasons?

7) How is prayer, in Merton's words, a "waste" of time, not to be measured in terms of usefulness?

SUPPLEMENTARY MATERIAL

Catholic Updates: "An Invitation to Prayer: A Guide for Deepening Our Prayer Life," by Father Edward Hays; "Pathways of Prayer," by Jack Wintz, O.F.M.; "Pray the Our Father With the Pope" [excerpted from *Jesus of Nazareth,* by Pope Benedict XVI].

Scripture From Scratch: "The Bible: Our Wellspring of Prayer" and "The Lord's Prayer," both by Leonard Doohan; "How Jesus Prayed," by Michael Patella, O.S.B.

Books: *101 Inspirational Stories on the Power of Prayer,* by Patricia Proctor, O.S.C.; *Paths to Prayer,* by Robert F. Morneau; *Praying Alone and Together* by Mary Sue Taylor; *Thresholds to Prayer,* by Kathy Coffey.

DVD: *Teach Us to Pray,* one disc; *Living From the Center: How to Pray,* by Richard Rohr, O.F.M. (Each is one disc with a study guide.)

PART FOUR

THE SAVING WORK
OF JESUS IN THE WORLD
TODAY

CHAPTER 13

JESUS LIVING IN HIS MEMBERS:
THE CHURCH

"THE CHURCH IS A KIND OF SACRAMENT OR SIGN AND INSTRUMENT OF INTIMATE
union with God, and of the unity of the whole human race...." (*Dogmatic
Constitution on the Church*, 1)

Vatican II shocked some Catholics who hadn't done their history homework. They thought the church was a tightly run ship, all orders from the
captain strictly carried out, perfect discipline and order. There were
obstreperous and sinful members, of course, but they were really "out,"
walking their own gangplank.

Then the church saw two thousand bishops assembled in Rome,
engaging not only in dry discussion but in heated debate. A mischie-
vous priest-reporter with the pen name of Xavier Rynne published
accounts of behind-the-scenes maneuvering that would have done
credit to a Democratic convention. People began to hear about a group
of experts called theologians with varying and even contradictory opinions who seemed to have the ear of the bishops.

More surprising still, the bishops told the laity, "You're the church too.
Speak up!" And they did—with all the variety of Pentecost, but not always
the peaceful spirit.

This variety of opinion was not really a new phenomenon in the church,
just more publicized. But this revelation of humanness in the church
made some people sad.

The greatest achievement of the Council was its opening of the church
to the world—the great theologian Karl Rahner called it a revolution that

can only be compared to Copernicus's proving the earth goes around the sun, not vice versa—and its *deepening of the church's consciousness of who we really are.* The Council painted a very idealistic picture. But, just as the bickering was nothing new, neither was the vision. It was a spelling out for our day of the implications of the gospel, the most challenging document ever written. What is different, or "modern," is the open and courageous way the church listens to all that is good in today's world and its applying the gospel to the concrete conditions of that world.

The greatest document of the Council was the *Dogmatic Constitution on the Church,* and it is that document we want to call upon to emphasize the heart of the matter: *The church—all of us—is the sacrament of Christ* (see *Catechism,* #775–776).

The opening words of the document could have been printed as poetry:

Christ is the Light of the world; his radiance brightens the face of the church!

Is that a description of the people you were with last Sunday at Mass? It is. It is, indeed, and all the sour cynicism about "hypocrites" and "I don't get anything out of it" does not change the fact. For Jesus was there, and his people were around him.

That's the greatest thing God ever had in mind for us. Certainly the Bride of Christ is not yet the unwrinkled beauty Saint Paul speaks of (see Ephesians 5:25–27). Christ's bride gets younger, not older, and there are some blemishes that only the future will erase.

But Christ was not *visible* last Sunday. He disappeared a long time ago. Angels told his bewildered followers to stop looking up into the sky for him (see Acts 1:11).

Jesus had come as the sacrament of God. If anybody wanted to know how God loved, forgave, yearned for human love, waited for erring children, all they had to do was look at Jesus. "Whoever has seen me has seen the Father" (John 14:9).

Jesus as sacrament was visible, touchable, hearable, flesh and blood: "an outward sign." But when you touched him or looked at his face, you touched God, you saw the radiance of divine love: "inward grace."

It hadn't been absolutely necessary for God to do this, but God wanted to be this close to us, to show our eyes as much as they could possibly see.

But the sacrament disappeared. What now? Wasn't it still terribly important, if not absolutely necessary, that we still be able to "see" God?

It was, and Jesus took care of it. He left a new sacrament called the church. The church is the sacrament of Jesus just as Jesus was the sacrament of God. Jesus' radiance must shine on the face of the church (see *Catechism*, #932–933).

All the words of Jesus about the union of his people with himself, the mission of the apostles and all his followers to proclaim the Good News, the promise of his presence to the end of time, the power to forgive and heal—all his words are describing something visible, hearable, touchable: namely, that "body" of human beings whom God calls together to be the Body of Jesus (see *Catechism*, #738).

There is no exclusiveness about this body. It is meant to include every human being on earth (see *Catechism*, #849). Today it is a minority in the world. Perhaps it will always be. But it is an open community, lifted up among the nations to be the sign and instrument of Jesus' continuing work of salvation.

There is a momentous implication here: If Jesus said, "Philip, whoever sees me sees the Father" (see John 14:9b), then the church—that is, all who are gathered in unity around Jesus—must be able to say to the world in general and to each individual, "Whoever sees us sees Jesus."

That statement sounds arrogant, and none of us likes to say it. It's too great a responsibility, we're not worthy and so on—all beside the point. No matter how we distort his face to each other and to the world, Jesus has chosen to come visibly to the world through us. That's what church means. We might even say Jesus can't help coming to the world through us, because he has joined his life to ours.

We have never shown Jesus to the world very well, but we have done it. Not only great saints but countless ordinary Christians, assembled for Eucharist or working in the marketplace, have brought Jesus visibly and effectively to each other and to the world. We have no choice, actually. There are no private cells in the Body of Christ where we can withdraw and enjoy private salvation. To be alone is to be a dead member.

Some people, however, scandalized by what they see as sin in members of the church, say they can get along without the "organized" church. They are just "Christians."

This is comparable to Jesus' saying, "My body isn't really important. My touching people, my words, my blood spilled, my flesh offered up, my risen body—forget all this and just concentrate on my *spirit.*"

But we can't get to Jesus' spirit except through his body. To be human is to be both spiritual/physical and visible/invisible. The church is people, and people have bodies. These bodies have to say Christ-things, do Christ-things. And Christ-things are loving things, forgiving things—so the Christ-people must be a community, a called-together people, a visible Body.

This opens the door to all sorts of messy failures: lying words and money-grabbing, sexual abuse and cover-ups, letting people starve and getting drunk. But it's the human condition. We couldn't strike each other if we had no fists, but we could not hold each other if we had no arms. There would be no slander or insults if we had no lips, but no comforting either, or sharing of feeling and need.

So Vatican II said the church is "both human and divine, visible and yet invisibly endowed, eager to act and yet devoted to contemplation, present in this world and yet not at home in it" (*Constitution on the Sacred Liturgy,* 2).

NAMES FOR THE CHURCH

1) *The Mystical Body of Christ:* This is a concept developed by Saint Paul. Christ and his followers form one Body: Christ is the Head, we are the members (see *Catechism,* #787–789). All light, guidance, strength come from the Head. The Holy Spirit can be called the soul of this Body, provided we do not forget that the Holy Spirit is the Spirit of the one God.

Here is an attempt to picture the Mystical Body: When we receive Holy Communion, we each receive the living Jesus, body and soul, God and man. Now, imagine a whole parish, or a whole diocese, receiving Communion at the same time. Each person receives Jesus, yet only one Jesus is received in all. The one Jesus exists in all his members. He forms them into a living Body with him and with each other (see *Catechism,* #1396). Just as there is only one bread, so there is only one Body.

Each member of the Body has a function, just as in the human body. For Paul's striking application of this doctrine, see 1 Corinthians 12; also Colossians 1:15–24 and Ephesians 4:1–16.

An amazing conclusion follows from this idea of the church: Jesus needs us. We are the only way his hands can touch the sick or give bread to the starving. We are the only way people can see forgiveness in his eyes. Our feet are the only way he can walk the roads of modern civilization and proclaim the Good News.

2) *The Vine and the Branches.* This is Jesus' own comparison, spoken at the Last Supper (see John 15). The metaphor of the vine, in the sense of a supporting stem, may be a better one to express the place and function of Jesus than "head." The strong stem seems a greater support to the clinging tendrils than the head of a body, though obviously one must not be too literal (see *Catechism*, #755). Jesus said:

> Remain in me, as I remain in you. Just as a branch cannot bear fruit on its own unless it remains on the vine, so neither can you unless you remain in me. (John 15:4)

But also:

> By this is my Father glorified, that you bear much fruit and become my disciples. (John 15:8)

3) *God's Family.* "…[Y]ou are fellow citizens with the holy ones and members of the household of God" (Ephesians 2:19b). The greatest revelation of God is that he is Father (Matthew). He makes us sharers in the life of his own "family" of Father, Son, Spirit. He gives us a brother, Jesus. Just as family members need and help each other, so do we. And those who need the most—the little ones, the crippled, the senile, the sick—receive our greatest care.

4) *God's Building.* Jesus was the stone that was rejected, but that turned out to be the cornerstone (see Psalm 118:22). On this divine/human rock God laid the foundation—the apostles and Peter (see Matthew 16:18; 1 Corinthians 3:11). "Through him [Jesus] the whole structure is held together and grows into a temple sacred in the Lord; in him you also are being built together into a dwelling place of God in the Spirit"

(Ephesians 2:21–22). Peter calls us "living stones" built into this temple (see 1 Peter 2:5).

5) *Jesus' Little Flock*. The Good Shepherd tells us, "Do not be afraid any longer, little flock" (Luke 12:32).

> ...I know mine and mine know me, just as the Father knows me and I know the Father; and I will lay down my life for the sheep. (John 10:14b–15)

6) *The People of God*. Vatican II chose to emphasize this title. God makes people holy and saves them "not merely as individuals without any mutual bonds but by making them into a single people, a people which acknowledges him in truth and serves him in holiness. He therefore chose the race of Israel as a people unto himself" (*Dogmatic Constitution on the Church*, 9).

The Council chose this title to emphasize the *community* aspect of the church. It is a "fellowship of life, charity and truth" (*Dogmatic Constitution on the Church*, 9). The term *people* reminds us that we do not "join" the church. Rather, we are called. The word *ecclesia* means "called out": The church is the "called-together people," the assembly of God (see *Catechism*, #751).

THE CHURCH AND THE KINGDOM OF GOD. The Kingdom of God is the power of God present to all human beings. This power offers salvation and also achieves salvation for those who respond.

God "rules" us by possessing our minds and hearts—and giving us the power to *choose* this self-surrender. God comes to us gently; we might almost say politely. God will not intrude. "But to those who did accept him he [Jesus] gave power to become children of God" (John 1:12a).

This gift of the Kingdom was given to the world in Jesus, in a way that can never be reversed. He inaugurated the Kingdom on earth, calling together a people made up of Jews and Gentiles, making them one in the Spirit.

By his death and resurrection, Jesus entered into the glory of the Kingdom, but he remains in his church to the end of time. Then he will hand over the Kingdom to his Father, forever (see 1 Corinthians 15:24).

The church is the initial budding forth of the Kingdom, though the Kingdom is broader than the church. The saving power of God may be in many who have never heard of Jesus or God, those who through no fault of their own have no explicit knowledge of God but who sincerely seek "God," striving to do God's will as it is known to them (see *Catechism*, #847–848).

The Kingdom is "already" here, and it is "coming." Every day we pray, "Thy Kingdom come." The "Good News" (the literal meaning of *gospel*) is precisely the coming of the Kingdom, finally and perfectly in Jesus, then and now.

ENTERING THE KINGDOM. We have been talking about the church as if it were a thing, something "out there." But, though God's action is primary, the church and the Kingdom involve flesh-and-blood people. The Kingdom is for sinful people who want to be forgiven, purified and enlivened. And since everybody is more or less sinful, every human being on earth is invited.

To be a member of the Kingdom, the first essential is interior conversion, a change of heart, repentance for sin and the determination to lead a new life.

"Born" Catholics may have trouble getting their minds around this. Converts have "conversion"; but many Christians are baptized as babies. How can there be a whole new life when one receives God's life at the beginning?

This is a real problem and there is no easy answer. What all of us must realize is that our whole life is an *endless conversion*. We are trying to become real converts. Whether or not we are baptized as babies, we must sooner or later—gradually (probably) or suddenly—come to the mind-shattering realization that Jesus is the Lord. We must come, as well as we can, to an Easter experience of knowing and being touched by the risen Jesus and then enter into a personal and conscious relationship of friendship-love-intimacy with him.

Most people don't think they've done this—though they probably have in a substantial way. But we must not let this "humility" distract us from the urgent and gentle pressure of Jesus for a total self-giving.

The fundamental attitude of membership in the Kingdom is twofold: *poverty in spirit* and *wholeheartedness.*

First, members of the Kingdom are "the poor in spirit"—those nobodies drinking in the words of Jesus on the shores of the lake:

Blessed are the poor in spirit;
for theirs is the kingdom of heaven. (Matthew 5:3)

The "poor" have nothing, and they know it, so they accept everything from God. They believe Jesus when he said that only little children can enter the Kingdom (see Matthew 18:3).

Second, members of the Kingdom have, or keep trying to receive, wholeheartedness. Jesus said, "But seek first the kingdom [of God] and his righteousness, and all these things will be given you besides" (Matthew 6:33). Members of Christ base their lives on no other protection but this final saving Kingdom of God.

Nowadays someone is always telling us what something is "all about." Jesus is telling us that the Kingdom is what our life is all about.

CHURCH: GOD'S IDEAL MADE REAL. The church has plenty of problems and faults, and we must face them. But, happily, we can and must fall back on the ideal vision of the church described in this chapter. If ever there was an impossible dream, it is the church. God had the dream from eternity; it becomes reality in Jesus and in all who try to follow him or who, not knowing him, follow the true and the good as best they can.

At the Last Supper Jesus prayed for all who believe in him, present and future. In his prayer he described the church:

And I have given them the glory you gave me, so that they may be one, as we are one, I in them and you in me, that they may be brought to perfection as one, that the world may know that you sent me, and that you loved them even as you loved me. (John 17:22–23)

REFLECTION/DISCUSSION STARTERS
1) Reflect on the statement, "The church is the sacrament of Jesus just as Jesus was the sacrament of God." Has the church been a sign of Jesus for you? In what way(s)?
2) Discuss the different ways to speak about the church: as the Mystical Body of Christ, the Vine and the Branches, God's Family, God's Building,

Jesus' Little Flock, the People of God. Which is/are most meaningful to you? Why?

3) Is the church identical to the Kingdom of God? What is the relationship between the two?

4) Interior conversion is essential for membership in the Kingdom. For each of us, life is an endless conversion but, as the author says, "We must sooner or later...come to the mind-shattering realization that Jesus is the Lord." What has your own interior conversion experience involved? At what point on your journey of "endless conversion" do you find yourself right now?

SCRIPTURE READINGS

Acts 14; Ephesians 5:25–27; 1 Corinthians 12; John 15; Psalms 118:22; Matthew 16:18; 1 Corinthians 3:11; 15:24; Matthew 18:3.

SUPPLEMENTARY MATERIAL

Catholic Updates: "Ten 'Peak Moments' of Church History: From Pentecost to Vatican II," by Alfred McBride, O. PRAEM.; "Treasures of Vatican II: Our Compass for the Future," by Edward Hahnenberg; "Vatican II: The Vision Lives On!" by Leonard Foley, O.F.M.; "What Does It Mean to 'Be Church'?" by Greg Friedman, O.F.M.

Vatican 2 Today (a twelve-issue newsletter): "Called to Holiness: Lay Ministry," by Karen Sue Smith; "Called to Holiness: Ordained Ministry," by Robert F. Morneau; "Catholic Discipleship," by Jack Wintz, O.F.M.; "Marriage and Family: The Domestic Church," by Brennan and Marie Hill; "The Mass: Our Greatest and Best Prayer," by Thomas Richstatter, O.F.M.; "Road Map for the Future: Teachings of Vatican II," by Jack Wintz, O.F.M., and John Feister; "Sacred Scripture: Food for Our Souls," by Dianne Bergant, C.S.A.; "Seven Sacraments, One Mystery," by Thomas Richstatter, O.F.M.; "Sharing Our Legacy of Faith," by John Roberto; "Today's Church: A Look in the Mirror," by William Shannon; "Today's Church: Signs of Joy and Hope," by William Shannon; "Vatican II: Catholicism Welcomes the World," by Virginia Smith.

Books: *The Compact History of the Catholic Church,* by Alan Schreck; *The Story of the Church: Peak Moments From Pentecost to the Year 2000,* by Alfred McBride, O. PRAEM.; *Vatican II Today: Calling Catholics to Holiness and Service,* edited by Judy Ball and Joan McKamey; *Vatican II: The Crisis and the Promise,* by Alan Schreck.

DVD: *Introduction to the History of Christianity,* by Thomas Shelley, Mary Martin and William Franklin, two discs with study guide

. | CHAPTER 14 | .

TRYING TO MAKE JESUS VISIBLE:
THE "OUTSIDE" OF THE CHURCH

THERE'S A HANGOVER FROM THE ANCIENT GREEKS—CERTAINLY NOT FROM THE
biblical Jews—that still makes some people apologize for their bodies.
Wouldn't it be nicer, they say, watching football mayhem on TV and
munching on Fritos, if we were not subject to such biological embarrass-
ments as digestion (or indigestion), elimination, reproduction, coughing,
sweating, muscle strain and ingrown toenails? Perhaps we could advance
to being bionic men and women.

That same discomfort with personal bodily existence translates into a
discomfort with the *bodily*, visible, organized—and, therefore, imperfect—
life of the church: Why can't we have a church without "Sunday
hypocrites"—a favorite harangue of non-goers. If only all Christians were
like Mary and Joseph, all kids as obedient as Jesus, all popes like John
XXIII (or Mother Teresa!), all bishops like the beloved disciple, all priests
like the Curé of Ars and all religious like Clare and Francis.

Unfortunately—rather, inevitably—we've had Peter, Judas and Ananias
the liar; indulgence peddlers and popes who led armies; bishops who
made Madison Avenue look shabby; priests who "ran" their parishes like
Marine sergeants; and laity who have gouged the poor, stolen each other's
spouses and relegated the gospel over to Trappist monks.

We've had Christians—all of us, from first communicant to pope—who
are more or less a scandal to each other and to the 70 percent of the world
that doesn't even profess to be Christian.

Hopeless? No, just human. Not right, but understandable. We can't see the loving God directly, and God isn't always able to get through others to us or through us to others. We face imperious demands from our instincts for self-preservation and self-interest, from our feelings and flesh, from our questioning minds and restless wills. Chaucer has us right, more or less, in the *Canterbury Tales.*

If all this sounds like an apology for the church, it is. Like every other human group, we are weak and sinful, always in need of healing, forgiveness, reformation. As Vatican II put it:

> While Christ, holy, innocent and undefiled, knew nothing of sin...the church, embracing sinners in her bosom, at the same time holy and always in need of being purified, follows the endless way of penance and renewal. Christ summons the church to continual reformation as she goes her pilgrim way.... (*Dogmatic Constitution on the Church,* 8) The church will reach perfection only when Jesus returns to establish the Kingdom in all its fullness (see Catechism, #769).

The amazing fact is: God knows all about us and loves us anyway. The ironic thing is: We the sinful are called to be Jesus' instrument for healing all sin. We are, as in the title of Henri Nouwen's classic book, "wounded healers."

We are, as human beings, the Body of Christ—and we have an "outside" for all to see. We are part of the "scandal" of the Incarnation. Jesus took our human nature; he joined us. He is gladly "stuck" with us, and he is willing to suffer all the bad publicity we give him.

For, in spite of "the gates of hell"—that is, the power of evil—the church, soul and *body,* is succeeding because it is the Body of Christ.

This chapter should not really be separated from the preceding one—as if the good and holy church were the Body of Christ, and the visible, "organized" church is really something else. There is only one church, just as there is only one Jesus, God and man.

In order to understand why the "outside" of the church—the visible, organized part—is important, we have to ask the question: What is the church for? The church's purpose is to do in *flesh and blood* what Jesus did and does. Jesus is Priest. Jesus is Prophet. Jesus is King (see *Catechism,*

#436). So the church has the commission and the power to *continue the priesthood of Jesus*—in all its members, each according to his or her vocation. The church has the commission and the power to *continue the prophetic* (speaking for God) work which Jesus did and does—again, in all its members: the hierarchy in its way, the laity in its way, all in Christ's way. And the church has the commission and the power to *continue the kingly rule of Christ*—the most problematic of the three, because it includes washing others' feet as well as "binding and loosing."

Since the laity have received a new birth of freedom from Vatican II, let's consider how they fit into this scheme first.

THE LAITY. *Layman* has a negative meaning, and changing to *laypersons* doesn't help much. Even the dictionary contributes to the conspiracy. A layman is someone who is not: not a clergyman, or—second meaning— not an expert in some field.

The Council tried to counteract this notion by a fundamental statement: "All the faithful of Christ of whatever rank or status are called to the *fullness* of the Christian life and to the perfection of charity" (*Dogmatic Constitution on the Church*, 40). "One and the same holiness is cultivated by all" (*Dogmatic Constitution on the Church*, 40, 41).

In other words, there are no second-class citizens in the church. A priest is not holier because he is a priest; a layperson is not less holy because his or her vocation is to be involved in secular affairs. We are all called to receive the one and only holiness: God's.

All Catholics learn somewhere along the line that the church's job is to teach, sanctify and rule. This is what is meant by "sharing in the three offices of Jesus: Prophet, Priest, King." Now the Council reminds all laypersons that popes and bishops and priests are not the only ones who do this (see *Catechism*, #901, 904, 908).

As Saint Peter said, we have all been made into a "royal priesthood, a holy nation" (see 1 Peter 2:9). This is not a denial of the ministerial priesthood—that of ordained priests—but an affirmation of what baptism does. The baptized can offer spiritual worship. Ordinary Christians' prayers, work and sacrifices are offered with Christ's Body and Blood (see *Catechism*, #901). Thus they have the privilege of being able to participate

in the Mass in a special way—unlike, for instance, a non-believing specta-
tor who happens to wander into church.

Laypersons are prophets, not necessarily in the pulpit, but at home, at
the hairdresser's, at the union meeting, at cocktail parties and funerals.
Christ's word comes through them in a way it may never come through
bishops and priests.

Christ's kingly mission is to "subject" all to himself. He does this not by
force but by service. So laypersons serving their fellow human beings can
lead them to the King through their humility and patience.

The Council emphasized that "a secular quality is special to laypersons.
By their very vocation, they seek the Kingdom of God in temporal affairs"
(*Dogmatic Constitution on the Church*, 31).

The laity are now exercising greater influence in the church and taking
their rightful place in ministry. Laypersons serve as religious education
directors, lectors, ministers of the Eucharist, members of parish councils
and members of the various committees that advise these councils.

But lay ministry is not a totally new movement. We have always had multitudes of laypersons teaching in and running Catholic schools, or being
quietly prophetic in public schools; serving in parishes as ushers and
members of various church societies or organizations to aid the poor; and
bearing powerful witness as just plain everyday Christians living their lives
in the world.

THE APOSTLES AND THEIR SUCCESSORS. Jesus chose twelve leaders for the
new Israel, the fulfillment of the promises to the twelve tribes of old. He
sent them as his visible representatives, first to his own people and then to
the world (see *Catechism*, #857).

As the apostles began to die, a structure to replace them gradually
developed (see *Catechism*, #877). The New Testament names "overseers,"
"elders" and "deacons" ("those who serve").

In varying degrees, these three orders of ministers (bishops, priests and
deacons) have the power and authority of Jesus backing them up:

All power in heaven and on earth has been given to me. Go, therefore, and make disciples of all nations, baptizing them in the name of
the Father, and of the Son, and of the holy Spirit, teaching them to

observe all that I have commanded you. And behold, I am with you always, until the end of the age. (Matthew 28:18–20)

And in John's Gospel:

And when he had said this, he breathed on them and said to them, "Receive the holy Spirit. Whose sins you forgive are forgiven them, and whose sins you retain are retained." (John 20:22–23)

Sternly, Jesus described the characteristics of authority in the church: "If anyone wishes to be first, he shall be the last of all and the servant of all" (Mark 9:35b). And, still more pointedly, at the Last Supper, he said: "If I, therefore, the master and teacher, have washed your feet, you ought to wash one another's feet" (John 13:14).

So the leaders of the church are to proclaim the Good News, teach all that Jesus commanded, bring Jesus' forgiveness of sins and guide the church on its way ("bind and loose")—and be servants of all. They are to make disciples by being witnesses of Jesus' power, love, forgiveness still visible in the world.

THE POPE. It is evident from the Gospels that Jesus gave Peter a special place among the Twelve (see *Catechism*, #881), so much so that one antipapal writer has said that the "unwarranted power" of the pope began in the New Testament itself!

Jesus said to Peter alone, after his strong statement of faith in Jesus as the Messiah:

Blessed are you, Simon, son of Jonah.... And so I say to you, you are Peter, and upon this rock I will build my church, and the gates of the netherworld shall not prevail against it. I will give you the keys to the kingdom of heaven. Whatever you bind on earth shall be bound in heaven; whatever you loose on earth shall be loosed in heaven. (Matthew 16:17b–19)

At the Last Supper, even as he foretold the denial of Peter—and thus accepted the fundamental weakness of the man (and men) in the office—Jesus said, "I have prayed that your own faith may not fail; and once you have turned back, you must strengthen your brothers" (Luke 22:32).

Finally, after his resurrection, Jesus singled out the penitent Peter, asked him three times if he loved him, and three times commanded him to "feed my sheep" (see John 21:15–17).

Jesus gave a general commission of evangelization and witness to the whole church, a special commission to the apostles and a singular commission to Peter. He is the *visible* center around which the unity of the church can be maintained. He is the unique feeder of the sheep, the unique source of strength for his brothers and sisters (see *Catechism*, #882).

There have been 264 popes or successors of Saint Peter (the word *pope* is from the Latin *pater* or father) and there will be more, because the service Peter performed is necessary until the end of time. A relative few were a disgrace (and their sins have been amply publicized!), but the great majority have served the church and the world well. Even a world that is touchy about any kind of authority has expressed admiration for the leadership, wisdom, graciousness and service of our recent popes: John Paul II and John Paul I, Paul VI, Blessed John XXIII and Pius XII.

The style of any one of them may not be congenial to all Catholics. They have their normal share of human weakness and temperament; they are unable to shake all the dead weight of entrenched custom. But they have done Peter's work for Christ, and they have done it well.

PAPAL INFALLIBILITY. While the climate of ecumenism has softened religious tensions considerably, infallibility remains an interdenominational problem, not only on the theological level—where there is hope—but also on the emotional level where our egos shout, "Nobody tells *me*."

Let us first be very clear what we are talking about when we say "infallibility." It extends as far as the church's doctrine and moral sense—to all the "truths of faith" (see *Catechism*, #2035). All that far, and no farther.

Infallibility certainly does not mean impeccability—that is, freedom from sin. The pope goes to confession like anyone else. And he can be as wrong as anyone else about the weather, the future of the dollar and the outcome of the Rome-Milan soccer game.

Let's take a look at history. We have this Spirit-guided group of people who can't wander too far off the track because Jesus has promised to remain with them and enlighten them by his Spirit. But they do manage, being human, to get picky or opinionated and back themselves into tight corners. Someone has to speak with enough authority to settle the argument, to respond to an error serious enough to throw the church off the track. Jesus *is* truly God. Jesus *is* truly man. God *does* absolutely forgive our sins. And so forth.

Back in Jerusalem the primitive church trusted the apostles to come to some kind of agreement as to whether or not circumcision—a tremendously sacred law of the Jews—should be required of Gentile converts. Throughout history, the Bishop of Rome, usually with those of his brother bishops who could attend a council, was trusted by the church to settle things. The Reformation made the question of papal authority (not to mention infallibility) a burning issue. But it was not until the year 1870 that the doctrine of papal infallibility was finally defined.

The First Vatican Council said that, within the faith of the whole church, the infallible teaching of a pope is the concrete expression of that faith *in certain very restricted circumstances.* The pope speaks infallibly when (1) he means to use his authority for the whole church, (2) and definitely decides, as a matter of obligation of faith for the whole church, (3) a matter of faith or morals, (4) using words which expressly say he is calling upon this power promised by Christ to Peter.

Pope Pius XII met these requirements when he defined the Assumption of Mary in 1950. The same can be said retroactively of Pius IX's 1854 declaration on the Immaculate Conception.

Notice that Vatican I spoke of the pope having "that infallibility with which our divine redeemer *willed to endow his church* in final decisions." The whole church is infallible in its faith.

How would any pope exercise this function? He is obliged to do what every other human being must do: exercise the virtue of prudence. With the utmost intensity he must use all human means of discovering the true faith of the church: study, prayer, consultation, deliberation (see *Catechism,* #2033). He does not receive any private revelation. He does not take a Gallup poll, but neither dare he ignore the long tradition of faith in all the members of the church. He teaches them, but also makes concrete what is already their fundamental belief.

It is also the teaching of the church that the *whole body of bishops, in union with the pope,* can exercise infallibility in teaching (see *Catechism,* #2034). Such teaching would normally take place in church councils. But Pius XII defined the Assumption of Mary apart from a council.

It is necessary to begin the discussion of infallibility with all these *ifs, ands* and *buts* because of the controversial nature of the doctrine. We begin like lawyers, which is fine, but we must end the discussion as believers. We will never "prove" infallibility to be true in a debate. Protestant and Catholic theologians are meeting each other to discuss the subject in charity and honesty, and that is the best hope we have.

But Catholics believe that the positive side of infallibility is the Holy Spirit, who cannot be tied down in lawyers' or theologians' language. We simply presume that the Spirit of Jesus fills the church, head and members, and illumines the faith of all.

The infallibility of the church is something positive and beautiful, something to be thankful for.

Magisterium. Obviously there is another kind of teaching which does not fall within the strictly defined area of infallibility (see *Catechism,* #890–892).

This is called the "ordinary teaching" (magisterium) of the church. In our day this will usually be found in papal encyclicals (letters to the whole church on important matters). In recent decades, for instance, great emphasis has been placed on social justice in encyclicals from Leo XIII (*Rerum Novarum*) to John Paul II's encyclical celebrating its one-hundredth anniversary, *Centesimus Annus.* Paul VI also issued *Humanae Vitae* (Human Life), stating the church's teaching on sexual morality in marriage. Benedict XVI's first encyclical was entitled *God Is Love.* The second one is *In Hope We Are Saved.*

BISHOPS. Except for infallibility, a bishop is for his "church" or diocese what the pope is for the whole church. A bishop cannot function apart from the church and the pope, of course, but he is not merely a delegate or helper. He is one of the successors of the Twelve, an authentic teacher of faith, the sign and center of unity in his diocese. He is not independent of the rest of the church, or its faith and law, but he is the "local apostle" (see *Catechism,* #886).

Catholics do not belong just to the worldwide church; they belong to a "local church," a diocese: the church of Denver or Pittsburgh, Sioux Falls or Santa Fe. Any community around an altar under the ministry of the bishop is a symbol of the oneness and the love of the Body of Christ. Vatican II says, "In these communities, though frequently small and poor, or living far from any other, Christ is present" (*Dogmatic Constitution on the Church*, 26).

Like the pope, the bishop exercises the priestly, prophetic and kingly office of Christ. He cannot be in every church of the diocese, but "every legitimate celebration of the Eucharist is regulated by the bishop" (*Dogmatic Constitution on the Church*, 26).

The bishop of a diocese is assisted by a presbyteral council, or a priests' senate. He is responsible for not only the spiritual but also the temporal welfare of the diocese. Like the pope, he must delegate some functions to others.

Priests are assistants to the bishop (see *Catechism*, #1564). They too are meant to be centers of unity and charity in the ultimately "local" community where the "whole" church is present when the Eucharist is offered. We will consider their office in chapter twenty-two on the sacrament of Orders.

LAWS OF THE CHURCH. All societies have laws. Families have rules and regulations (in by midnight, no snacks before dinner, homework before TV). The purpose of law, including the law of the church, is to guide people to a growth in love of God and neighbor (see *Catechism*, #2041). Law safeguards the rights and privileges of each person. Law also directs people to their duties and obligations.

The body of church law is called Canon Law. Just as family rules change when circumstances change, so do the laws of the church. The most recent update of church law occurred in 1983.

Many Catholics were shocked in 1966 when Pope Paul VI repealed the law of Friday abstinence for much of the year. (They should have read the whole document, which was a restatement of the continual need of all Christians for penance.) They had equated this church law—made by the church and therefore changeable by the church—with the law of God.

On the other hand, one sometimes hears Catholics speak of some laws of God as "church rules" which should be changed. When the church presents its teaching on abortion or contraception or divorce, it is not pushing its own regulations, but what it believes to be the law of God. Pope Paul did not ban contraception the way the Senate once banned TV in its chambers. Rather, he saw the law of God demanding certain conclusions.

Like it or not, the church is not a democracy. It is a visible community with a visible head. The pope is neither a dictator nor a counter of opinions. Like any prudent person he must listen to anyone who can help him come to awareness and insight; but he is the single leader who must uniquely serve all.

WHO BELONGS? We learned a new word from Vatican II: *ecumenism.* Strictly speaking, it refers only to the movement toward unity among Christians (see *Catechism,* #820–822). But the spirit of Vatican II also reached out in welcome to non-Christians.

The Council said, first, that the unique church of Christ *subsists* in the Catholic Church, although holiness and truth can be found outside its visible structures. In some real way, all Christians are joined with Catholics by the Holy Spirit, whose gifts and graces are given to all the baptized. Therefore, those who "believe in Christ and have been properly baptized are brought into a certain, though imperfect, communion with the Catholic Church" (*Decree on Ecumenism,* 3).

The bishops of Vatican II also recognized others related in various ways to the People of God. First, the Jews, "the people to whom the covenants and the promise were given.... This people remains most dear to God." Next, the Muslims, who "along with us adore the one and merciful God who on the last day will judge mankind" (*Decree on Ecumenism,* 16).

The term *anonymous* Christian is not used, but the Council did say, "Nor is God himself far distant from those who in shadows and images seek the unknown God, for it is he who gives to all men life and breath and every other gift, and who as Savior wills that all men be saved." Further, "those also can attain to everlasting salvation who through no fault of their own do not know the gospel of Christ or his church, yet sincerely seek God and, moved by grace, strive by their deeds to do his will as it is known to them through the dictates of conscience. Nor does divine providence deny the help necessary for salvation to those who, without blame on their part, have not yet arrived at an explicit knowledge of God, but who strive to live a good life, thanks to his grace" (see *Dogmatic Constitution on the Church*, 16).

And most importantly, returning to those who belong to the visible Body of the church: "A person who does not persevere in charity, however, is not saved, even though incorporated into the church" (*Dogmatic Constitution on the Church*, 14).

The greatest ecumenism, and the greatest witness to the genuineness of the church, always rests on Jesus' words:

This is how all will know that you are my disciples, if you have love for one another. (John 13:35)

Love within the church cannot be held within its visible boundaries. The simple love its members display is the greatest apology for their faults and the strongest argument for the unity Christ desires.

REFLECTION/DISCUSSION STARTERS

1) What do you see the role of laypeople to be in the church? What is their role in the wider society?
2) Describe the kind of authority Jesus conferred on the church. How do you see authority being exercised in the church today?
3) How can the position of pope be traced back to Jesus' words?
4) Discuss the concept of infallibility. How has it been defined? When has it been invoked? Does it mean that church leaders can never err in any position or statement?
5) Can a person dissent in clear conscience from the magisterium or "ordinary teaching" of the church? Discuss some instances of dissent of which you are aware.
6) In what way are all Christians joined to the Catholic church? How are non-Christians related to the People of God?

SUPPLEMENTARY MATERIAL

Catholic Updates: "Being Truly Catholic Today," by Rembert Weakland, O.S.B.; "The Christian Family Tree," by Thomas Bokenkotter; "Forgiveness in Our Church Today: Key to Healing," by Thomas Richstatter, O.F.M.; "Infallibility and Church Authority: The Spirit's Gift to the Church," by Kenneth R. Overberg, S.J.; "Lay Ministry: Not Just for a Chosen Few," by Thomas Richstatter, O.F.M.; "The Roman Curia: How the Church Is Run," by Pat McCloskey, O.F.M.; "Tradition in the Catholic Church—Why It's Still Important," by Monika K. Hellwig; "Vatican II: The Vision Lives On!" by Leonard Foley, O.F.M.; "What All Catholics Should Know About Eastern Catholic Churches," by Phyllis Zagano.

Scripture From Scratch: "First Among Disciples: Peter's Primacy in the New Testament," by Pheme Perkins.

Books: *Catholic Questions, Wise Answers*, edited by Michael Daley; *A Concise Guide to the Documents of Vatican II*, by Edward Hahnenberg; *The Compact History of the Catholic Church*, by Alan Schreck (rev. ed.); *The Story of the Church: Peak Moments From Pentecost to the Year 2000*, by Alfred McBride, O. PRAEM.; *Why Be Catholic? Understanding Our Experience and Tradition*, by Richard Rohr, O.F.M., and Joseph Martos.

Document: *The Lay Members of Christ's Faithful* (1989 post-synodal apostolic exhortation by Pope John Paul II).

CD: *Rebuild the Church*, by Richard Rohr, O.F.M., five discs; *Richard Rohr on Church*, four discs.

CHAPTER 15

JESUS WORSHIPS IN HIS CHURCH: EUCHARIST, THE RADIATING CENTER

IT IS NECESSARY AND HELPFUL TO TALK ABOUT "GRACE" AND "THE SUPERNATURAL" and "the sacraments." But we must beware of making them *things* existing by themselves. Going to confession to "get more grace" can have beautiful meaning; it can also sound like gathering some extra gold bars.

In order to de-emphasize this almost unavoidable view, I would like to begin our consideration of the sacraments by talking about actual living persons acting together, consciously and faithfully. After we have made their experience our own, we can speak about what all sacraments do.

EUCHARIST IN THE IDEAL CHURCH. Forty or a thousand or five people smile at each other as they take their places around a simple altar. A woman has lost her husband during the past week, and those near her embrace her silently, one by one. A baby cries; an old man is helped forward and given a seat next to the altar. A priest who has been moving through the group stands at the altar, and silence falls. After a minute or two, he extends his arms as if to hold us all and says, "Father, we thank you for calling us together to praise you with Jesus. We thank you for bringing us again to his saving death and resurrection and for renewing your Spirit in us. Nourish us again, heal the wounds of our sin, deepen our love and for-giveness for each other. Open our hearts, now, to your living Word. We pray through Jesus our Lord."

The whole group answers "Amen!" and looks expectantly to a young man who goes to the altar, reverently picks up a Bible and reads slowly and confidently. Again a relaxed silence falls.

A woman sings a short refrain, "This is the day the Lord has made," and we repeat her words. Then she sings, softly at first, several stanzas of a psalm: "I will bless the Lord at all times…," pausing a little between verses. The group sings the refrain after each verse.

The Gospel is Jesus' words about the seed that must die in order to bear fruit. After its proclamation, the priest sits down, leans forward and seems unable to find words. Then he looks all around him and says, "When John died last week, we sang with hope, because he had loved and prayed with us, and we knew his lifelong willingness to be joined to Jesus' death and resurrection. Today, Jesus asks us again to continue our dying and rising. He gives us power to die to everything that is not his work and to rise in faith and hope and love to be with him. This is his gift to us. We offer it, in him, to the Father."

A husband and wife bring bread and wine to the altar. The priest prays that they may become the Body and Blood of Jesus.

"Lift up your hearts!" And the answer comes, strongly, "We have lifted them up to the Lord!"

"Let us give thanks…."

The "Holy, Holy" rises joyfully. The simple words of the Eucharistic Prayer go on: "Let your Spirit come upon these gifts….Take this, all of you, and eat it. This is my body which is given up for you….The cup of the new covenant is my blood. Drink it, all of you." There is a little pause. Our heads bow with Jesus on the cross, and we see his face radiant with Easter glory.

"Christ will come again!" The last words are prolonged, as if no one wants to part with them.

"Father, we offer you Jesus, we offer ourselves in Jesus' childlike trust and obedience. Bring us closer together with him and with each other, so that we may be the one Body and show your kindness to the world.

"Bless all your people, who span the earth making you visible under our earthly father, the pope, and our bishop. Take to yourself brothers and sisters who ate at this table and have gone through the veil in faith. And make us, gathered here, worthy to be with Mary and all your children who are gathered with you, in Jesus.

"It is through him and with him and in him that we who are one in your

Spirit can offer you this perfect gift of honor and glory."

"Amen! Amen! Amen!" We sing our faith. Yes, that is what we want: to be the one Body, each concerned for every member, always dying with Jesus, always rising, joyful in offering his trust, his obedience, his worship.

He taught us to pray. Children around a table, we call to our Father and bless his name. The bread we ask for, the nourishment that will keep us alive forever, already lies before us. "Save us in the great trial."

The loaf is broken, a piece for each person present. The Body is not broken, but shared. Its separate pieces come together in the bodies and spirits of all present, making us the living Body. It is a fearful responsibility, a divine generosity. We sing our faith, our love for each other, our trust and our joy. Then it is over, quickly, and we go back—perhaps to our cells in a Roman prison, or to the kitchen for coffee and cookies, or home for breakfast. The Mass is over, the Mass has just begun. The pain of dying and the assured peace of rising thread our days.

WHAT HAPPENED? There are people who are irked at idealistic presentations. Better to be practical. What really happens to all those people who crowd into churches on Sunday? What kind of books do they need? When does one stand, sit, kneel? When is it a mortal sin to miss? How close together can we schedule Masses and be sure the parking lot isn't a mess?

Thank God for practical people. They save their communities from buying mythical oil wells in Cincinnati, from attempting Handel's *Messiah* at the 7:30 AM Mass and from trying to build a church with local elm trees.

But there is no need to apologize for the idealistic. We are personally involved in an event that reaches far beyond idealism. We are part of a divine action. We don't go to Mass to watch but to act. And our acts are the least: God acts first, right now, in Jesus. To be very practical, we shouldn't miss the point.

LIVE AND IN PERSON. We have seen what Jesus did: lived, died, rose. What does he do now, today? At this Mass?

The Jews cherished a saying which shows what a liturgical-sacramental celebration does: "Not with our fathers did he [God] make this covenant, but with us, all of us who are alive here this day" (Deuteronomy 5:3).

They certainly weren't denying what God had done in the past. They were saying that the past is present. God acted back there in history. But there is no "back there" with God. There is only *now*.

When Jesus said at the Last Supper, "Do this in memory of me," he was not inviting a sort of wistful remembering of something long ago, like pleasantly basking in the memory of a childhood picnic or of a kindly doctor, long since dead, who saved our life.

Jesus does not die and rise at each Mass. Calvary and Easter are not repeated. Rather, his one sacrifice and victory are made present. We are brought into union with them; time is annihilated. As the Mass is repeated throughout history, this happens to more and more people at more and more times.

At the Easter Vigil, one light is struck from flint in the darkness. This symbolizes the Resurrection. Then the flame runs through the church as through stubble, as all the candles of the people are lighted from the one source. *It is one fire.*

Fire is a good word here. We may tend to think of "presence" as something factual, impersonal, dead. All the kids may be "present" in class on the day of the first snowfall, but their eyes are on the window. Two people can be seated at the same table and cut off from each other. In the room where you are, chairs and pictures and lamps are present, but they are not present to you.

It is the living risen Jesus, raised above all human limitations and pain, who is present with us: not like a visiting official, but as our closest friend; not impersonally, but sharing an intimate meal; not condemning, but forgiving (see *Catechism*, #1373–1377).

This Jesus, eternal God and our brother, shows us the heart of Calvary and Easter through his attitude, his spirit, his trust, obedience, generosity, total love of the Father. Eucharist is to make us, as a body and as individuals, like him.

LORD, SAVE YOUR PEOPLE. Jesus does not save us as individuals, but as members of his Body. We are not just people—unconnected and isolated arms and legs. We are a people—in fact, the People of God.

God saves the world by undoing Babel, which happened when a people became just *people*, all doing their own thing. They did not love each other so they did not love God. They did not love God, so they did not love each other. Babel babbles—no communication because no community.

"God was reconciling the world to himself in Christ" (2 Corinthians 5:19c). The whole world is meant to be one family in Jesus. Jesus came to bring all of us "into the circle," which is what *re-concile* means. (We pull our chairs back from the circle; we don't want any part of the meeting. We're not interested in *them*, just in ourselves. Jesus re-forms the circle, inviting us to pull up a chair again.)

In the first burst of enthusiasm after Pentecost, we find an "ideal" Christian community—a model, so to speak, of Jesus' whole purpose. As Luke reports in Acts:

> The community of believers was of one heart and mind, and no one claimed that any of his possessions was his own, but they had every-thing in common. With great power the apostles bore witness to the resurrection of the Lord Jesus, and great favor was accorded them all. There was no needy person among them, for those who owned prop-erty or houses would sell them, bring the proceeds of the sale, and put them at the feet of the apostles, and they were distributed to each according to need. (4:32–34)

(There's no denying some troubles in that community. The selfishness of Ananias and Sapphira [see Acts 5:1–2] pops up today, too. But this is still the authentic picture of church.)

God calls a people together. *Ekklesia*, the Greek word from which we get English words pertaining to church—*ecclesiastical*—meant an assembly of citizens called together by the town crier. We do not "go to church," as if it were our idea. We are privileged to be called. We have received an urgent message from the King.

Jesus makes us into his people, again and again. But he doesn't start from scratch each time. At our initiation into the church, we are brought into an existing community, the Body of Jesus. The Mass is the expression of a love already existing among us; it nourishes and reconfirms that love. And as we visibly converge on the altar, like spokes of a wheel, we "make" the visible Jesus today, his Body. Only he can give us the power to love and forgive each other, and as we do that together at Eucharist, we discover he is in our midst.

THE LAST SUPPER. Jesus has consciously and willingly accepted his death. He has deliberately come to Jerusalem to die. It is his choice, the final, perfect giving of himself to his Father. Now, before the agony begins, he celebrates his death and resurrection in the family meal his people have celebrated for a thousand years (see *Catechism,* #611, 1337).

His spirits are high. In a few hours the coming horror will rise to the surface, and he will shrink into the earth at Gethsemane. But now he says, "I have eagerly desired to eat this Passover with you before I suffer" (Luke 22:15).

Passover is the most sacred time in the Jewish year. At the meal, a child ritually asks, "Why is this night different from all other nights?" The answer is a grateful recalling of the greatest moments of Jewish history— until now.

When they were slaves in Egypt, God gave the Jews a special meal: an unblemished lamb. Some of its blood was to be put on their doorposts; then they were to eat the lamb with loins girt, sandals on their feet and staff in hand, like those who are in flight (see Exodus 12:11).

The angel that struck the firstborn of the Egyptians "passed over" the homes marked with the blood. Then God led the people out of slavery— the Exodus, the escape, the way out, the rescue—and brought them to the desert. God fed them with manna. And on a sacred day at Mount Sinai, God ratified a new covenant with the people: "If you...keep my covenant, you shall be my special possession, dearer to me than all other people....You shall be to me a kingdom of priests, a holy nation" (Exodus 19:5–6).

Moses offered the sacrifice that ratified the covenant in a dramatic liturgy. Taking the blood of animals, he poured half onto a stone altar which represented God. Then he sprinkled the other half on the people saying, "This is the blood of the covenant" (Exodus 24:8b). Blood meant life: By God's gracious gift, God's life was joined to the life of the people.

Now the Lamb of God is about to pour out his blood on the altar of the cross. In an amazing irony, "His blood be upon us and upon our children" (Matthew 27:25b) will come true. The new Moses will pour his own life-giving blood out of his crucified body to give his life to his people.

Jesus carefully follows the Passover ritual. But when the time comes to eat the unleavened bread, he speaks words never heard before:

> Then he took the bread, said the blessing, broke it, and gave it to them, saying, "This is my body, which will be given for you; do this in memory of me." And likewise the cup after they had eaten, saying, "This cup is the new covenant in my blood, which will be shed for you." (Luke 22:19–20; also see Matthew 26:26–28; Mark 14:22–24; 1 Corinthians 11:23–26)

The constant faith of the church has always taken the words of Jesus literally. "It has always been the conviction of the Church," said the Council of Trent, that there is a "marvelous and extraordinary change of the whole substance of the bread into Christ's body and the whole substance of the wine into his blood, so that only the species [external appearances] remain." Or simply: What was bread and wine is now Jesus.

But the meaning is essential to the fact. The Last Supper made present the reality of Calvary and Easter even before they happened in time. The body that would die and be glorified, the blood that would become the life of his people, already lies in the hands of the disciples and touches their lips. Jesus is irrevocably committed to his death and resurrection. The Eucharist of the ages is already before the Father.

In the same way, our Eucharist is Jesus' making present the fact and the meaning of his death and resurrection (see *Catechism*, #1104). It is always, as it was then, a new Exodus, led by a new Moses. It is a new and transformed Passover meal, a holy sacrifice uniting God and the chosen people. It is the new and perfect covenant, eternal and unshakable. "The Eucharist, as Christ's saving presence in the community of the faithful and its spiritual food, is the most precious possession which the Church can have in her journey through history," wrote John Paul II in *Church of the Eucharist* (9).

THE TRANSFORMATION OF THE COMMUNITY. It is not just bread and wine that is changed. We are changed, transformed, purified, enlivened. It may not always be possible to feel the fire that runs through the assembly, but we must be open to its transforming power.

Jesus certainly doesn't want a group of bored "disciples" standing outside the door while he goes in and makes arrangements for our release. We're not just getting out of prison; we're getting out of human slavery to evil, untruth, greed, lust, cruelty, mindlessness, boredom. We're being rescued from human suffering.

But this process is not merely negative. There's no way we can be forgiven without being made more fully human. So Jesus has to make us fully human—loving, thirsting for truth and wisdom, open, forgiving—in order to have something to "sacrifice" to the Father in authentic worship.

Jesus, of course, is the perfect Adorer of the Father. But the only criterion of how I love God is the way I treat my neighbor. So the sign of true adoration is true community. Jesus can only be our "Amen" to God if we join his "Amen" as sincerely loving brothers and sisters.

In a certain community of priests, a maverick homilist once said, "We do not dare to continue this Mass if we don't intend to stop treating each other like strangers!"

ONE LOAF, ONE CUP. In an ancient eucharistic hymn the first Christians prayed: "Just as this bread which was once scattered grains on the hillside has been gathered into one loaf, so may the Church be gathered into one Body" (*Didache*).

Like the gathered grain is the one cup of wine, the product of many grapes. Wine is the symbol of festivity and fellowship. We are nourished, but we are also delighted.

Bread and wine—it is the meal of the deathly poor, indeed, but also the banquet of the children of God, a foretaste of the eternally happy table of the Messiah: "Learn to savor how good the Lord is" (Psalm 34:9a).

As for the physically poor, Eucharist moves us to help them. We cannot welcome the Lord in bread and wine if we refuse to welcome him in the poorest of his brothers and sisters (see *Catechism*, #1397).

A HOLY SACRIFICE. The popular notion of sacrifice centers on giving up something valuable; often it has a note of penitential discipline. But the understanding of sacrifice in the Bible—and in early Christian theology—centers on the literal Latin meaning of the word: "to make holy."

Saint Augustine's definition of sacrifice was "every work done in order to achieve unity with God in holy communion." Saint Thomas Aquinas says that the suffering of Christ is a sacrifice precisely because it is the expression of his love for us and for his Father. Sacrifice is primarily a matter of the heart and involves total self-offering. And Jesus was wholly open in love to his Father.

So the Mass is the one perfect sacrifice in the world. Jesus offers himself and we are offered with him. Sacrifice is the way Jesus makes us holy. By his blood we have divine life (see *Catechism*, #1359–1366).

The Mass is both meal and sacrifice. Jesus is both priest and victim—if we remember that the meaning of the latter word is "set apart, holy." The whole purpose of his sacrifice is to unite us with him. Paul says, "I have been crucified with Christ; yet I live, no longer I, but Christ lives in me..." (Galatians 2:19b–20a).

Jesus makes us holy by standing before us and saying, "I hand you my life. I hand you this bread and wine to be your life. I want you to know what it is to die that others may live."

CHRIST WILL COME AGAIN. At the beginning of this chapter we spoke of an ideal Mass. This straining toward the best is implicit in the Eucharist: We are—perhaps unconsciously—straining toward the Kingdom in its perfect fulfillment, the way it will be in heaven. Heaven begins on earth, in the union of Jesus and his people. We are already the community of the faithful joined to the heavenly Eucharist Jesus celebrates with all who have gone before us in faith (see *Catechism*, #1107, 1130). They are gathered around the Father in happiness—and we are that same gathering. When Jesus spoke of himself as Bread of Life, he said, "Whoever eats this bread will live forever" (John 6:51b).

Forty, or a thousand, or five people smile at each other as they leave the altar to become a widening circle of Jesus' presence in the world. They go back to their cells in Buchenwald, strengthened and peaceful against the day of their being offered up; back to the kitchen for coffee and klatsch; back to a thousand homes where life will have hope and courage and dignity.

...[L]ive in love, as Christ loved us and handed himself over for us as a sacrificial offering to God for a fragrant aroma. (Ephesians 5:2)

REFLECTION/DISCUSSION STARTERS

1) The Eucharist can be described in many ways: making present the fact and meaning of Jesus' death and resurrection; a new Passover meal; the transformation of the community; the one perfect sacrifice. Which of these is/are most meaningful to you? Why?

2) Reflect on the "marvelous and extraordinary change" of the bread and wine into Christ's Body and Blood. What does this change mean to you?

SCRIPTURE READINGS

Luke 22:19–20; Matthew 26:26–28; Mark 14:22–24; 1 Corinthians 11:23–26; Acts 5:1–11.

SUPPLEMENTARY MATERIAL

Catholic Updates: "Eucharist: Heart of the Church," John Paul II's encyclical *Ecclesia in Eucharistia* in condensed form; "Eucharist: Understanding Christ's Body" and "The Liturgy of the Eucharist," both by William H. Shannon; "Finding Jesus in the Eucharist: Four Ways He Is Present" and "From Passover to Eucharist: God's Liberating Love," both by Lawrence Mick; "God's Love Is Free: The Banquet Says It All," by Richard Rohr, O.F.M.; "How 'All of Us' Celebrate the Mass," by Sandra DeGidio, O.S.M.; "Real Presence: Jesus' Gift to the Church," by John Feister; "Sacraments of Initiation: God's 'I Love You,'" by Thomas Richstatter, O.F.M.; "Sunday Mass: Easter All Year Long" (shortened form of *Celebrating the Lord's Day*), by Pope John Paul II; "A Tour of a Catholic Church" and "A Walk Through the Mass: A Step-by-Step Explanation," both by Thomas Richstatter, O.F.M.; "Ten Reasons for Going to Mass," by Leonard Foley, O.F.M.

Books: Fire of God's Love: 120 Reflections on the Eucharist by Mike Aquilina; *The Mass: A Guided Tour* by Thomas Richstatter, O.F.M.; *A Short History of the Mass,* by Alfred McBride, O.PRAEM.; *201 Inspirational Stories of the Eucharist,* by Patricia Proctor, O.S.C.

Encyclical: Church of the Eucharist.

. | CHAPTER 16 | .

THE ONE JESUS IN ALL THE
SACRAMENTAL ACTIONS

THE EUCHARIST AS DISCUSSED IN THE LAST CHAPTER CAN BE TAKEN AS A MODEL of all the other sacramental actions of the Church: baptism and confirmation, reconciliation and anointing of the sick, marriage and orders.

For a working definition, which will be expanded, let us say that the sacramental actions of the church are visible signs of God's saving love (see *Catechism*, #774). Jesus "makes" these signs by means of his community, the church. Faith-filled entrance into these signs is the means of salvation and holiness of individuals and, therefore, of the community.

GOD ALONE BRINGS US TO THE ALTAR. Our human tendency is to congratulate ourselves on the great things we do for God—such as faithfully going to Mass on Sunday. The fact is, we could not approach or partake in the Eucharist if we were not invited and empowered by God. Our covenant-friendship with God is God's gift, not our achievement.

We have the privilege of being born again into God's own life. "Going to confession" is possible only because God calls to us. Christian marriage is God's special consecration, not merely something comparable to what a justice of the peace can effect.

GOD ACTS IN JESUS. Recall the tremendously important fact that Jesus is the sacrament of God. In him we see God in human flesh. We know what God is like by looking at Jesus, by listening to him.

But Jesus is no longer visible. So he gave the world the *sacrament* of Jesus, his visible Body, the church—a group of people who *do what he did*, not simply in imitation, but with his power acting through them. They continue his saving actions today (see *Catechism*, #774).

Each Christian around the altar represents Jesus in a unique way. The priest has been given the vocation of representing Jesus as the Head and Center, a visible center around which the church can gather. Every man and woman and child there, by baptism, is a sharer in Jesus' priesthood, enabled and called to full, conscious and active participation.

If sacramental life begins to pall from repetition, faith can revive the astounding fact at the center: Jesus meets us personally and applies now, through his Spirit, the healing and enlivening power of his death and resurrection.

JESUS ACTS THROUGH SIGNS. The traditional definition of sacraments is that they are "outward signs of inward grace instituted by Christ."

These sacramental signs are not dead signs, like "Albuquerque, 46 miles," or "Luebering's Paint Store." They are *people-signs*—that is, living, conscious, faith-full persons entering into the meaning of certain visible actions.

Sacraments can be called *symbols* (even though many people think of something that is "just a symbol" as not very important). A symbol is a sign-with-feeling: a kiss, an embrace, sharing a birthday cake, putting a live plant at a convalescent's bedside. Things are symbols only if someone *means* them: wedding rings, an American flag, a flower pressed between the pages of a prayer book.

The first and greatest sign Jesus uses, we must always repeat, is the church gathered in faith and love. Within this fundamental sign, however, Jesus and his church chose other signs. First, in the Eucharist, Jesus chose the oldest "natural sacrament" of the human race—a family meal. For baptism there is water, the symbol of cleansing and, more importantly, of life and death—we cannot live without it, but we can drown in it. Anointing with oil suggests the suppleness and strength of athletes' muscles as well as the healing ointments put on the bodies of the sick. Hands laid on people in orders is a kind of embrace, showing the desire to share power, love, healing. The vows of a bride and a groom are the sign of their lifelong and exclusive commitment to each other.

WHY SEVEN? Every person, every action, every thing in the world can be a sign, a symbol and a "sacrament." Words are symbols. Emily Dickinson speaks of the "sacrament of summer days." Every Christian is called to be a sacrament of Jesus' love and healing today.

The seven sacraments, however, are the events in which the *crucial moments* of salvation history are brought to bear on *critical situations in our lives* (see *Catechism*, #1210): in the Eucharist, a summing up of all salvation; in baptism, birth; in confirmation, facing up to responsibility; in penance, the terrible human need for forgiveness; in anointing, facing the inherent weakness of the body; in marriage, the forming of the essential building block of society; in orders, the need for a center of unity and proclamation of Jesus' words.

One final purpose of a determined set of visible signs as we have in the seven sacraments is this: *We can be sure.* Of course we know God loves us— as you might "know" your spouse or friend loves you. But if he or she gives no external sign of love—if there were never any word or touch or gift or smile—you would conclude there is no love. Once deeply loved, we may be able to go on if we are forced into loneliness or isolation. But just being human means we need to be *reassured* all the time.

The signs of God's love made by his community in the sacraments are absolute assurances of God's love. I am absolutely certain God welcomes me at the eucharistic table or forgives my sin because the church does.

We may get some idea of the assurance of the sacraments by recalling an expressway trip. We are fairly sure we're on I-75. We saw the sign when we started. We couldn't have missed a turn, could we? But there hasn't been a sign for a long time...Ah, there's one—I-75!

But this is a mere "dead" sign. Sacramental actions are living signs, like embracing, holding someone's hand, comforting a sick child. They "contain" human and divine action and feeling.

SACRAMENTS DEMAND COMMUNITY. The church is never so much the church as when it is gathered together for the liturgy. In fact, that is the only time one can find the church; otherwise it is invisible, merged with the world. Liturgy is our public action, the way we carry on Jesus' work of redemption in plain sight (see *Catechism*, #1069).

By the sacraments Christ acts with and in us *now*. The words and signs we use, by the power of the Spirit, make real and effective what they signify (see *Catechism*, #1084, 1108).

We have already stated many times that the community of the church makes Jesus visible. What needs to be stressed, further, is the presence of the community for the celebration of *all* the sacraments. Just as no one can live completely alone, no one can believe in total isolation. We believe because we have seen the effects of belief in lives around us; we inspire others to belief in the same way. We are, each of us, links in a great chain of believers (see *Catechism*, #166).

Sometimes only a priest can be present to an individual for the sacramental action—a lonely sick person, the only person who comes to confession. Or the baptism of a baby may be attended only by two sponsors. These circumstances may be unavoidable, but they are not the normal way the church should act. A genial priest may be able effectively to communicate a whole parish's welcome. But in any case it is the whole community's love that needs to be made visible.

In baptism the *whole* parish—at least the part represented by all who are, say, at one of the Sunday Masses—welcomes the new member. In confirmation those who have already given witness in the Spirit—and perhaps have some scars to show for it—add their own "confirmation" to that of the Spirit. In penance the sinner is joyfully received back by a community which continues the forgiving spirit of Jesus; in anointing, at least family, friends and neighbors represent the great community of the church, which asks the sick person to join his or her suffering to the ongoing dying and rising of Jesus. In marriage the community is happy to see a new "little church" beginning and promises its support and encouragement. At an ordination, the congregation welcomes one sent to proclaim the Word to them.

The spirit and attitude of the priest and all the other members of the community is very important. A listless priest and/or a bored community can make the individual sacramental actions look like magic mumbo jumbo. If a number of individuals come to the same Mass, but show no interest in each other, they certainly do not give the "sign" of the loving Jesus continuing his work. If a priest is mechanical with a penitent, if the parish shows no interest in a new baby's baptism or a young couple's marriage, the impression can be given that something merely official or magical happens.

A word must be said here about a phrase that has caused a lot of misunderstanding about sacraments: *ex opere operato.* This means that the worst priest in the world, provided he has at least a minimum intention of exercising his priesthood, cannot stop the love of God coming to his people through sacramental actions. In other words, the *worthiness* of the minister is not an essential factor (see *Catechism,* #1128). Nevertheless, the sign-value of the minister and the worshipping community is important if the fullness of God's saving action is to be experienced.

It is the ongoing community which makes possible sacramental action. We do not start from square one every Sunday. We come to express the faith and love which God has already developed within us, and we come to *be renewed and strengthened* in that life. Hence the sacraments are both causes and effects. A celebrating community is alive when it comes and more alive when it disperses. In all the sacramental actions—not just Eucharist—unity and charity are of the essence.

GOD SPEAKS. An important new emphasis in sacramental celebration is the reading of God's Word. This was always done at Mass, of course, and at anointing. Now it is an integral part of the other sacraments as well.

For instance, readings similar to those in the Liturgy of the Word at Eucharist are now part of communal penance celebrations. Even at the reconciliation of just one penitent, a reading from Scripture is to be made. Why?

It is a reminder, at least, that we are not the prime movers. This is God's sign, and God wants to tell us the meaning of the sign. God's initiative is heard in the word. God's gentle assurance—or unavoidable warning—are part of the divine call.

"INWARD GRACE." Grace is at the heart of Christianity and should be as clearly understood as anything divine—and therefore mysterious—can be.

First of all, grace is not an "it," even though we refer to "it" that way. There is no such thing as "grace" stored in a vast heavenly container, from which God sends out various "amounts." It is a shame that we human beings think of grace that way, because we thereby reduce "it" to a measurable commodity like money or ice cream.

Grace is actually the loving God offering to us a relationship of friendship. God offers us a sharing in the divine life, whereby our love becomes possessed by divine love and our consciousness (faith) by divine wisdom. God's grace is not something separate from God, as a person's gift is separate from the person. Grace is God calling us into the Trinity's own intimate life—not just to any kind of relationship but into God's very nature (see *Catechism*, #260). Grace is God personally coming to us. This God-life is hidden now (though its effect, in good people, is beautiful to behold). But someday it will blossom into face-to-face vision and union with God.

The "it" problem comes from the fact that we speak of grace as the *result* of God's coming—our accepting the relationship, our "allowing" God to enter into our lives. (But even this is God's doing. As the *Sacramentary* says, "Our desire to please you is itself your gift.") From this viewpoint, then, we think of grace as something "in" us. Yet it is not a something so much as a *quality* of our being. It is God's loving gift of the power to be united with God, the power to choose to accept and continue a loving relationship. Truly, grace enables us to be "born again" into a "new" life infinitely superior to mere human life.

In Jesus we have unparalleled grace. That is, as a *man*, he allowed himself to be totally possessed by his Father's love. His very food was to do the Father's will. He was totally graced. He was the primary sacrament of God's gracious loving.

Each sacramental action means the pouring out of the one love of God in accordance with the particular purpose of that sacrament. The sacraments separate out the one love of God into its various aspects as a prism separates light into the colors of the rainbow. So we see the one love of God as life-giving, healing, reconciling, strengthening, enabling.

But we must not make the sacraments the only source of God's grace. These are the peak moments, the high points in the Christian community's life. They are moments, as it were, of *visible* grace, of assured grace.

But God simply loves all people *all the time.* As Gregory Baum has well said, the first means of grace is life. Every moment, every person, every situation is a kind of sacrament. Coming through each one is God's offer of strength, God's reassurance, God's call to truth and love—to God's own self.

It is our *life* that is graced. We are never without the presence of the saving God.

WORSHIP. Do we think of getting married as worshipping God? Or going to confession? That is the emphasis the church is trying to get us back to.

The sacraments are indeed God's signs. If God did not "make" them, we would be helpless. But we must enter into them, and into their *meaning.* And when God acts, it can only be to bring us to the only source of life and happiness: God. When that happens, what is the obvious thing to do? To thank God, to *treat God as God*—that is, as the only Good, the only Love, the source of all, Father and Savior. This is worship.

When God leads us through sorrow to a new dedication to total trust and faith and obedience, this is the worship of our lives. When anointing calls upon the sick person to put complete trust and hope in God, or when Christian marriage places a lifetime into God's hands—this, too, is worship.

This is not just staid, somber, "official" worship, but the joyful worship of those who are fully aware of the privilege of being God's people, who can come with a deep joy and peace even to the funeral of a loved one, and who can go away from the altar, if necessary, to the ovens of Auschwitz.

Someone has suggested that a very simple definition of any sacrament is *saving worship.* The love of God comes "down" to us, and our perfect worship goes "up" in Jesus.

STRAINING TOWARD THE FUTURE. In the back of our minds, at least, we realize that any sacramental action of Jesus comes from eternity where he is already "at the right hand of the Father." Yet the life of the church can only be lived today, of course. To live in the past or in the future is to miss the grace of the present moment. But it is still true that "…here we have no lasting city" (Hebrews 13:14a).

We may not neglect any possible improvement of the human condition, in medicine, science, education, art, and so on. But we are straining forward to the day when we will see God face-to-face, when we will see the risen Jesus and be united to all our families and friends and the whole people of God.

Those who have "gone before us" are part of every liturgy. The praise of the earthly community is the same as that of Mary and the saints in heaven.

Summing up, then: God calls us to sacramental acts. They are the acts of God, in Jesus and in the Spirit; they are acts of the church; they are acts of each individual. They are acts of faith and worship. They are the acts of a visible sign, a community, using visible signs itself. God speaks to us in human words, and our hearts are filled with divine life, called grace. We worship and we are saved. We face the present with peace and the future with hope.

So the Christian community is called to give "signs of life." From a human viewpoint, it is a fearful responsibility. Only God gives our sacramental actions meaning. If the first "sign"—the union of loving Christians—is not an evident sacrament, many will feel that the seven particular sacraments are meaningless ritual.

It is easy to describe Sunday Mass as a bore. Thousands of people do. But Jesus came to make, not to find, the perfect community. He found sinful men and women and offered them forgiveness, healing, new life, faith. It doesn't happen magically, and it doesn't happen instantly. The last day a Christian community gathers around an altar, there will be something awry. There will still be a ferment of resentment in some hearts. Not everybody will be "open" to his or her neighbor.

But it will still be the Mass. All the glorious things said of it will be true.

And for the people there, painfully on their way to becoming "Christ come to full stature" (see Ephesians 4:13), it will be a *sign*—of hope.

REFLECTION/DISCUSSION STARTERS

1) Name some signs or symbols in daily life that are especially meaningful to you.
2) What are some of the signs used in the sacraments?

3) Reflect on the most significant or crucial moments of your life. In what ways do the sacraments mark significant moments in a person's spiritual life?

4) How do you understand grace? How have you experienced grace in your life?

5) Reflect on the statement that "every moment, every person, every situation is a kind of sacrament." How is that true? Is it true for you?

SUPPLEMENTARY MATERIAL

Catholic Updates: "How Catholics Understand Grace," by John Feister; "Sacraments: It All Starts With Jesus," by Thomas Richstatter, O.F.M.; "Sacramentals: Embracing God Through Creation," by Joanne Turpin; "The Seven Sacraments: Symbols of God's Care," by Sandra DeGidio, O.S.M.

CHAPTER 17

JESUS WELCOMES STRANGERS INTO HIS COMMUNITY: BAPTISM

SUPPOSE A STRANGER HAPPENED INTO THE PLACE WHERE THE EUCHARIST WAS being celebrated by the same group we met in chapter fifteen. Suppose, further, that this man or woman was moved by the obvious love present. The stranger might sense the peace of the assembly, perhaps an atmosphere of humbleness as well as joy.

What would the community do for the stranger?

Again, let us paint the ideal picture. The gathered Christians would first of all welcome the stranger as a person with respect and ease. They would then offer anything possibly needed: food, clothing, shelter.

If the outsider sooner or later asked, "What is it that you have? Why do you act the way you do?" they would say, "Stay with us and see."

In this way the "catechumenate" would begin (or rather, in this case, the "pre-catechumenate"). The word *catechumenate* comes from the Greek and means "instruction." Earlier generations of Catholics learned in their "catechisms"—the same word—that far back in church history the first part of the Mass was called "the Mass of the Catechumens." Catechumens were people being prepared for baptism.

Because a time came when infants were almost the only ones being baptized, the catechumenate faded for a time from the experience of the church. "Taking instructions" to become a "convert" replaced the catechumenate. An individual (sometimes a class) would meet with a priest weekly for two or three months for instruction in the doctrines of the church. If all went well, baptism followed.

The bishops at Vatican II called for the restoration of the catechume-nate and, after years of preparation, the new rite was given to the church in January 1972. It is "something new again" for many Catholics. Their instinct is right, for the respected liturgist Father Aidan Kavanaugh, O.S.B., has said: "This document may well appear to a writer a century from now *as the most important result of the Second Vatican Council for the life of the Church.*"

Why? Because it will—or should—bring home to both catechumens and "born Catholics" the radical and shattering implications of what it means to be "born into Christ." It points to the only possible way of approaching the Christian life: total, lifelong, deepening "conversion."

In Christian countries the most frequent celebration of the sacrament, obviously, will still be for infants. We will return to this matter later. But the emphasis on the catechumenate will serve to point up what must be the lifelong process whereby these baptized infants are brought to full commitment to Christ.

The catechumenate takes place within the Christian community. Special people are of course involved—bishop, priest, deacon, sponsors. But the whole community (parish) is called to be concerned for this iden-tifiable group of catechumens. The catechumens are a designated group; they are known and loved for who they are, new "children" coming to birth. They are the object not only of the prayers but also the personal attention and encouragement of the community.

The Rite of Christian Initiation of Adults (RCIA) directs the faithful to "be ready to open up the spirit of the Christian community to the candi-dates, to invite them into their families, to engage them in private conver-sation, and to invite them to some community gatherings." Community members should be present at the various celebrations of stages in the process of being brought to baptism, especially the special lenten cere-monies. As the new Christians are baptized at the Easter Vigil, Christians "should renew their own baptismal promises in their hearts." In the time after baptism they should welcome the newly baptized with charity and help them to sense the joy of belonging to the community of the baptized.

Each candidate has a sponsor who knows and helps him or her. The sponsor is the witness to the community of the "morals, faith and intention" of the candidate. It is the sponsor's responsibility to "show the cate-chumen in a friendly way the place of the gospel in his own life and in society, to help him in doubts and anxieties, to give public testimony for him, and to watch over the progress of his baptismal life."

The bishop or his delegate admits the candidates. Priests attend to the pastoral and personal care of the catechumens, providing for their cate-chesis with the help of deacons and catechists.

The preparation of catechumens covers several periods. The first is a period of inquiry (the *pre-catechumenate*). The community—priests and laypersons—begins to introduce its belief and its life to an interested person.

The *catechumenate* begins with a public ceremony in which the catechu-mens profess their intention to become a part of the community. The community, in turn, welcomes them to the church. During this time, cat-echumens are instructed more deeply in the faith, grow more familiar with the community's way of life, participate in the Liturgy of the Word and begin to take part in the community's activities.

The third stage (*election*) begins the day the catechumen is chosen for baptism by the church. It usually coincides with Lent, a period of intense purification and enlightenment for all believers, but especially for those preparing for baptism. Special rites are celebrated within the Sunday liturgy, offering the catechumens the support of the community's prayers and introducing to them the words Christians cherish: the Creed and the Lord's Prayer. The culmination is the high point of the church year: the celebration of baptism at the Easter Vigil.

Finally, the period of *mystagogia*, or post-baptismal catechesis, draws the newly baptized into full participation in the community.

SACRAMENTALS OF BAPTISM. At various points in the process of the catechu-menate, special ceremonies unfold the meaning of the sacrament (see *Catechism*, #1667, 1671–1673). The Sign of the Cross is made on the fore-head of the candidates by the priest and sponsors or catechists when they are accepted as catechumens. They may take a new name. The candidates are welcomed into the church building. Special oil is blessed for anoint-ing the catechumens, a sign of strength. Special ceremonies are held for them on the third, fourth and fifth Sundays of Lent.

After baptism each new Christian is anointed on the crown of the head as a sign of new dignity shared with Christ as priest, prophet and king. A white garment is placed on each, and the priest prays, "You have become a new creation and have clothed yourselves in Christ. Take this white garment and bring it unstained to the judgment seat of our Lord Jesus Christ, so that you may have everlasting life."

Finally, the sponsors light a candle from the Easter candle, representing Christ newly risen, and hand it to the newly baptized. "You have been enlightened by Christ. Walk always as children of the light and keep the flame of faith alive in your hearts."

Evidently something very serious is going on here! And "born Catholics" are moved to say, "If so much is asked of these catechumens, what should I be asking of myself? What does it mean that I am a baptized Christian?"

What *does* it mean?

New Life in Christ. Saint Paul speaks of the Gentiles being grafted onto the vine who is Christ. A grafted branch bears leaves and fruit from a new "rich root" (see Romans 11:17). The new Christian begins an entirely new life. He or she is a "new creation" (see 2 Corinthians 5:17), called to be as different from the old self as the new Adam was from the old.

Another word not familiar to us has a powerful meaning: *incorporation.* Baptism makes us members of the Body (*corpus*) of Christ. We become living members through which the life of Jesus flows and acts.

The stranger who wandered into our ideal community soon felt the warmth of Jesus in his members and heard his call. Baptism is the concrete assurance of that acceptance. It is the stranger's personal decision to be accepted and become no longer a stranger, but one who is joined to the whole community of Christ—both this visible one right here and the community of Jesus in the whole world—a living member, needing and needed.

Another word seems somehow unworthy of baptism: *initiation.* But it means more than joining a club; it means to make a beginning. There are three sacraments whereby one is fully initiated into the Body of Christ: baptism, confirmation, Eucharist (see *Catechism,* #1212). The new

Christian celebrates all three of these sacraments with the community at the Easter vigil.

Baptism is a "*Christ*-ening," a beautiful word we have flattened into "christening." It means being made able to grow to the maturity of Christ. Each of us is unique, and has a unique, unrepeatable relationship with Christ—a source of the infinite variety and beauty of the church. In Jesus we enter into the life of the Trinity, baptized "in the name of the Father and of the Son and of the Holy Spirit."

We are the "adopted" children of the Father because, unlike in a legal adoption, God begets in us a sharing in divine life. Beyond all understanding, we become "sharers of the divine nature" (see 2 Peter 1:4). We live and move and have our being in the very life and love and power of God. Saint John exclaims:

> See what love the Father has bestowed on us that we may be called the children of God. Yet so we are.... [W]hat we shall be has not yet been revealed. We do know that when it is revealed we shall be like him, for we shall see him as he is. (1 John 3:1a–b, 2b)

Baptism is the concrete assurance of these gifts of God. It is also our acceptance of God's love. It is our declaration of unconditional self-giving. We become God's property. We always were, of course, but now we make it joyfully voluntary.

The voluntariness is a gift. We do not "decide" to come to Jesus; he calls us to him. This is dramatically expressed in the ritual dialogue at the very beginning of the catechumenate:

> *Celebrant*: What do you ask of God's church?
> *Candidates*: Faith.
> *Celebrant*: What does faith offer you?
> *Candidates*: Eternal life.

Being "in Christ" becomes the prime value of life. No one and no thing is more important. Now there is only one way to look at all Christians: They are all graced by Christ. Everything else—being pope, working miracles, having children, being crucified—is secondary. As Paul says, for all who have been baptized into Christ, "There is neither Jew nor Greek, there is neither slave nor free person, there is not male and female: for you are all one in Christ Jesus" (Galatians 3:28).

WATER: DEATH AND LIFE. Whether baptism is administered by means of immersion or by pouring water over the candidate's head, its meaning is the same: We die and rise again. In the early church baptism was conferred by immersion (as in many churches today). After the long period of preparation, the climactic moment came. The candidates were led, one by one, down the steps of a baptismal pool and immersed beneath the surface of the water. They disappeared, "drowned." Then they were raised up, literally and grace-fully, and led up the steps on the other side of the pool—new Christs.

This transformation is what Paul is referring to when he says: "How can we who died to sin yet live in it? Or are you not aware that we who were baptized into Christ Jesus were baptized into his death? We were indeed buried with him through baptism into death, so that, just as Christ was raised from the dead by the glory of the Father, we too might live in newness of life" (Romans 6:2–4).

We are close to divine mystery here. We are brought into the dying and rising of Jesus himself. We are enabled to join his willingness to lose everything, even life—in total trust of the Father. With him we are raised to new life—he to glory, we to grace now and glory ultimately. When Paul says, "I have been crucified with Christ," he is not speaking of physical suffering (though that finally became a result of his union with Christ), but of a death to everything that was not the attitude of Christ, as his next words indicate: "I live, no longer I, but Christ lives in me" (Galatians 2:20a).

FORGIVENESS OF SIN. The stranger who came to our Eucharist is a symbol of all the alienation in the world. To sin is to become a stranger to God, wandering like Cain in a vast and empty wasteland. But in baptism, received in faith, God forgives all sin.

In the beginning the human race estranged itself from God by deliberate sin. As a result, we are all born in the condition of "original sin" (see *Catechism*, #387–389). It is as if our grandfather once owned the state of California and lost it in a poker game. It is not our fault we will not inherit the property, but we have no claim to it just the same. Likewise, our earliest ancestors lost the spark of divine life that was given them at creation.

Being born in the state of original sin does not mean we are being deprived of any "rights" by God. It is the mystery of human solidarity that no one person can do anything without affecting everyone else. If that condition seems unfair to us, let us remember that God's love surrounds every human being more powerfully than the condition of belonging to an alien race.

God wills the salvation of every human being. What God wills, God effectively achieves. Nothing—not the death of a baby before baptism, not ignorance, not living in a place where Jesus' name has never been heard—nothing can stop God from offering salvation to every human being. How? We don't know. We are simply sure that if we are concerned, God is infinitely more so—and will take care of it admirably.

What of those who through no fault of their own do not know Christ or God or who conscientiously reject a distorted concept of God that has been offered them? The bishops spoke clearly at Vatican II: "Nor does Divine Providence deny the help necessary for salvation to those who, without blame on their part, have not yet arrived at an explicit knowledge of God, but who strive to lead a good life, thanks to his grace" (*Dogmatic Constitution on the Church*, 16).

Almost certainly, God's grace-life enters a catechumen months or years before the actual hour of baptism, through what is called "baptism of desire."

God does not have moments. The Father of Jesus does not decide he will forgive someone next Tuesday; he is forgiveness. So the moment anyone accepts the healing love of God, all sin is forgiven.

Why, then, the sacrament? Because we need external signs. This is the whole rationale of all sacrament and ritual. We need to see and feel and experience concretely what we are sure of in our heart, but which is not yet fully human because it has not been expressed in the flesh. The sacrament is the absolute assurance, through the action of the church, of God's forgiveness.

Forgiveness is the first part of the Good News, the first result of Jesus' dying and rising: "This is my blood..., which will be shed on behalf of many for the forgiveness of sins" (Matthew 26:28). The first forgiveness the church brings is not that of reconciliation but baptism.

When Paul encountered Jesus on the road to Damascus, Jesus told Paul to go to the Gentiles, "to whom I send you, to open their eyes that they may turn from darkness to light and from the power of Satan...and an inheritance among those who have been consecrated by faith in me" (Acts 26:17b–18a, c).

In Peter's Pentecost discourse forgiveness is the first effect of baptism he cites: "Repent and be baptized, every one of you, in the name of Jesus Christ for the forgiveness of your sins; and you will receive the gift of the holy Spirit" (Acts 2:38).

Conversion—reform—is a lifelong process. Baptism is not a once-and-for-all completion of our union with God. It is a beginning, just as the birth of a baby is a beginning. It is a decisive and unrepeatable moment, indeed, but it needs to be filled out in literally millions of moments to follow. We are not "converts" but "people being converted." In baptism God reveals our true (final) image, and we begin to let our Creator make that image real in ourselves.

INFANT BAPTISM. The ongoingness of baptismal conversion is precisely the argument for baptizing infants. If the church could have started with the adult candidate at the moment of birth, it would have done so, for this would have meant twenty, thirty, forty more years of training and example.

The important factor in infant baptism is the community and, within the community, the parents and sponsors (see *Catechism*, #1119–1120). They share the responsibility for bringing this baby to the point where full Christian commitment will be his or her totally voluntary choice.

Appealing as it may seem at first, the argument that it would be better to wait until the age of say, twenty-one, seems to lose all force when the question is pressed: "Wait for what?" No child can be brought up in a value-free atmosphere. Parents' and society's values are constantly being impressed on the child.

It would be unthinkable to wait until a child is twenty-one to insist on bathing, eating properly, being honest and caring. So it is unthinkable to Christian parents that Jesus be kept a stranger from their children. They want them to experience, gradually and according to their capacity, the meaning of God's gift of eternal life.

This is a delicate process, of course. Religion should not (and cannot) be rammed down the throat of anyone (see *Catechism*, #160). Faith cannot be taught; it can only be "caught" from others in whom it burns bright. Children are the "catechumens" of home and school and, gradually, the "big" church.

Infant baptism has one other advantage: It is a clear statement that salvation is entirely God's work (see *Catechism*, #1996). His love is freely bestowed before the child can possibly do anything to seem to deserve it. Long before a baby has come to know the Christian community, the community says, in Saint Paul's words: "So then you are no longer strangers and sojourners, but you are fellow citizens with the holy ones and members of the household of God, built upon the foundation of the apostles and prophets, with Christ Jesus himself as the capstone" (Ephesians 2:19–20).

Strictly speaking, the RCIA is organized for catechumens, for people who have never been baptized. Many who participate in the RCIA, however, are candidates for full communion with the Catholic church, that is, people who have already been baptized but who now wish to be in full communion with the Roman Catholic church. Their needs are similar to, but not identical with, those of catechumens. At the Easter Vigil, these candidates make a Profession of Faith—having received the sacrament of reconciliation prior to the Easter Vigil. Appendix B of this volume has a section entitled "Special Resources for Candidates for Full Communion with the Roman Catholic Church."

REFLECTION/DISCUSSION STARTERS

1) What does it mean to see the Christian life as one of "total, lifelong, deepening 'conversion'"? Do you experience your spiritual life in that way?
2) How does the RCIA demonstrate that view of Christianity?
3) What does water represent to you? How does it symbolize dying and rising?
4) How does the view of conversion as a lifelong process support the argument for baptizing infants?
5) If God's grace has entered your life already, why is the sacrament of baptism needed?

Supplementary Material

Catholic Updates: "Infant Baptism: Gift to the Parish," by Thomas Richstatter, O.F.M.; "A New Look at the RCIA," by Rita Burns Senseman; "A Quick Look at the New Catechism," by Carol Ann Morrow; "The RCIA: The Art of Making New Catholics," and "The Sacrament of Baptism: Celebrating the Embrace of God," both by Sandra DeGidio, O.S.M; "Sacraments of Initiation: God's 'I Love You,'" by Thomas Richstatter, O.F.M.

Cathecism for Us: Breaking Open the U.S. **Catechism for Adults:** This twelve-issue newsletter by Joan McKamey and Gerard Baumbach has contributions from Archbishop Donald Wuerl and Karen Sue Smith.

Books: Your Child's Baptism, by Carol Luebering.

DVD: A Lenten Journey With Father Michael Himes, one disc with study guide and four programs (What Is Temptation Really?; Danger and Desire; God Sees Into the Heart; Endless Possibilities).

. | CHAPTER 18 | .

THE SPIRIT OF JESUS SENDS FORTH WITNESSES: CONFIRMATION

CONFIRMATION IS THE SECOND OF THE THREE SACRAMENTS OF INITIATION. ITS focus is the Holy Spirit, already given in baptism, but "now" given for a special purpose.

The two words *already* and *now* point up a minor difficulty in understanding the sacrament: How can the Holy Spirit be given twice?

The difficulty did not exist for the first Christians. In the early church (as in the restored catechumenate), baptism, confirmation and Eucharist were one celebration, one rite of receiving new members into the community.

In later history entire cultures became Christian and most baptisms were of infants. Christian initiation was divided into two parts: baptism with water by a priest and anointing by a bishop (see *Catechism*, #1312–1313). Since the bishop obviously could not be present at all baptisms, the anointing gradually was seen as separate and postponed (along with First Eucharist) to later life.

Obviously, God cannot be parceled out in time capsules. One who is baptized becomes a temple of the Spirit, the home of the indwelling Trinity. No "part" of the Holy Spirit is held back at baptism to be given in confirmation. Every celebration of a sacrament is a sign from the one God of the one continuing, infinite love that is poured into our being (see *Catechism*, #1289).

Neither is confirmation a sign of Catholic adulthood (see *Catechism*, #1308). Its celebration does not mark a mature commitment to Christ.

Reaching such a commitment is a lifelong process; it can neither be delayed until twenty-one nor "finished" at seventy-one.

Baptism and confirmation are still almost impossible to separate in meaning. Each happens only once; each calls for a continuing unfolding of the Christian life. We probably have to be satisfied with the general statement that baptism makes us alive in Christ, members of his family, given holiness and called to holiness. This implicitly calls for the activity that confirmation stresses: witnessing to this faith with courage, in the power of the Holy Spirit.

SEALED WITH THE SPIRIT. When confirmation is celebrated, the bishop takes fragrant oil (chrism) on his thumb and makes the Sign of the Cross on the forehead of the one being confirmed, saying, "Be sealed with the gift of the Holy Spirit" (see *Catechism*, #1295–1296).

The perfumed oil (olive or any suitable plant oil) is the sign both of what the Pentecost prayer calls the "sweet refreshment" of the Spirit and of the strength the Spirit gives. (Oil may not immediately suggest strength to us today, but athletes still use "rubdowns" to make their bodies limber and strong.)

To be "sealed" is to be authoritatively marked or stamped as the property of someone. In confirmation the Spirit claims and empowers a Christian as a responsible and, if you will, "official" representative of the church before the world. He or she is to take responsibility for bringing Jesus to the ends of the earth.

The newly confirmed Christian now says what Jesus said of himself:

The Spirit of the Lord is upon me,
    because he has anointed me to bring glad tidings to the poor.
He has sent me to proclaim liberty to captives
    and recovery of sight to the blind, to let the oppressed go free,
and to proclaim a year acceptable to the Lord. (Luke 4:18–19)

Paul sums up what we are celebrating in this way: "But the one who gives us security with you in Christ and who anointed us is God; he has also put his seal upon us and given the Spirit in our hearts as a first installment" (2 Corinthians 1:21–22).

Thus confirmation stresses the power of the Spirit to make Christians witnesses of Jesus to the world. It turns the Christian *outward* to face the world with courageous testimony—in whatever way—to the Good News of Jesus.

Confirmation is to baptism what Pentecost is to Easter. Again we should not make too great a separation: John tells of Jesus conferring his Spirit on the evening of Easter Sunday; Luke sets the event fifty days later. It is one and the same giving.

In Acts, written by Luke, Jesus tells his apostles to wait in Jerusalem for "the promise of the Father about which you have heard me speak; …in a few days you will be baptized with the holy Spirit…. But you will receive power when the holy Spirit comes upon you, and you will be my witnesses in Jerusalem, throughout Judea and Samaria, and to the ends of the earth" (Acts 1:4b, 5b, 8).

Luke describes the transforming Pentecost experience in terms of fire and wind—the way the Old Testament describes the coming of God, for example, at Mount Sinai. Something like a strong, driving wind filled the house where the disciples were. "Tongues as of fire" descended on each one. "And they were all filled with the holy Spirit and began to speak [witness] in different tongues, as the Spirit enabled them to proclaim" (see Acts 2:2–4).

The rest of the Acts of the Apostles is the story of this bold proclamation under the guidance and power of the Holy Spirit. We might almost say that Acts is the "confirmation book" of the New Testament, and that the sacrament makes Pentecost a permanent event in the life of each Christian.

WHAT DOES IT MEAN TO WITNESS? An entire document of Vatican II, *The Pastoral Constitution on the Church in the Modern World*, might be used by confirmed Christians as a textbook on witnessing to Christ: "Inspired by no earthly ambition, the church seeks but a solitary goal: to carry forward the work of Christ himself under the lead of the befriending Spirit. And Christ entered this world to give witness to the truth, to rescue and not sit in judgment, to serve and not to be served" (3).

To mention just a few examples of Christian witness to the world might suggest nonexistent limits. Any genuine activity for the benefit of others can be done only with the power of the "befriending Spirit." A mere skimming of the topics treated in *The Pastoral Constitution on the Church in the Modern World* shows the unlimited field for action: the problem of change, humanity's deeper questioning, the dignity of the person, the problem of atheism, social justice in the world community, marriage and the family, the proper development of culture, economic development, politics and the church, war and peace, the international community.

Catholics can find many groups for activity, both local and private as well as church-wide and formal. But no one needs to do anything special—except to do the special thing which his or her talent and circumstances call for. The person dying of cancer witnesses to Christ as well as the pope; a child who prays in innocence is breathing in the Holy Spirit. Couples who "simply" love each other faithfully and courageously and endure the joys and sorrows of family life are telling the world of the Spirit's presence—and the world hears, even when it seems to be looking the other way.

Christians are daily telling the world that there is Good News. They are making visible the reconciliation God works in Christ and the transforming of creation into the kingdom.

PERSONAL EXPERIENCE OF THE SPIRIT. In biblical symbolism the number seven stands for fullness, completeness, perfection. Hence to speak of the "seven" gifts of the Holy Spirit is to emphasize not the number, but the fullness the prophet attributed to the promised Messiah:

> The spirit of the LORD shall rest upon him:
>   a spirit of wisdom and of understanding,
> A spirit of counsel and of strength,
>   a spirit of knowledge and of fear of the LORD,
>   and his delight shall be the fear of the LORD. (Isaiah 11:2–3)

(Translating the first mention of "fear of the Lord" as piety made the gifts seven in number.)

Likewise, Saint Paul's list of the *fruits* of the Holy Spirit is his tumbling of words upon words to express the limitless benefits of that Spirit: "The fruit of the Spirit is love, joy, peace, patience, kindness, generosity, faithfulness, gentleness, self-control" (Galatians 5:22–23a).

Gift in Greek is *charisma*, which means grace, favor, kindness and gift. In recent years the "charismatic renewal" has become a prominent and sometimes bewildering part of Catholic life. This renewal stresses certain particular gifts (charisms) of the Spirit (see 1 Corinthians 12:4–11), especially speaking in tongues and prophesying.

Charismatics speak of "Baptism of the Spirit": an intense religious experience of the Spirit. This is not the first baptism of the Spirit which all Christians receive sacramentally, but a felt release of the Spirit's power, a deeper realization of the presence of Jesus, greater strength in prayer and greater zeal to witness.

Like all renewal movements, this one has not been without its problems —the place of authority in charismatic communities, the danger of fundamentalism in Bible teaching, the temptation to elitism. But you can tell a tree by its fruit (see Matthew 7:20), and the church can rejoice that thousands of lives have been dramatically changed by the charismatic experience.

Those who find the charismatic renewal either threatening or excluding them have to look to their own willingness to be open to whatever gifts the Spirit may give them—particularly, as the Council says, those which are less dramatic and more ordinary. Saint Paul reminded the charismatics of Corinth that the litmus test of the Spirit's presence is the gift which "surpasses all the others"—love (see 1 Corinthians 13). Church leaders must discern charisms, seeking to coordinate diverse and yet complementary gifts, helping them to work together for the good of the whole Body of Christ (1 Corinthians 12:7; see *Catechism*, #801).

Every Christian is called to experience the presence of God as fully and consciously as possible. But it is also a commonplace of all Christians' experience—the saints' especially—that this can mean many difficult days and dark nights. Faith lives on trust.

REFLECTION/DISCUSSION STARTERS

1) How are baptism and confirmation related in terms of their meanings and purposes?

2) Why is anointing used in confirmation? What does it signify?

3) What does it mean to you to say we are called to Christian witness in the world? How do you see this happening in your life? How have you experienced the Christian witness of others?

4) How would you explain the "Baptism of the Spirit" of which charismatics speak?

SCRIPTURE READINGS

1 Corinthians 12:4–11; 13.

SUPPLEMENTARY MATERIAL

Catholic Updates: "Confirmation: Anointed for Fuller Witness," and "The RCIA: The Art of Making New Catholics," both by Sandra DeGidio, O.S.M.; "Sacraments of Initiation: God's 'I Love You,'" by Thomas Richstatter, O.F.M.

Books: *Charismatic Spirituality: The Work of the Holy Spirit in Scripture and Practice,* by Stephen Clark; *An Introduction to the Catholic Charismatic Renewal,* revised edition, by John and Therese Boucher; *Your Child's Confirmation,* by Carol Luebering.

DVD: *Sacrament of Confirmation: Sealed With God's Spirit,* by Thomas Richstatter, O.F.M., and Bishop Kenneth Untener, one disc with study guide.

CHAPTER 19

JESUS BRINGS SINNERS BACK TO THE FATHER: RECONCILIATION

"NOTHING IS A SIN ANYMORE!" HAS BECOME THE WORRIED COMMENT OF A significant number of Catholics. The church seems to have become very lenient—or at least many Catholics have decided to be rather lenient with themselves.

One cause of the new outlook, among many contributing factors, is this: While the "requirements" for mortal sin are still the same (serious matter, full awareness, full free consent of the will; see *Catechism*, #1857–1859), these have now come to be seen in their full depth of meaning. "Full awareness" means at least an implicit knowledge of the fact that my sin is actually rupturing my relationship with God; "full consent" means that, knowing this, I go ahead anyway with a freedom that is not seriously damaged by emotion. Mortal sinfulness is seen as a kind of life-choice. It isn't something people can "zigzag" in and out of.

Pope John Paul II called a synod of bishops in 1983 to consider the problems facing the church in the sacrament of reconciliation ("confession" is only part of the sacrament). They wrestled with the subject for weeks. Later the pope issued an exhortation that summed up his own conclusions and those of the bishops.

As if answering the complaint that "nothing is a sin anymore," he describes the evil that is rampant in the world: the trampling of the rights of persons, above all the right to life and to a decent quality of life; the attack on freedom, especially that of professing one's faith; racial discrimination, violence, torture, terrorism; the piling up of weapons in an arms race which spends billions that could ease the undeserved misery of many human beings. The pope sees divisions in a shattered world: between individuals and groups, nations and blocs of nations. And he says that the root of all these things lies in our inmost self. In the light of faith we call it sin.

The pope uses two Bible stories to illustrate the meaning of sin: (1) In erecting the tower of Babel, humanity sought to be powerful without God—a rival of God, in fact. (2) We find the same rivalry in Eden, when human beings set themselves up as being somehow self-sufficient, as powerful as God.

All through history this has been sin, in all its forms: exclusion of God, the rupturing of relationship with God. Sin is the disobedience of a person who by a free and knowing act does not recognize the sovereignty of God over his or her life, at least when the sin is committed.

All Christians need, in view of all this, a renewed sense of sin—a spiritual thermometer whereby we are sharply aware of the seeds of death contained in sin as well as the thousand disguises under which sin hides itself.

THE MEANING OF SIN. In chapter fifteen we tried to describe the church at its best at Eucharist. The community returns to try to re-create that ideal every Sunday. At the same time, it is a community that always needs to be saved because it is always a weak and sinful community. Some members of the Body may have become lifeless; others are seriously ill; all may have at least a slight fever.

How does sin happen in the very Body of Christ? A gradual lessening of warmth between members occurs, aided by repeated experiences of the limitations and faults of others; a willingness not to look too hard for the truth or at the truth grows. One by one people slip into a life that is partly a lie, a disorder they will not face; they are overtaken by the heady wine of freedom, the satisfaction of pleasure divorced from purpose. Things become little gods instead of creations; people become things for use and enjoyment apart from the great purposes of life.

And so it is possible gradually to move back from the circle of the community and from the Lord who gives that circle a center.

Sin is a way of life (see *Catechism*, #1863, 1865). It is an attitude that grows—just as love develops in giving and receiving. Nothing human is instantaneous. What happens at 12:00 was already begun at 11:59 and at 9:00, growing toward fullness yesterday and last week and perhaps last year. The growth is not unnoticed—for then there would be no fault—but it is not admitted.

Often I choose sin by default: I do not do the right and reasonable thing. I need not stamp my feet and shake my fist at God; I just don't decide to do the good thing. I will not do what the words of Jesus are call-ing me to do. His meaning is obvious, but I refuse to hear. There is a ter-rible scene in the book and movie *Leave Her to Heaven*, in which a woman sits calmly in a rowboat, her eyes hidden by sunglasses, watching a rival drown. She sits very still, watching, doing nothing.

Sin-*fullness* becomes this *sinful* act, gradually, just as one can become drunk by letting his glass be filled again and again and never objecting.

It really isn't serious for a while. This is literally true but has led to the foolish view that something is "only" a venial sin. But nothing is just "a" sin; it is a point along a ramp going down. All sin is a gradual slipping from life to death, so gradual that when one crosses the line it is scarcely noticed—for the willingness to cross the line was present long before. The woman who watched her rival drown had come to be a murderer by many slow, sly steps.

So the community we spoke of is not ideal because there are empty places at the table. Some may have moved their chairs to private cliques (Paul had trouble with that at Corinth). Some, in John's words, must hear Jesus say, "You have lost the love you had at first" (Revelation 2:4b).

CHURCH: THE RECONCILING COMMUNITY. By the very fact that Jesus joined people into a visible Body to be his sacrament, he "automatically" created the sacrament of reconciliation. For the church is the sign of Christ's love, and therefore of God's endless willingness to forgive. The church is given the ministry of reconciliation not just for the rebirth of baptism, but—such is the "bind" God gets into by being God—for the seventy times seven times one may lose the life once gratefully received (see Matthew 18:22).

The words of Jesus, "Whose sins you forgive are forgiven them, and whose sins you retain are retained" (John 20:23), affirm the community's power to reconcile sinners. reconciliation with the church means recon-ciliation with God.

The community—somebody—must carry out the ministry of reconciliation in such a way that sinners can first be sure they are welcome back. To the sinner—miserable and alone in the most crowded room, caught in the trap of greed or hate, cold stubbornness or pride, lust or mere self-sufficiency—someone must bring back the memory of the Father's table.

If sinfulness is a way of life, so is the life of grace. A new—the former—way of life must be entered.

First, and hardest of all, must come the admission of sinfulness: not a "mistaken judgment" or a "forgetting" or an "I didn't think...," but a simple, factual statement, with the Prodigal Son, "Father, I have sinned...; I no longer deserve to be called your son" (Luke 15:21a, c).

Real sorrow must follow—not just remorse for the self-inflicted pain and misery (for punishment is built into sin itself) but a genuine sorrow that God's love has been ignored, God's trust betrayed. Something holy and valuable has been spoiled. A consecrated body-spirit, a mind made for truth, freedom made to love, a body made to share and show the spirit's faith, a heart meant to experience the beauty and purity of life—all have been infected, abused, prostituted.

The sinner turns back to God for healing and new life. "...God was [and is] reconciling the world to himself in Christ" (2 Corinthians 5:19a). God brings the sinner back to the table, knowing how he or she has hungered for that place. God gives the determination to change, the power to take the necessary steps, to leave the foreign country where the inheritance was squandered, to do practical things like repairing and restoring and apologizing.

The sacrament of reconciliation is the sign from God that the sinner is absolutely forgiven. The sign is the welcome of the community, the kindness of the priest, the certainty of acceptance, the grace of God made visible.

CONFESSION. One who has been truly guilty of mortal sinfulness must ordinarily confess the sinfulness to a priest, individually and privately, even though God's forgiveness has already been given and experienced (see *Catechism*, #1456–1457, 1484). (Ordinarily—unless, for instance, one is unable to confess because of physical or moral impossibility such as sickness, the danger of being overheard or the like.)

This is a sticking point for many—once for Protestants, now for some Catholics. Why go to a man, the argument goes, when God has already acted? Or, in the words of the more liturgically minded, why do we need anything more than the community's forgiveness, expressed in its welcome?

We are speaking, remember, of one who truly separated himself or herself internally from the Body of Christ. It seems only common decency that one does not resume a place at table as if nothing had happened. Even the most loving of families would expect something more than that.

Confessing, like any external physical act, makes the interior act fully human. If a resolution or feeling is genuine within me, it will out. It may not even be fully *mine*—of me, this body-spirit unity—until I have done something external, until I have created words that make me realize what I truly mean.

Confessing is a "public" statement (even in the privacy of the confessional or reconciliation room) that (1) I am truly a sinner; (2) only God can forgive my sinfulness; (3) I want and accept God's forgiveness; (4) I mean to do something about my sinfulness.

Confessing involves saying the three most difficult words in the human language: "I was wrong"—not just "in error" but *sinful.* It is not meant to be a humiliation—the priest goes to confession too—but a healthy statement of fact. Once said, the words are lost in the mercy of God. True confession means the end of guilt and guilt feelings.

Most important of all, the voice of Christ himself becomes audible in confession—speaking to us individually about our individual sinfulness. It is the sign which, being human, we desperately need.

The actual words of absolution said as the priest holds his hands on or over the head of the penitent are:

God, the Father of mercies, by the death and resurrection of his Son, has reconciled the world to himself, and sent the Holy Spirit among us for the forgiveness of sins. By the ministry of the church, may God give you pardon and peace. And I absolve you from your sins in the name of the Father, and of the Son, and of the Holy Spirit.

THE NEW RITE. Vatican II called for a revision of the rites of the sacraments to make their nature and purpose clear. In the case of the sacrament of reconciliation, the revisions are not all that new. There is a new emphasis, however, on three things: (1) the internal—the full, deep meaning of sinfulness and grace; (2) the word of God; (3) the community. Let us begin with the last.

On a particular day the community gathers to celebrate the sacrament of reconciliation (a communal penance service; see *Catechism*, #1482). The sinner who has been away comes back. It is no humiliation to return, for now the pain of self-imposed isolation is over. The sinner confesses privately to the priest in the course of the sacramental celebration, and God gives the assurance of forgiveness through the priest's words of absolution. The community welcomes the sinner back to the table.

But even when only priest and penitent meet (in private confession), the community is there. The priest represents the reconciling community. The confessor must make a judgment for the church. Ninety-nine times out of a hundred the judgment is that the penitent is truly sorry. But it is possible that a priest may be forced to conclude that a given person is nowhere near real sorrow or purpose of amendment. The priest has the great responsibility to try to show the sinner the love as well as the truth of God; but he cannot make a mockery of the words of absolution and pretend the sinner has really returned to community life when in fact it may merely be a case of empty ritual.

Besides this emphasis on community, the revised rite insists that the word of God be an integral part of every sacramental celebration. The Bible is a kind of sacrament of God's actual living word to us *today*. It is not a collection of choice sayings, an interesting religious anthology. The reading of Scripture in sacramental celebrations is, or should be, a striking emphasis on the fact that the sacraments are God's actions, God's self-communication, and involve some definite expectations of us.

So the reading of Scripture focuses our minds on God's presence and *action*. The words of Scripture are a communication from God, and a personal response must be given. In this sacrament, it is God giving reassurance, healing, forgiveness—but, insofar as necessary, a restatement of the divine will and a wholesome warning.

Finally, there is a renewed emphasis in the new rite on deepening our awareness of the full meaning of sin and grace. Confession need not be made face-to-face, but this method gives priest and penitent a better chance to get beneath the surface of sin to its roots and to make the reconciliation a felt and grace-full experience.

The priest is not a psychiatrist. He is a fellow Christian who can help the penitent see things in faith again and make personal the present love of God. He can sympathize as well as speak the unyielding truth (see *Catechism*, #1466).

It is easy to make fun of the old "grocery list" confession, but who knows what depths of real sorrow and full awareness of the grace of reconciliation and of the need of penance accompanied that list? At any rate, the emphasis today is where it always has to be—on the motives and attitudes that run beneath the surface, the traits of temperament that are the filter of both sin and virtue.

It is hoped that the sacramental rite can help even so-called "venial sinners" sense the seriousness of sacramental reconciliation (see *Catechism*, #1458). Even if I have not left the table, I may have pulled my chair back: I can't stand this person, or I don't want to share with that one, or I don't want to have to adapt to that one. I am thereby refusing to love my neighbor, and the life of the community is made a little less healthy. The pulse and flow of the life of the Body has been restricted.

When a community gathers for the sacrament, each member is saying to all, "I have hurt you by what I have done and by what I have not done. Show me the forgiveness of Jesus." And each member also says to all the rest by the very coming together, "I offer you the forgiveness of Jesus, who calls us to be one in him." This is reconciliation, turning away from sin and turning to God by joining the community again or joining it more generously.

PENANCE. Finally, there is a "penance" to be done by each individual after celebrating the sacrament. It is not "satisfaction" in the sense of "making up" to God for our sin, for we can never do that. We can only accept divine forgiveness.

Penance is letting God change my life, particularly in the area in which I have sinned (see *Catechism*, #1459–1460). An individual's "penance" is balm for his or her particular needs and difficulties: to learn charity by performing an act of kindness for a person the penitent dislikes, for instance.

Thus the healing of Christ is given to all who have thrown aside their baptismal garment or have soiled it, who have let their candle go out or burn low, who have wiped the oil of their dignity off their brow (see *Catechism*, #1421).

If we acknowledge our sins, he is faithful and just and will forgive our sins and cleanse us from every wrongdoing. (1 John 1:9)

RECONCILIATION IS WORSHIP. The celebration of the sacrament ends with a proclamation of praise to God. Sacraments are worship, and the most natural thing for a reconciled sinner to do is to be happy about the mercy of God. This is not like leaving a courtroom where one was barely acquitted and perhaps subjected to humiliation. Rather it is the celebration of the family, especially the reunited members. No longer does it matter what I was or what I did. Shame and scandal are forgotten. Joy comes from what I am: loved to life by God.

REFLECTION/DISCUSSION STARTERS

1) Discuss the concept of sin as a way of life, an attitude that grows, a gradual slipping from life to death.
2) Reflect on times when you wanted someone to forgive you. Did you receive that forgiveness? If not, how did you feel?
3) Reflect on times when you have forgiven someone. Was it difficult? Did you feel better afterward?
4) Why should reconciliation be part of the church's ministry?
5) If God forgives us, why do we confess to a priest?
6) What is the purpose of a "penance" to be done by a person after celebrating the sacrament?

SUPPLEMENTARY MATERIAL

Catholic Updates: "Forgiveness in the Church Today," and "How to Celebrate the Sacrament of Reconciliation Today," both by Thomas Richstatter, O.F.M.; "The Sacrament of Reconciliation: Celebrating God's Forgiveness," by Sandra DeGidio, O.S.M.; "Why Confess My Sins?" by Leonard Foley, O.F.M.

Books: *How to Go to Confession When You Don't Know How,* by Ann M.S. LeBlanc; *Meeting the Merciful Christ,* revised edition, and *Why Go to Confession? Questions and Answers About Sacramental Reconciliation,* both by Joseph M. Champlin; *101 Inspirational Stories of the Sacrament of Reconciliation,* by Patricia Proctor, o.s.c.; *Your Child's First Penance,* by Carol Luebering.

DVD: *The Church Celebrates the Reconciling God; The God Who Reconciles; Preparing Your Child for First Reconciliation.* Each one-disc program has a study guide.

. | CHAPTER 20 | .

JESUS HEALS THE WHOLE PERSON: ANOINTING OF THE SICK

SIN IS NOT THE ONLY FLAW IN OUR IDEAL COMMUNITY; SICKNESS OF EVERY KIND also exists there. We are not spirits who merely drag our bodies along, but amazing creatures whose total well-being and happiness is physical-emotional-spiritual.

Our bodies are really a part of us, and so, therefore, is all the sickness and suffering that bodies entail. No part of God's wise and generous creation can be ignored.

The body was certainly not beneath the notice of Jesus, as if he came to speak only "spiritual" things. Almost the first thing he did in his public life was to go down the street and heal the sick. Much as we may shrink from using the phrase, Jesus is the "faith healer."

Health—wholeness—remains a prime Christian concern. As the bearers of Jesus' ministry, we must reach out to those who are in pain. If we must wait to go to Mass because we are needed at a sickbed, then the Mass must wait—for an hour, or a day or a week.

Taking a broader view for a moment: Just as it would be un-Christlike to tell a man in terrible pain to wait for his medicine until we finish the Eucharist, so it is a contradiction in terms to celebrate the saving death of Jesus and be unconcerned about the pain of our brothers and sisters anywhere in the world: the starving, the malnourished, the prisoners of

199

tyranny, the poor crushed under greed. (Suffering can be borne gracefully only after the experience of God's love visible in others, not before.)

Our physical, emotional and spiritual health is one. If there is a disorder in one area, there is a disturbance in all. Physical sickness can be, to say the least, a great distraction. It may present great temptation to discouragement, bitterness or even loss of hope. When the body is trussed up with tubes and bottles and wired like a machine while the person's feeling and agony are ignored, sickness is dehumanizing.

With the mindset of the Old Testament, Jesus approaches a human being as a unity. He came to save us, not just our souls. (That is why bodily resurrection is part of salvation.) When he sent his disciples out to proclaim the Good News and the corresponding need for repentance, they also "drove out many demons, and they anointed with oil many who were sick and cured them" (Mark 6:13).

Besides the general mission of healing which Jesus gave the church, the particular sacrament of anointing is described in the Letter of James: "Is anyone among you sick? He should summon the presbyters of the church, and they should pray over him and anoint [him] with oil in the name of the Lord, and the prayer of faith will save the sick person, and the Lord will raise him up. If he has committed any sins, he will be forgiven" (5:14–15).

As we have seen, "sacramental grace" is the one love of God applied to a particular situation. Serious illness is one of life's most critical situations. Salvation must be brought about in these circumstances, too.

Faith says that suffering can be a spiritual experience, a time when God draws us closer and when we understand our whole life more deeply. Suffering by itself, however, is worthless. The whole plan of God is to rid us of every kind of pain.

Yet suffering seems not only inevitable but even the noblest part of many people's lives. Obviously, only faith can reconcile these opposites, making suffering a test but not a temptation. Only the power of God's love can enable us to share the trust and generous love of the suffering Jesus.

DOES JESUS STILL HEAL? Before we go on, we must face the nagging questions: Does Jesus heal the sick today? Are the healings by people like

Kathryn Kuhlman and Oral Roberts genuine or imaginary or hypnotically induced? Why have most of us never heard of, still less experienced, a miraculous healing?

We might as well admit it: We may not have enough faith. Notice James says that "the prayer of faith" will reclaim the sick person. Jesus did not work miracles in his hometown because of the people's lack of faith (see Matthew 13:54–58). If we really don't expect God to do anything, nothing will happen. If we expect mere magic, nothing will happen. Genuine faith, even if it can only repeat, "I do believe, help my unbelief!" (Mark 9:24), sees God working in the world through the Body of Christ. It is not surprised at anything.

But after admitting that we may be wanting in faith, we must also realize that this is not the only reason why prayer and sacrament fail to effect miraculous cures. Mother Teresa no doubt prayed with great faith every day for many sick people, even particular sick people. We all know people with pure, humble faith who pray for the sick and "nothing happens." What can we say?

The anointing of the sick is a sign of God's absolute victory over all evil in the death and resurrection of Jesus. Looking at the total history of the world "from eternity," we can be absolutely sure that all evil will be destroyed: sin, death, suffering, sickness. We have no doubt whatsoever about this. Is it watering down the sacrament to say that the physical healing may not occur until the Lord raises the body of the sick person from death to eternal and total "health"? The anointing of a sick person's body is the signed promise of God that Jesus' healing will come. We may wish and hope and expect that it come immediately, but we need not be disturbed if healing is delayed.

WHAT THE SACRAMENT DOES. As the body of a sick person is anointed, the church prays:

Through this holy anointing may the Lord in his love and mercy help you with the grace of the Holy Spirit. May the Lord who frees you from sin save you and raise you up.

Through the sacrament the whole person is brought to health— now or ultimately.

The essential first healing is forgiveness. Suffering and death are the result of sin—humankind's sin, not the sin of the sick person (though my sickness may sometimes be the result of my abusing my body, my emotions or my mind). The great Healer always heals the worst sickness first (see *Catechism*, #1420–1421).

The sacrament gives the strength to face the temptations and anxieties of sickness. Serious sickness brings us face-to-face with the fact that we are fragile creatures. Even though this sickness may pass, ultimately we will fail to save our bodies from death. Facing that knowledge, we can either be depressed or we can put ourselves with trust into God's hands, knowing God will give us the strength to suffer, to die and to rise when the time comes. Grace creates in us confidence, trust and peace in spite of pain and a gloomy prognosis by the doctor.

The sacrament joins us to the suffering and victorious Jesus. We are given the light and strength to make Paul's words our own: "Now I rejoice in my sufferings for your sake, and in my flesh I am filling up what is lacking in the afflictions of Christ on behalf of his body, which is the church" (Colossians 1:24).

Nothing is really lacking in the sufferings of Christ. But he has left a place beside him for us to join his *spirit* in suffering, his absolute trust of the Father and therefore his redeeming power. We can no more think of suffering as our particular punishment than we can imagine a vindictive God "satisfied" by Jesus' suffering. Suffering is unavoidable. Ours is to win over it by maintaining our peaceful faith. If we do that, the "prayer of faith" will indeed save us.

The sacrament is God's absolute assurance that this pain, this desolation has been transformed in the suffering and death of Jesus and that we are already joined to his resurrection and victory. The complete concrete fruits, healing and joy, will infallibly come. When we shall taste them, we leave in God's hands. Hence the words of Vatican II to the sick, exhorting them "to contribute to the welfare of the People of God by associating themselves freely with the passion and death of Christ" (*Dogmatic Constitution on the Church*, 11).

The sacrament should be celebrated in conditions that are as "normal" as possible. Being sick is not normal, of course. But the time for the sacrament is as early as possible in the sickness, not when death is close and the patient is sedated almost beyond consciousness. The sacrament is not some kind of magic to be mumbled over an unconscious person. The sick man or woman should be given the best opportunity to exercise faith consciously and to be aware of the support of family and friends.

AGAIN, THE COMMUNITY. In the ritual of anointing, the church repeats what it says of all sacraments: The presence of the community is very important, not only for psychological reasons of support, but for the loving reassurance that makes Christ visible. "The family and friends of the sick and those who take care of them have a special share in this ministry of comfort" (*Rite of Anointing*, 34).

Sometimes it is impossible to gather the community: A priest may be called to the hospital bed of one who has no immediate relatives; nurses are busy; no friends or other parishioners can be found. The priest is the comfort of the whole church. But normally "the church" should be more visibly present.

DEATH. It will take perhaps two or three generations to eradicate the notion that when the priest is called to anoint the sick, it is also time to call the undertaker. The old name of the sacrament was Extreme Unction, the last anointing, "the last rites." Vatican II asked that the sacrament be called "The Anointing of the Sick."

But the old name was not without foundation. Serious sickness is a signal, perhaps decades ahead of time, that our hold on life is precarious. Humanly speaking, we are alone and helpless before death. Mortality is part of our inheritance.

But Jesus made even death a beautiful and deliberate act of trust and love. Death was the symbol of the fatal power of sin until Jesus made it the focus of the opposite power—God's power to create and recreate, to heal and raise. Jesus' death was the most voluntary act he ever made. It summed up his life of absolute trust in the Father. He literally handed himself over in the dark to his Father. His Father embraced him and he was alive again, fully free and whole, victorious and all-powerful.

Some psychologists say we begin to come to terms with death early in life. As Christians we try to rise above the natural fear of dying by a life that is basically love and trust. We would do well, though, deliberately to make an act of trustful dying far ahead of time. One way of doing this is expressed in a prayer I found on a well-worn piece of notepaper in a saintly old lady's prayer book: "Lord Jesus, trusting in you, I now at this moment willingly accept whatever death you may send me, with all its pain and darkness, for I know it is my coming to be with you forever."

Here we see the full meaning of healing. We may be restored to health now, in view of a longer preparation for our final salvation; or healing may be a holy death in the Lord, who is our final health and salvation, and who will infallibly give us total health forever.

REFLECTION/DISCUSSION STARTERS

1) "The whole person is brought to health" through the sacrament of anointing, says the author. Discuss the kind of healing, the strength that the sacrament offers. Have you known anyone who has received the sacrament? What effect did it appear to have on the person?

2) How can you explain the fact that, though physical healing is prayed for, it does not always occur?

3) Why is the presence of the church community important for the celebration of the sacrament of anointing?

SCRIPTURE READING
Matthew 13:54–58.

SUPPLEMENTARY MATERIAL
Catholic Updates: "Anointing of the Sick: A Parish Sacrament," by Thomas Richstatter, O.F.M.

Books: Men and Women Are From Eden: A Study Guide to John Paul II's Theology of the Body, by Mary Healy; *Men, Women and the Mystery of Love: Practical Insights from John Paul's* Love and Responsibility, by Edward Sri.

DVD: Sacrament of Anointing: The Church's Prayer for the Sick, by Thomas Richstatter, O.F.M. One disc with a study guide.

. | CHAPTER 21 | .

JESUS AT THE HEART OF
MARRIED LOVE: MARRIAGE

A MIDDLE-AGED WOMAN ONCE CAME TO ME IN SHOCK. AFTER THIRTY-THREE years of marriage, her husband had just announced that he was leaving her. This was his response to their teenage daughter's pregnancy. (Life is always stranger and crueler than fiction.)

Now these two blows were tragic enough. But this woman expressed another worry, vivid in her feelings in spite of the greater sufferings: Should she stop being a minister of Communion in her parish?

She was sure, from her experience, that some would think it improper for her to continue, even though she was completely innocent as far as the divorce was concerned. I was reminded of a case in which another mother received three poison-voice phone calls berating her for allowing her pregnant and unwed daughter to remain at home!

These are examples of a total absence of community and total ignorance of what a parish is called to be. They reflect an externalism that has no heart—only legalistic observance.

The community aspect of the sacraments is doubly important in the case of marriage: First, there would be no community if there were no faith-full married Christians; second, married Christians need the support of the community to remain faith-full.

We know this instinctively. Baptism may unfortunately be celebrated with only a few people present, and reconciliation may, also unfortunately, be an isolated experience. But weddings always bring a crowd of friends and relatives. In a sense, this is the church community giving approval and support. It is a kind of natural "parish" for the couple.

But perhaps the friends live far on the other side of town and relatives return to Coshocton and Seattle. What then? Perhaps nothing but what is described by a rather ominous term: "the nuclear family," husband and wife and children alone in a sea of strangers. Perhaps they do not even know the names of the people in the next apartment.

So, let us go back to that community gathered around the altar for Eucharist. Today we are celebrating the wedding of Jim and Helen.

What do we *mean* when we celebrate the sacrament? What do we say to them—and to all the husbands and wives struggling to communicate their feelings to each other, to put their lives on the line each new day, to maintain love and patience when the fire burns low? What do we say to those deserted by their spouses or hurt by infidelity? What do we say to all the fathers and mothers present, those with children pulling straight A's and those whose sons are already crippled by drugs and whose daughters reject the faith that was "rammed down their throats"?

We again say something *ideal, impossible, Christian.* We say that sacramental Christian marriage is like the human-divine life of Jesus himself: Godlike love flowing into (and through) the limited "container" of our human nature.

In Jesus there were no limitations of selfishness, no moral obstructions— only the physical limitations of flesh, space, time. In married Christians there are also moral limitations, the not-always-successful struggle to love freely and generously. But the similarity to Christ's life is there. Day by day, "for better or worse, in sickness and in health," the patient effort of Christian couples to be faithful to each other and to the ideals of Christ is the constant making of the Church, the body of Christ. Christian couples' love gathers into itself all that is beautiful about "natural" love and transforms it in a personal couple-relationship to Jesus (see *Catechism,* #1617).

It is possible that a couple wants to be married without considering the Christ-relationship. They would just as readily be married by a justice of the peace, except that their Catholic families would be upset, or because they like the church or the reception hall.

Now, this may be a "good" marriage. The couple may love each other very deeply just as, say, two atheists may love each other. We are not ridiculing this love; we are just saying that if it has no relationship to Jesus it is not *Christian.*

We are all at different stages of faith. Perhaps that couple has a glimmering of what they are called to do in faith. Perhaps their love will develop, and they may "catch on" to what it's all about. We cannot judge the interior disposition of anyone. But we cannot water down the sacrament, either.

THE PRESENCE OF THE DIVINE. All genuine love is divine. For if it is genuine, it springs from the presence of God at the heart of all who love.

God is love, and whoever remains in love remains in God and God in him. (1 John 4:16b)

We have to say that if love fills one's whole life, it is fully graced love, even though it is not consciously Christian because of ignorance or immaturity.

But Christian married love is called to be *consciously* Christian, *consciously* Jesus-related, *consciously* divine. The grace of the sacrament is the one love of God enabling a couple to live a Jesus-conscious life in all the circumstances of marriage.

Veteran marrieds may smile at this—tolerantly or cynically. But Christians can say no less.

It took a while for the church to realize the depths of Christian marriage, it is true. At first Christians were married by whatever secular form was in use. But gradually it became evident that there was something special about the love of Christian husbands and wives. The sacrament was not created, then, but discovered.

Some Catholics have heard Saint Paul's words about Christian marriage so often that they flow over them like water off an oilskin: "This is a great mystery, but I speak in reference to Christ and the church" (Ephesians 5:32). It sounds "tacked on" to what everybody knows is the "real" and thoroughly human experience of marriage.

Again we must say: We are not talking about just any marriage, no matter how beautiful, but Christian marriage. And again it must be said: No condemnation of couples who have not reached even the most minimal stage of Christian awareness is intended. God bless them, but let's not talk about the sacrament as if it is something that happens magically by repeating the words "I do" in front of someone who happens to be a priest or a deacon.

THE MEANING OF CHRISTIAN MARRIAGE. What has our (hopefully ideal) community (with the help of the couples' parents, of course) taught Jim and Helen over the years about marriage?

They have taught them, by the example of daily living and sometimes in words of faith, that Jesus is the inspiration and the empowerment of married love; that all the pleasure and pain of marriage, the highs and the lows, have a part in the redeeming love of Jesus that is saving the world. They have demonstrated that the deeper their faith is, the more they can love each other; that the more they open themselves to the unknown depths to which God is leading them, the more they can be willing to venture with trust into the mysterious growth areas of human relationship. They have professed that communion with each other is communion with God, and communion with God is enriched by the experience of human love in all its forms (see *Catechism*, #2204–2205).

Jim and Helen realize that Jesus' love is a love for individual persons, not just a generic love spread thinly over all. The whole church is made up of families, and the love within families is the symbol and actuality of Jesus' love for the church, and the church's love for Jesus. One feeds the other; one is impossible without the other.

Most of all, they realize that they cannot maintain their love without being inwardly possessed by the love of Jesus. That is, they know that if they had to find fulfillment *only* in each other, they would not find it.

FAITHFULNESS IN MARRIAGE. The greatest thing the Jews could say about their God was that Yahweh loved them with a steadfast covenant love. They might change, or sin, or abandon God, but God could not abandon them.

To put it in the lowest terms, God is "stuck" with us. It's God's choice, but it is a choice that calls for a lot of forgiveness, patience, that marvelous attribute called "long-suffering" and waiting. But God loves us anyway, not reluctantly or with a love that has grown merely official from the wear and tear of our unfaithfulness, but with both the fireworks-love of the young and the steady-burning love of the mature.

The essence of any Christian marriage is to reflect God's love in a lifelong commitment. If the worm of tentativeness is in the apple on the wedding day, there is no real marriage—only a tryout.

So the Christian couple is undertaking a fearful thing: to have and show and share the very love of Christ to each other for life, and to "create for God"—pro-create—faith-full children.

We used to use a horribly inadequate word for Christian marriage: *contract*—something that is possible between the bitterest enemies. *Covenant* is a better choice because in that we are imitating God, who "wedded" us for eternity and who will not turn back. Jesus' humanity is the pledge of that. Married couples enter into God's eternal faithfulness because there is no other way for their love to be divine and complete.

This means infinitely more than not committing adultery. It means making life together a shared adventure with intimations of eternity. Everything has eternal value, everything is "for good."

The word for this quality of Christian marriage is "indissoluble" (see *Catechism*, #1644). This does not mean love cannot die, but that the very nature of living Christian love simply makes "another" married love as impossible as having two heads. This is not merely an external law, but a condition of having Christian married love in the first place.

Jesus himself said it: "But I say to you [in contrast to the former permission to divorce], whoever divorces his wife (unless the marriage is unlawful) causes her to commit adultery, and whoever marries a divorced woman commits adultery" (Matthew 5:32).

Jesus is not just talking to people who have reached the stage where adultery becomes appealing. He is saying that married love can think of nothing less than having the faithfulness of God.

Bible scholars have long puzzled over Matthew's exception, once translated "except for lewd conduct." Now, Jesus is certainly rejecting the easy-divorce principles of some of the religious teachers of his day. He is not "allowing" remarriage because of immoral conduct on the part of husband and wife. He must mean, the scholars point out, a marriage that is not a marriage—an illicit union, a mere living together or perhaps a marriage of very close relatives. Gentiles were not as strict about this as Jewish people were.

"ANNULMENTS," SEPARATION, PAULINE PRIVILEGE. When a marriage is not fully a marriage, as in the case of an unconsummated union, the church has always claimed the right to annul. What is often *mistakenly* called "annulment" today is something quite different. Technically, it is called a "declaration of nullity," that is, a church court finds that there was "nullity," no sacramental marriage, from the beginning (see *Catechism*, #1629). True marriage never did exist, for one or more reasons: for example, because of force or fraud, psychological immaturity, emotional disorder—whatever did, in fact, prevent the "consent" from being the full and free consent required for the lifelong covenant of Christian marriage. The church in these cases is not changing its doctrine, merely deciding about facts.

Separation is sometimes legitimate (see *Catechism*, #1649). Uncondoned adultery is such a reason—though forgiveness is always an option. If life becomes intolerable because of physical, moral or emotional abuse, there is no obligation to continue living together. It may be necessary, in some cases, to obtain a civil divorce, so that the innocent party can be assured of obtaining his or her rights. This does not, of course, mean freedom to remarry since the previous marriage bond still exists.

The following words of Saint Paul are the basis for the church releasing a person from a non-sacramental marriage for the sake of his or her faith:

> ... [I]f any brother has a wife who is an unbeliever, and she is willing to go on living with him, he should not divorce her; and if any woman has a husband who is an unbeliever, and he is willing to go on living with her, she should not divorce her husband.... If the unbeliever separates, however, let him separate. The brother or sister is not bound in such cases; God has called you to peace. (1 Corinthians 7:12b–13, 15)

So, when a partner in a non-sacramental marriage will not live "peaceably" with the other party, who is thereby kept from practicing the faith, the church invokes these words of Saint Paul to annul the marriage.

SACRAMENT OF DAILY LIFE. One professor of theology used to treat marriage first in his course on the sacraments because it so fundamentally enters into all aspects of life. That is to say, God's love enters the lives of husband and wife in every kind of situation (see *Catechism*, #1644). The particular "crisis" or "decisive point" to which this sacrament looks is *all life*. One might say this of baptism, in that the life of God is given simply for living.

But the grace of marriage focuses that baptismal power on the day-to-day, nitty-gritty, earthly-divine elements of life which married persons face.

No offense to the single. One can lead the full baptismal life without being married—and do so devotedly, heroically. The very nature of sexuality—"male and female he created them" (see Genesis 1:27)—shows the essential incompleteness of every person, absolutely needing to be filled by love and friendship, whether in marriage or in single life. But, obviously, married life, with its tremendous responsibility for children and its intimate, exclusive and lifelong relationship, involves experiences which singles do not have.

God's gracing of matrimony is a pointed reminder that everything human has been consecrated—making a living, going on a picnic, holding a sick child, exploring all the pleasures and enrichment of sexuality, building a new home, putting up with the old car, facing emotional, physical and moral problems, failing and succeeding, forgiving and starting all over again.

WHEN BEGINNINGS ARE SHAKY. In the United States the diversity of churches inevitably leads to marriages between Catholics and Lutherans, Jews and Episcopalians—even atheists and Christians.

Leaders of all faiths, I believe, must say that it is better for a person to marry within his or her own faith. If marriage is the sharing of life, it should include the sharing of the deepest values of life. It is hard to imagine a fully Christian marriage where husband and wife do not share the Eucharist. Perhaps two Christians will not be affected by differences on matters like papal authority, infallibility, some of the sacraments, church tradition—but it seems impossible to do this without a quite vigorous faith (which of course should be there in the case of any Christian marriage).

But there may be a bigger problem than that of difference of belief— the *apparent* absence of much Christian belief at all. The priest must sometimes agonize over whether or not to concur with a couple's decision to marry. He cannot celebrate a sacrament that is almost certainly not a sacrament in any real sense of the word; for instance, when the only reason a couple wants to be married at St. John's is the fact that it is a "stylish" church. On the other hand, he cannot demand full maturity in those who by definition are called to grow.

That leaves a large gray area in between where he must weigh the possible harm of a commitment that has very shaky foundations and the possible benefit of a beginning surrounded by a supporting, praying community.

EQUALITY IN MARRIAGE. Poor Saint Paul has been lumped together with the male chauvinists, and it's not really fair. He did reflect the culture of his time, as we all do. (Future ages will be horrified at our blithe abuse of natural resources.) He certainly did not see women as inferior to men: "For all of you who were baptized into Christ have clothed yourselves with Christ. There is neither Jew nor Greek, there is neither slave nor free person, there is not male and female, for you are all one in Christ Jesus" (Galatians 3:27–28).

In marriage he counsels husbands and wives to give themselves equally —wholly—to each other. "A wife does not have authority over her own body, but rather her husband, and similarly a husband does not have authority over his own body, but rather his wife" (1 Corinthians 7:4). Even the often quoted verse, "Wives should be subordinate to their husbands as to the Lord" (Ephesians 5:22), is preceded by a word to all: "Be subordinate to one another out of reverence for Christ" (Ephesians 5:21). And no less is demanded of husbands. They must love their wives "as Christ loved the church" (Ephesians 5:25b).

CHILDREN. Mutual communion in love is so intimately connected with that other purpose of marriage, the procreation of children, that it is impossible to separate them (see *Catechism,* #1652). Love is by nature creative— otherwise we would not be here. This divine instinct makes people who truly love each other want to see that love embodied and shared. Only because mother and father love each other is there any hope they will have children who can experience life as God made it to be.

It is as important to help children experience being Christian, if only in a minimal way, as it is to teach them Christian concepts and definitions. This of course is part of the whole "change" in the world and in the church from an emphasis on the objective to an emphasis on the subjective, from "what" to "why," and from external form to internal meaning.

Fathers and mothers can never delegate their responsibility to others. Everyone else—priest, nun, teacher—is a helper for them. Parents have the primary privilege and responsibility of "teaching" religion to their children (see *Catechism*, #1653). Actually, they succeed or fail at this "automatically," or rather, inevitably. That is, they are exposing their children to day-long experiences, and these experiences are either Christian or they are not. If they are, then the child has experienced the meaning of Jesus before any words or definitions are learned. Those experiences of love and forgiveness, respect and sharing, a common table and common prayer—are the greatest (and really the only) "education" parents can give their children. Parents must trust that their marriage in Christ gives their lives power.

The day may come when their children will either sinfully or misguidedly reject these values. So be it. They must take their lives into their own hands and decide. Parents can only do what God does: offer truth and love and ultimately allow freedom to make its choice. The community shows the concern of Jesus in helping parents in this task.

AND STILL THE COMMUNITY. The law of the church requires that Catholic couples be married before a priest or deacon and two witnesses. This sounds very cold and legalistic. It means that marriage is a great concern of the community. The priest or deacon is to make a judgment—and he can be helped by any number of community members—as to whether the couple is indeed free to marry and whether they are prepared to live a Christian married life.

Every new marriage is a new unit of the church beginning—for there would be no "big" church without all the little "domestic churches" of family life (see *Catechism*, #2204–2205)—and the community is concerned that it be a responsible unit, not just a couple whom civil law declares to be married. The two witnesses stand up for the community, but there should be many more than two. Again, not just to "make it legal" but to show the support and prayer and welcome of the community—and to promise that support for the future: in warm friendship, for every Sunday, for times of financial or emotional strain; when children come or tragedy strikes through death or disgrace or desertion.

The deserted wife mentioned at the beginning of this chapter must not have received (or noticed) the message of community love from her parish. All those "little churches" of Christian marriage should have given most when she needed it most. Marriage—and those suffering broken marriage—can only survive by feeding on and passing along the divine love at the heart of the sacrament.

REFLECTION/DISCUSSION STARTERS

1) Discuss the role of the church community in Christian marriage. Why does the community care about the marital union of two people?
2) Why is marriage a sacrament? Why is it considered "a sacrament of daily life"?
3) Not every marriage is a Christian marriage. What distinguishes a Christian marriage from one that is not?
4) Discuss why covenant may be a better word to use than contract to describe Christian marriage. If you are married, do you think your relationship is more like a covenant or a contract?
5) Discuss the reasons for annulments, or declarations of nullity. Explain how the church might judge that no sacramental marriage existed from the beginning.
6) Of the marriages you know, does there appear to be equality or inequality between husband and wife? Which seem to be happiest? Do you believe there are certain roles in a marriage that a husband should fulfill? That a wife should fulfill?
7) If you are married, are you and your spouse becoming "more married" each day? If so, how?

SUPPLEMENTARY MATERIAL

Catholic Updates: "Bringing Your Marriage Into the Church: Convalidation of Civil Marriages," and "10 Questions About Annulment," both by Joseph M. Champlin; "Interchurch Marriages: How to Help Them Succeed," by Elizabeth Bookser Barkley; "Natural Family Planning: Key to Intimacy," by Fletcher Doyle; "Sacrament of Marriage: Sign of Faithful Love," by Thomas Richstatter, O.F.M.; "10 Tips for Married Couples" by Susan Vogt; "Why the Church Is Granting More Annulments," by Jeffrey Keefe, O.F.M. CONV.

Books: *Catholics, Marriage and Divorce: Real People, Real Questions,* by Victoria Vondenberger, R.S.M.; *Good News About Sex and Marriage: Answers to Your Honest Questions about Catholic Teaching,* by Christopher West; *Life-Giving Love: Embracing God's Beautiful Design for Marriage,* by Kimberly Hahn.

CD: *A Daring Promise: A Spirituality of Christian Marriage,* by Richard Gaillardetz, five discs.

DVD: *Planning Your Wedding Liturgy.*

CHAPTER 22

JESUS CONTINUES HIS PRIESTHOOD: ORDERS

THE IDEAL COMMUNITY OF JESUS, THE CHURCH, CONTAINS AN AMAZING VARIETY OF individuals. The love of God shines through them like colors through a prism. But the richness can be sustained only if there is community. Jesus must be the Center, the Head, the only source and model of Christian life.

The whole church makes Jesus visible. The priesthood makes Jesus visible as Head and Center. The unity of the church gets its visible support from the gathering of Christians around his visible representatives in the priesthood. (In this chapter we use the word priest to include bishops, who have the fullness of the priesthood, priests and deacons, within the limits of their sacramental function [see *Catechism*, #1536].)

Recall that a sacrament is first of all a *sign*. The sacramental ordination of a priest is a sign Jesus makes through the action of his church. In this case it is the public "sending" of a person to make Jesus visible in the church as Head of his body, a center around which the church can find its unity (see *Catechism*, #1548–1549).

In a culture where the only authority usually recognized is that of competence, not appointment, the ordination of a man may seem to say that he is "better" than the rest of the church. A priest should be a true disciple of Jesus. But, to put it crudely, Jesus has to have *somebody*, so he picks this man! It could be anyone, but it must be *someone*.

The church is not a group of unrelated individuals, but a Body, a living organism, a unity which needs a center. The priest is, for his eucharistic community, a public center from which Jesus wants the Good News proclaimed, a visible center around which the community gathers for Eucharist and other sacramental celebrations, and a center from which unified guidance can come. The priest is the means of sacramental union with Jesus.

No one knows better than a priest that he is unworthy to make Jesus visible as Head of the church. But it must be done. The church must hear "This is my Body" and know that it is Jesus truly speaking. A sinner must know that Jesus is personally forgiving and healing him when he hears, "I absolve you from your sins."

WHAT PRIESTS DO. Jesus sent his apostles and their successors and helpers to proclaim the Good News in his name, to celebrate the Eucharist and the other sacraments, and to guide and shepherd the People of God (see *Catechism*, #1587). This "sending" is the origin of the new Christian priesthood, and these three functions of the priest are the three great offices of Jesus: prophet, priest, king.

Vatican II reminded priests that their *primary* duty is the proclamation of the gospel of God to all. In this way they fulfill the Lord's command, "Go into the whole world and proclaim the gospel to every creature" (Mark 16:15). Through this word the spark of faith is struck in those who do not yet believe, and it is fed in the hearts of the faithful. The Council lists four ways in which priests proclaim the word: by their own "honorable behavior, by actual missionary preaching, by handing on and explaining the faith, and by their trying, in the light of Christ, to deal with contemporary problems." Priests do not teach their own wisdom—but God's word, issuing "a pressing invitation to all men and women to conversion and to holiness" (*Decree on the Ministry and Life of Priests*, 4).

If the primary task of the priest is to proclaim the gospel, the *source* of that preaching *and its apex* is the celebration of the Eucharist, "the very heartbeat of the congregation of the faithful over which the priest presides" (*Decree on the Ministry and Life of Priests*, 5).

Radiating from the eucharistic celebration in the midst of the community, the priest's office of pastor, guide, shepherd is concerned above all with peaceful unity—in charity, in doctrine, in service. "They gather the family of God as sisters and brothers endowed with the spirit of unity and lead it in Christ through the Spirit to God the Father" (*Decree on the Ministry and Life of Priests*, 6).

He has the responsibility of handing on the authoritative teaching belief of the church, and thus sometimes of pointing out doctrinal error.

In specific detail there is almost no end to what a priest may be called to do. Nowadays, he is collaborating more and more with the laity, as is proper. In a changing world, he can only try to be open to changing needs in the spirit of the Good Shepherd.

BISHOPS. Priests, though they work fairly independently, are helpers of the bishops, who represent the apostles whom Jesus sent as his primary representatives. Bishops have the fullness of the priesthood. Sacramentally, the main difference between bishops and priests is that the former can ordain other bishops and priests and are, by their office, *the* official proclaimers of the word in their dioceses. A bishop is *the* spiritual father of the church over which he has been placed to serve and a member of the worldwide college of bishops.

DEACONS. Deacons share in the office of Jesus the priest "in the ministry of the *liturgy*, of the *word*, and of *charity*." The Second Vatican Council listed these offices of a deacon: to administer baptism, to care for and dispense the Eucharist, to assist at marriages, to bring Holy Communion to the dying, to read the sacred Scripture to the faithful, to instruct and exhort the people, to preside at the worship and prayer of the faithful, to administer sacramentals and to officiate at funeral and burial services. He is also dedicated to duties of charity and administration (*Dogmatic Constitution on the Church*, 29).

PROBLEMS. Wherever there is authority, there is going to be trouble. The priesthood has the problem of involving two totally different kinds of authority: first, what might be called jurisdictional, that which has to do with government and law in the church. We discussed this in chapter fourteen (see page 190).

In this area popes and bishops have usually been at the storm center, either because of their own faults or because of the human aversion to being told what to do. But pastors, too, are now learning the joys and sorrows of democracy from parish councils and worship commissions. And even ordinary priests are more and more frequently hearing that new imperative mode in the English language: "Father, would you like to use these readings today, and this Prayer of the Faithful?"

A second problematic kind of authority is that connected with the "power of orders." Just what authority belongs to a sacramentally ordained bishop, priest or deacon?

Among Protestants, the names of denominations indicate their solution to the problem. Congregationalists hold that Christ is the only head of the church, and all sovereignty rests in the congregation. Luther stressed the common priesthood of the faithful, and the doctrinal basis for Lutheran "ministering men" has not always been clear. Presbyterians (from *presbyter,* "elder") reject both episcopal authority and congregationalism. As the name implies, the Episcopal Church, as well as its Methodist offshoot, is under the authority of bishops. Baptists place authority in all the baptized in the local congregation.

In the Catholic Church the recognition of the dignity of the laity has naturally led to many questions about their function. How many of the functions of the priesthood today could or should be exercised by laypersons? Lay pastoral care programs are being sponsored by many dioceses. These are bringing more and more laypeople into such activities as teaching, counseling, spiritual care for the sick, hospital chaplaincies, administrative offices, spiritual direction, leadership of prayer groups. In the liturgy they are becoming increasingly active as ministers of Holy Communion, lectors, cantors and catechists. Some parishes have lay pastoral coordinators.

This can only be seen as a healthy development in the church. Many priests who exercised most of the years of their priesthood before the cultural explosion of the sixties found the transition hard. But, despite unavoidable blisters from the new shoes, most priests welcomed the "rise" of the laity. They were doing too many different things, anyway.

THE LAW OF CELIBACY. Priests of the Latin rite (as compared with the Eastern Catholic churches) are bound to celibacy, that is, not to be married. This practice began in the fourth century and was gradually extended to the whole Western church by the twelfth. Priests of the Eastern churches may marry, but usually they must do so before receiving the diaconate; they may not marry later.

The law of celibacy has no essential connection with priesthood. It is a law of the church, and the church could change the law if it wished. Individual priests may therefore be excused from the law and allowed to marry, having received permission no longer to be active priests. Married clergy from other churches have been accepted into the Catholic priesthood.

Why celibacy? If we start at the most practical level, it is a matter of time and possibly economics. There would no doubt be advantages to a married priesthood, but there is also no doubt that a celibate priest has time to be available, mobile and committed to a degree that no responsible married man could be. (See 1 Corinthians 7:32–34.)

On the level of witness, anyone (not just a priest) who lets himself or herself be thus publicly designated as freely and faithfully living a celibate life is giving a sign of the kingdom of heaven (see *Catechism*, #1579). The sign may not be impressive to many, and it may be obscured by human weakness and fault. But in itself, voluntary celibacy for Christ points to the need for every Christian to have one fundamental relationship before all others—with Christ. Gospel celibacy is not a putdown of marriage. It gives a different witness. Marriage glories in the holiness of the Incarnation, this life now; it is said to be an incarnational witness. Celibacy in faith is a witness to the other world, already present. It is, if you don't mind the big word, an eschatological witness.

THE DIVINE OFFICE. Bishops, priests and deacons are joined by members of religious orders and laity in what is called the Liturgy of the Hours or, in ordinary parlance, praying the Breviary or Divine Office. The purpose of this prayer, which is largely taken from Scripture, is to make the whole course of the day holy. The "hours" are Office of Readings, Morning Prayer, Daytime Prayer (at mid-morning, noon or mid-afternoon), Evening Prayer and Night Prayer. By thus distributing the prayer through the day (and in some monasteries and convents during the night), the church is "ceaselessly engaged in praising the Lord and interceding for the salvation of the whole world" (*Constitution on the Sacred Liturgy*, #83).

RELIGIOUS COMMUNITIES. A religious "order" or community—Sisters of Mercy, Dominicans, Brothers of Mary, Poor Clares—is a religious group of men or women who live in community, under a common rule, observing the vows of poverty, chastity and obedience with the approval of the church. Religious orders find their distinctive spirit from their founder: Ignatius of Loyola for the Jesuits, Francis of Assisi for the Franciscans, Teresa of Avila for the Carmelites. Some orders are "clerical," that is, composed entirely or largely of priests. (These are not the same as "diocesan" priests, those ordained to serve a diocese.) Others are entirely lay. A man may be a priest *and* a Benedictine, or he may be a Benedictine only. It is an unintended insult to such brothers, "regular" members of an order, to ask why they do not "go on" to become priests. They have a wholly different function. They are, among men, what sisters are among women.

Each religious institute may have a particular kind of work, but the fundamental purpose of all is to be living reminders of eternal values to the rest of the church. There is obviously a negative element to vows: One does not have property of one's own, one does not marry, one does not have absolutely free disposal of one's activities. But this "giving up," if done with a free spirit and buoyed by a joyful community life, is a reminder to all—like the celibacy of priests just referred to—of the "other world" whose values must underlie the most secular of activities. Religious brothers or sisters are not better than others. They just have a different function in the varied beauty of the church.

Three sacraments cannot be repeated: baptism, confirmation and orders. They are said to "engrave" upon our person a certain "character" or distinguishing mark. (The word *character* literally means a mark engraved on stone, or a mark to indicate ownership.) While the church has never determined the precise nature of this "indelible mark," theologians have generally taught that it has to do with priesthood—that of the laity and that of priests. A baptized person is simply different from, say, a good Muslim who happens to be at Mass. The Muslim may be far holier than the Christian at the moment. But he or she is not a member of the worshipping community. The Muslim has not been given the power to make the offering on the altar a sacred sign of the worship of God and of oneness in love with Jesus the High Priest. Without flaunting superiority, Christians are "set apart."

REFLECTION/DISCUSSION STARTERS

1) When has it been necessary for you or a group of which you are a part to elect someone to represent you? How did you choose the person?
2) Why does the Christian community need priests? What are the functions of a priest?
3) Lay ministry is a growing phenomenon in the church today. What functions or jobs do you see lay ministers performing that in the past were usually done by priests? Does this mean the role of the priest has changed?
4) Discuss celibacy for priests. What are its practical and sign values? Are there disadvantages? Should it be optional?
5) What do you see as the role of religious communities in the church?

SUPPLEMENTARY MATERIAL

Catholic Updates: "Creating a Culture of Vocation," by Janet Gildea, S.C.; "The Sacrament of Holy Orders: Priesthood in Transition," by Thomas Richstatter, O.F.M.

Book: 101 Inspirational Stories of the Priesthood, by Patricia Proctor, O.S.C.

PART FIVE

OUR GRACE-FULL RESPONSE TO THE COMMANDMENTS OF JESUS

CHAPTER 23

"WITH ALL YOUR HEART": MORALITY AND CONSCIENCE

Blessed are the poor in spirit, for theirs is the kingdom of heaven.

Blessed are they who mourn, for they will be comforted.

Blessed are the meek, for they will inherit the land.

Blessed are they who hunger and thirst for righteousness, for they will be satisfied.

Blessed are the merciful, for they will be shown mercy.

Blessed are the clean of heart, for they will see God.

Blessed are the peacemakers, for they will be called children of God.

Blessed are they who are persecuted for the sake of righteousness, for theirs is the kingdom of heaven.

Blessed are you when they insult you and persecute you and utter every kind of evil against you [falsely] because of me. Rejoice and be glad, for your reward will be great in heaven.

(Matthew 5:3–12a)

THESE WORDS ARE THE HEART OF JESUS' PREACHING, THE FULFILLMENT OF THE old Law. They point beyond earthly happiness toward the kingdom; they reveal the fullness of God's plan for us: sharing in God's own happiness. We were made to know, love and serve God, and to share Christ's glory and the life of the Trinity (see *Catechism*, #1716–1721).

What do you do when you have experienced someone's love for you? When deep within you are filled with peace and security because someone has given you trust and generosity and unselfishness?

You want to *respond* in a way that will give the other the same happiness you have. Love begets love, not by measuring who gives or gets more but by a simple, free *response.*

God calls us to holiness—to wholeness, perfection. "So be perfect, just as your heavenly Father is perfect," Jesus says (Matthew 5:48). Our life is a journey toward ever greater intimacy with God, ever closer union to that perfect human, Christ (see *Catechism,* #2013–2014).

As Jesus said: "You shall love the Lord your God with all your heart, with all your soul, with all your mind, and with all your strength" (Mark 12:30).

Jesus is quoting Deuteronomy (6:5; 10:12). This is no new commandment, therefore. It is, we might say, the most fundamental law of nature: that the creature turn back to the Creator with its whole being, with *everything.* God cannot ask for anything less than truth. And the truth is, we owe God, who has given us everything, absolutely everything. God cannot love half-heartedly, or even only 98 percent. Neither can God's children. The Great Commandment is not an arbitrary rule but the law of our own human nature.

The Bible uses four words to express our whole being: *heart, soul, mind* and *strength.* We all know what these words mean and imply in everyday life: "Put your heart into it!" "Have a heart!" *Heart* means generosity, enthusiasm, feeling, passion, compassion. We have "soul music" and someone is the "soul of kindness." *Soul* is life, spirit, breath. Our *mind* is something we make up or lose; it is our intention, awareness, purpose, decision. Finally, our *strength* is our power or our ability.

If we put all these things together, we know what we are called to be, and we know the elements that are involved in all human goodness and evil. Without too much forcing, we may even reduce the four terms to two: *heart-strength* to signify our feeling and our freedom; and *mind-soul* to express our consciousness, our awareness, knowledge.

HEART-STRENGTH

What does our heart have to do with responding or not responding to the love of God, with being morally good or morally evil, with being in the "state" of grace or mortal sinfulness? Obviously, everything.

Jesus had a lot of trouble with some of the Pharisees, as we have seen, because he kept emphasizing the heart, the interior, and they kept emphasizing external observance. He told them, for instance, "A good person out of the store of goodness *in his heart* produces good, but an evil person out of a store of evil produces evil; for from *the fullness of the heart* the mouth speaks" (Luke 6:45; emphases added). And on another occasion, again rejecting their excessive harping on external and ritual purity, Jesus said: "Woe to you scribes and Pharisees, you hypocrites. You cleanse the outside of cup and dish, but inside they are full of plunder and self-indulgence" (Matthew 23:25).

Notice that Jesus speaks of something already in the heart before the good or evil act is done: There is a "store" of something there, even a "fullness." Modern theologians have coined a phrase that says the same thing in more abstract language: *fundamental option,* a basic choice of a way of life.

What it all means is this: Each one of us gradually becomes consistent in our way of life—fundamentally good or bad. We multiply decisions and, gradually, these decisions become one big decision—our way of life, our "heart," our "fullness," our "store." On that basis alone can we judge ourselves, and on that basis it becomes impossible for us to judge others.

It should be obvious that our particular actions are influenced by our fundamental option (just as they formed it). Those who deny this were censured by Pope John Paul II in his 1993 encyclical, *The Splendor of Truth.*

The following may exemplify the influence of the fundamental option on individuals' actions. Imagine a mother who is dead tired. She hears her baby begin to cry. The dynamo of her love drives her. She is committed deep down, even though it is unreasonable, even though she *feels* like walking out and never coming back.

As the pope says, the fundamental option "engages freedom on a radical level before God. It comes from the core of man, from his 'heart'" (see *The Splendor of Truth,* #65–66).

The man or woman who has built up a way of living, responding, deciding that is aimed at total love of God—a fundamental option for God—is the one in whom all the glorious promises of God are being fulfilled. God truly lives in such a person; he or she is "in" the state of grace, is alive with God's life, has real faith, hope, love.

If we think of our lives as a line going from base-zero—an infant, neither good nor bad—to full life in Christ, we see the story of growth. When does one cross the line from being a non-moral infant or child to being a mature—better, *maturing*—person who freely and consciously chooses to accept God's love and life? It is as gradual and unmeasurable as the growth of a tree. This growth cannot be judged by anyone except the person involved—and God. What may look like the genuine thing from the outside may not be. What may look like its absence may be a false impression.

But it should be evident that our true goodness takes its root, as Jesus said, in our "heart."

MORTAL SINFULNESS. As with a good "heart," so with an evil one. One decision after another produces—gradually, then finally—a big decision that is a fundamental choice, a way of life, that represents our values. "For where your treasure is," Jesus said, "there also will your heart be" (Matthew 6:21). Mortal sin empties the store of love in a human heart (see *Catechism,* #1855).

Those who commit mortal sin make a decision. *Fully realizing* that what they choose (the object of their decision) is *seriously wrong,* they decide with *full freedom* to do what they know, at least subconsciously, is fatal to their friendly relationship with God (see *Catechism,* #1858–1859).

Since mortal sin is such a terrible act, it is not lightly committed. One who does not *realize* its full meaning is not guilty of mortal sin; one of the essential factors is missing. Likewise, a person who is not *fully* free in his or her decision is not guilty of mortal sin. Human freedom can be diminished or destroyed by fear or passion.

One only gradually slides into what Saint John calls the "second death" (Revelation 20:6, 14)—that is, the death of our relationship with God. We may still be doing externally good things but overlooking our "venial" sins. These "little" sins are not to be taken lightly. They slowly decrease our store of love for God and neighbor; they grease the slippery slope (see *Catechism,* #1863).

Before the adulterer does anything overt, Jesus says, "everyone who looks at a woman with lust has already committed adultery with her in his heart" (Matthew 5:28b). People on the verge of going over the line interiorly may still be going to church, but:

This people honors me with their lips, but their hearts are far from me. (Matthew 15:8)

It is very hard—indeed, it is impossible—to judge the interior guilt of others, precisely because we don't know where they are on the "ramp"—and whether they are headed up or down.

This is not to say that single acts are not sinful, or that external order, the keeping of laws, should not be a serious matter to any Christian. But no single act is committed in isolation from the rest of a life, apart from years of growth—or non-growth—in understanding and love. No one *suddenly* becomes an adulterer or an embezzler or a slanderer. Certainly no one enters mortal sinfulness abruptly. It is simply impossible psychologically and, therefore, morally.

Because this is so, I cannot judge the *guilt* of anyone's actions but my own (see *Catechism*, #1861). I can and I may judge the emotions and some of the reasons why somebody does something: Obviously this person wants to chair the committee so badly she can taste it; obviously this man has a bossy, domineering temperament; obviously this boy "likes" this girl. But I cannot judge the moral goodness or evil of any of their actions because I cannot see what is in their hearts.

Yet even while I cannot judge the guilt, I must deal with externals. Society cannot say, "Since we don't know the moral guilt of this bank robber, we will have to let him go." The bank robber can be convicted of a *crime* with complete certainty, but it is possible that he committed no serious sin. It is possible that his heart was drowned in fear or anger to such a degree that his fundamental goodness was temporarily blocked out.

MIND-SOUL

Separating mind and heart is dangerous. Like separating hydrogen and oxygen: You end up not having water. Each of us is one body-spirit, one free, intelligent, feeling being. Yet we speak of "knowing" as being different from "feeling" and "deciding."

Here we meet our conscience.

CONSCIENCE. Let us set aside for now two common usages of this term: We speak of "examining our conscience"—that is, remembering our past actions and considering their goodness or evil. Second, we speak of "forming our conscience"—thus taking it to be something that needs to be refined and sharpened for the future. Neither this past nor future orientation of conscience is the focus of our discussion here.

Conscience, rather, is our ability and our obligation to seek the truth and decide for the truth now. Ultimately, conscience is a decision or a judgment made in the light of our knowledge (see *Catechism*, #1778–1784). It is a decision about the *here and now*.

To sin is to be aware of what God is really calling us to do here and now and to refuse (or simply to omit) to do it. To be a child of God and a follower of Christ is to have *discovered* by serious *deliberation* what the loving and Christlike thing is here and now, *deciding* to do it and *doing* it.

Sometimes the impression is given that conscience is automatic. Sometimes it is: For instance, I have an impulse to take revenge, but the impulse is so alien to my love of God I immediately reject it. But more often the situation is cloudy: Should I stay with this sick person or not? How long? Should I move to a new job? Should I report this drug addict? Should I say this or that or nothing? When should I speak up against what seems to be unfairness? When should I be tolerant? How much money should I share with the poor?

Sometimes it is not even clear how the law applies, or if it applies. I may not bear false witness. But is it false witness to give good references to a person who desperately needs a job but who is not entirely competent? The commandment tells me not to kill. Must I let a maniac keep killing others if the only weapon I have to stop him will cause his death? I must not steal. Is it stealing to take home items from work when one gets less than the minimum wage?

Prayer is not enough when good advice, discussion, authority and expertise are available. One cannot expect the Holy Spirit to insert decisions into our mind. The Spirit floods all of life with the light of the great truth of God's relationship with us. We know with absolute certitude the spirit with which we are to proceed. But the Spirit must not be subjected to our itch for magic or made into a supernatural computer from which automatic answers can be obtained by pressing a few keys of prayer. Prudence is *our* job.

It has been suggested that there are four "Ds" that make up the act of conscience. The first is to *dig* for facts. What's involved? Who? When? Where? Why? What will be the results? What does Jesus say? The church? My friends? My enemies? The experts? Common sense? What do I sense through prayer? The other "Ds" are to *deliberate* among the alternatives, to *decide* one way or the other, to *do* what has been decided.

A judgment of conscience always involves a bit—or a lot—of risk, depending on the amount of certainty I can acquire. But God accepts my good will in seriously approaching the question. I may turn out to be "technically," or objectively, incorrect or imprudent. I really shouldn't have bought the Edsel, or moved to Hoboken, but my decision was prudent—that is, I did all the things that truth and love required. (To make a very long story very short, this means that "God's will" is what I prudently decide!)

Sometimes conscience can only choose the lesser of two evils. Sometimes I may have difficulty deciding whether the good result I seek is worth the bad that will incidentally accompany it. And always a higher law makes lesser laws stand aside: "The sabbath was made for man, not man for the sabbath" (Mark 2:27b).

Conscience is not very often automatic. It is the ongoing moral task of our lives. Just as our heart and strength is gradually built up to become a store and a fullness, so our mind and soul gradually acquire habits of making either morally good or morally evil judgments.

To do good, for a Christian, is to see everything (at least subconsciously, by habit) in him who is the Light of the world. To sin is to shut out the Light. Jesus quotes Isaiah to describe a sinful conscience:

> Gross is the heart of this people, they will hardly hear with their ears, they have closed their eyes, lest they see with their eyes, and hear with their ears, and understand with their heart and be converted and I heal them. (Matthew 13:15)

It has been said that Jesus merely brought the good or evil in people to the surface:

> For everyone who does wicked things hates the light and does not come toward the light, so that his works might not be exposed. But

whoever lives the truth comes to the light, so that his works may clearly be seen as done in God. (John 3:20–21)

THE CHALLENGE: MERCY. Our hearts and minds are mysterious, even to ourselves. We are not as free as we might be; we often obstruct the light. We can only keep trying to be liberated from all that enslaves us, from all ignorance and prejudice. That is salvation—being saved, freed, rescued.

But we must stand under both the judgment and the mercy of God: "God knows your hearts" (Luke 16:15b). That may be our greatest consolation—or our condemnation. We are not deceiving ourselves if we see that we were not entirely free in a certain thought or action, or we were not aware of the full meaning of the action. (And this holds for our good acts, too!) To reach the fullness of sin or goodness, we must be fully free and fully aware of the meaning of what we do.

And if we can be merciful to ourselves, we must be so to others. As far as they are concerned, only the "mercy" side—not the "judgment"—is available to us.

Many people are damaged both in their awareness and in their freedom. Perhaps denied love in childhood, or kept in a state of perpetual anger or fear by the injustice of others, they are simply not fully free. Emotional sickness can also cloud both mind and will.

Jesus takes note of the differences in people's awareness in this parable: "That servant who knew his master's will but did not make preparations nor act in accord with his will shall be beaten severely; and the servant who was ignorant of his master's will but acted in a way deserving of a severe beating shall be beaten only lightly. Much will be required of the person entrusted with much, and still more will be required of the person entrusted with more" (Luke 12:47–48). By the same token, less will be asked of one to whom less has been entrusted.

LAW

Emphasis on the interior may lead to de-emphasis on the exterior. But we are not angels. We are body-spirits, and our lives have sharp corners that may injure others, or take up their space, or consume their food. I am free, but so are you. Respecting each other's freedom imposes limits on both of us.

Laws are needed for organization in any society, even one of thieves. Laws try to ensure the peace and security of community life. They protect rights and define duties. They point out areas of moral danger.

But law, by nature, must be general and simple. It cannot take all circumstances into consideration.

This is the essential difference between civil law (at least in the United States) and the law of God and the church. There are no exceptions in Anglo-Saxon law. Even if you need the money to save your child's life, the Internal Revenue Service will penalize you for not paying your taxes. Even in the middle of the desert, with no other cars within miles, you can be ticketed for going through a red light.

But God's law is always directed toward the highest possible good, even if that means setting aside one of God's specific commands. Thus my neighbor's need for first aid on Sunday morning outweighs my obligation to attend Mass; my desperate need for food takes precedence over your property rights.

Even God's positive laws (those which command us to do something, rather than avoid evil) may be morally or physically impossible to observe: I simply cannot take care of this person any longer; I cannot fulfill a promise now; in these circumstances, I cannot take back the stolen purse. Why? Because I would suffer greater harm than the situation warrants. Jesus excused David for eating the holy bread which only the priests were permitted to eat, because "he was in need and he and his companions were hungry" (Mark 2:25b).

Under God's law, the higher good also supersedes any human law, ecclesiastical or civil, unless disobeying the law would cause harm to the whole community. For example, if my refusal to give up a job for which I am incompetent but which I desperately need would mean the loss of federal funds for a project, my job must go. Likewise, if my refusal would mean contempt for God or goodness (I may not engage in immoral acts even to save my life or that of others).

How big a reason do I need to be excused from the law *now?* My reason —my physical or moral impossibility—must be as serious as the law itself. For instance, I do not need to have something as serious as scarlet fever to be excused from Mass this Sunday, but soreness from yesterday's picnic doesn't excuse me either. I need not go through a blizzard to bring the evening paper to my mother, but I must run the risk of infection to save the life of an abandoned sick person.

In all this we see the need for a sensitive, humble conscience. To say that one may sometimes be excused from the law is not to say we should make a career of looking for excuses. On the other hand, to worship the law and neglect its purpose and the human needs of others is to fall into the legalism of the Pharisees, so angrily denounced by Jesus. "Woe to you, scribes and Pharisees, you hypocrites," he said. "You pay tithes of mint and dill and cummin, and have neglected the weightier things of the law: judgment and mercy and fidelity. [But] these you should have done, without neglecting the others" (Matthew 23:23).

WHOLENESS IN ACTION. Spirit and meaning are not enough; external rule-keeping is not enough. With our *whole* persons we are to love God—with our whole heart, our whole mind, our whole soul and our whole strength, and our neighbor as ourself.

We keep the highest law in mind *first*: following Jesus in total faith and trust and love for God and neighbor. Then we try our best to sort out all the tangled circumstances of life and bring the spirit of Jesus to bear. We want his light to shine on our whole life—all persons, all circumstances, all possibilities. We want our hearts to be ruled by the generosity of Jesus himself.

Our calling is to reflect God's image and to bear the likeness of the Son. This is not just a private matter; it also involves our life in the human community. We cannot exist alone. We need other people—the small communities of family and neighborhood, the larger communities of city, nation and world.

REFLECTION/DISCUSSION STARTERS

1) What does the concept of fundamental option as applied to sin and morality mean to you? What is mortal sinfulness?

2) Think of times when you have attempted to judge others' morality— their moral goodness or evil. Consider times when others have

attempted to judge you. Why is it impossible to judge someone else's moral goodness?

3) The author suggests there are four "Ds" that make up the act of conscience. Consider a moral decision you have had to make. Did you carefully work through the "Ds": *dig* for facts, *deliberate* between alternatives, *decide, do?*

4) Limited freedom or awareness can affect a person's moral choice. Give some examples of moral situations in which that would be so.

5) Think of a moral situation in which a higher good, God's love, might conflict with a human law.

SUPPLEMENTARY MATERIAL

Catholic Updates: "Adam, Eve and Original Sin," by Michael Guinan, O.F.M.; "The Beatitudes: Finding Where Your Treasure Is," by Leonard Foley, O.F.M.; "Your Conscience and Church Teaching: How Do They Fit Together?" by Nicholas Lohkamp, O.F.M.

Books: Conscience in Conflict: How to Make Moral Choices, by Kenneth R. Overberg, S.J.; *Twelve Tough Issues and More: What the Church Teaches and Why* and *Being Catholic: What We Believe, Practice and Think,* both by Archbishop Daniel E. Pilarczyk.

CD: Men and Women: The Journey of Spiritual Transformation, by Richard Rohr, O.F.M., three discs with study guide.

DVD: Making Sense of Christian Morality, by Richard Sparks, C.S.P. One disc with study guide.

. | CHAPTER 24 | .

JESUS' LIGHT ON THE FIRST THREE COMMANDMENTS

THERE ARE NO RULES TO DEFINE LOVE'S RESPONSES, THOUGH LOVE ALWAYS FINDS concrete expression. Those who have not yet experienced God's love need rules—guardrails—to keep them from hurting themselves until they catch on to what life is about.

So there are commandments for all of us who seem never to catch on completely to what God is about, to what God's love is all about. Sometimes we experience a transfiguration, a peak moment when we feel the awesomely tender love of God within us. At other times we need the guardrails, when we seem barely able to do the minimum.

So the Christian life is a strange combination of two things. On the one hand we experience the zeal of which John spoke: "...[T]he anointing that you received from him remains in you, so that you do not need any-one to teach you" (1 John 2:27a). On the other hand we need to be as hard on ourselves as the most cold-blooded business analyst: "Where are the results? What proof is there that you are Christian? Are you doing even the minimum—keeping the rules?"

These two outlooks may be behind the polarization in the church today. Some say that if you don't *mean* what you do, if there's no love in it, what's it worth? Others argue that if you don't do what you say you mean, what good is your airy talk about love?

Thus people complain, "They don't teach the Ten Commandments anymore," and call for more discipline, more authoritative teaching. And others plead for depth and spirit and deep personal relationships with God and with our neighbor.

At least these two groups may keep each other honest!

THE "COMMANDMENTS" OF JESUS

As Christians, we must base our lives primarily on the commandments of Jesus, which obviously include the Ten Commandments. Jesus said, "Do not think that I have come to abolish the law or the prophets" (Matthew 5:17a). But Jesus came to bring the Law—all law—to perfection.

The new law is his own Spirit and spirit. Jesus is our Law. And following that Law will take us miles beyond the Ten Commandments, which are only the minimum, the guardrails of morality.

The whole New Testament is the commandment of Jesus. His life, his spirit, his death and resurrection, his presence with us—that is our law of life, the standard whereby we make generous responses of love and conscientious decisions.

Spirit, not analysis, binds friends. That is to say, two people who love each other do not sit down and *chart* their love. One would never say to the other, "Today I will work on trusting you; tomorrow I will concentrate on being generous to you; Sunday I will zero in on faithfulness." Rather, they want to be all these things at once, as expressions of one spirit, one love. At times, they may send many words tumbling over each other, trying to express the one love: "I love you. I trust you completely. I will stay with you through thick and thin. You light up my life."

It is the same in our relationship to God. We speak of "different" virtues (faith, hope and charity), but they do not live in airtight compartments. One supposes the other; none can survive without the others.

So in this chapter we will discuss several things together, because they belong together and are all concerned with the one love that must fill our lives. That is, we will combine the *first three commandments* of God and the fundamental virtues of *faith, hope* and *love.* These first three commandments concern God directly; so do the virtues. And Jesus' "commandments" bring them to perfection. True, it is impossible to separate love of God and love of neighbor, to separate the first three commandments from the other seven. But since we cannot talk about everything at once, we think first of our relationship to God.

A MATTER BETWEEN FRIENDS. We begin, then, with the supposition that the commandments are a matter between friends. The fact that this friend is God does not affect the freedom of love. But in this case there is no equality between friends: God is the total giver and we are total receivers. The friendship begins when this loving God-man Jesus says to us, because he loves us, *"Follow me."*

"Follow *me.* Not just any one thing, not just any one teaching, not just any one rule. But *me,* as a person. Make my spirit your spirit, my attitude your attitude. You don't have to do what I did—be a carpenter, walk around Palestine. You will probably not have to die the same way. But I have no choice but to ask you to die to everything but me. I love you. I died for you and I live for you. Trust me."

Now the "greatest" commandment has a new meaning: "You shall love the Lord your God with all your heart, with all your soul, with all your mind, and with all your strength"—and now the "new" commandment of Jesus: *"And follow me in doing this!"*

In other words, Christians do not start with the law, even the Law of the Ten Commandments. We start with Jesus, and fulfill all law in his spirit.

Another "commandment" of Jesus is to believe that in loving him and our neighbor we are made part of the community of God, the Trinity. "Whoever loves me will be loved by my Father" (John 14:21b). He asks us to believe that "the love of God has been poured out into our hearts through the holy Spirit" (Romans 5:5b).

This is less a commandment than a reassurance. Jesus is saying, "Don't be afraid to believe that it is God, not just a man, who loves you. You are valuable, you are important, you are loved. Live with this assurance. Then all other things—all obedience—will be added to you."

The whole Christian life is a matter of responding to the love and friendship of God as we experience it in Jesus and through his Spirit. It is unthinkable—except when we let down our end of the friendship—that we should reduce friendship merely to "fulfilling our obligations." When friends start doing that, they become strangers fulfilling a contract.

The first thing Jesus asks—a commandment, if you will—is that we have a personal relationship, an "encounter," a friendship with him, and experience his love. How do we do that? Only by being loved by other human beings: family, friends, the Christian community.

WITH ALL YOUR HEART. Is there such a thing as a "minimal" friendship? Can you tell me how much I "have to do" to be your friend, or give me a list of obligations so that when I have fulfilled them I don't need to bother further? Anyone who has ever loved and been loved—in marriage, family, community—knows that this is the sign of a dying or dead friendship. *We make up the list*, not our friend—and we make it as long as we possibly can.

Love is like fire. It cannot be confined. If you put walls around it, with no outlet, it dies. Therefore the God who knows all about love can only ask us to love him *totally*. Jesus was not being domineering, only truthful, when he said, "[E]veryone of you who does not renounce *all his possessions* cannot be my disciple" (Luke 14:33; emphasis added). Nothing, no treasure of mind or body or bank, can be more important than our friendship with Jesus.

People may complain about the lack of absolutes today, but this is one absolute: "Love me absolutely." This is what love of God is.

There's a nameless saint in the Gospels, a poor widow with only two copper coins to her name. It was, in Jesus' words, "her whole livelihood." She put them into the temple's treasury, and Jesus loved her. "I tell you truly, this poor widow put in more than all the rest; for those others have all made offerings from their surplus wealth, but she, from her poverty, has offered her whole livelihood" (see Luke 21:1–5).

Isn't this unrealistic? Idealistic? Impossible? Yes, of course. How deep a friendship would you have to have to give up your last two pennies? Yet that is the kind of absolute trust Jesus asks of his followers.

This trust is like that of the birds of the sky and the lilies of the field. Birds don't have barns, and wildflowers don't have garment factories "yet your heavenly Father feeds them. Are you not more important than they? …Your heavenly Father knows that you need them all. But seek first the kingdom [of God] and his righteousness, and all these things will be given you besides" (Matthew 6:26b, 32b–33).

Notice that Jesus doesn't ask us to abandon our intelligence or our daily work. He just says that there must be an absolute priority in our lives: the Kingdom of his Father. Those who would follow Jesus must want absolutely to be possessed by the love of the Father and to live by the power and wisdom of God.

THE FIRST THREE COMMANDMENTS

FIRST COMMANDMENT. *"I, the Lord, am your God, who brought you out of the land of Egypt, that place of slavery. You shall not have other gods besides me"* *(Exodus 20:2–3).*

What has Jesus done to this commandment? We "keep" it now by having the absolute love of Jesus for his Father and an absolute trust in Jesus himself, who alone leads us out of every kind of slavery. Jesus tells us that his friendship must precede all other loves. Anything less than total love is a lie, love given to other "gods"—other sources of power, pleasure, love, happiness.

If we really have experienced friendship with Jesus, all the *details* of the commandment become obvious. No one thinks to *buy* a real friend's care or concern (magic, superstition), and the last thing to do would be to abuse or dishonor someone or something connected with the friend (sacrilege).

SECOND COMMANDMENT. *"You shall not take the name of the Lord, your God, in vain" (Exodus 20:7).*

In the biblical mind, the name is the person. ("My name is *me*," said a contemporary Arab to explain why he did not want me to write down his name, thus "possessing" him against his will.) Even for us it is unthinkable to use a friend's name to back up a shady deal or to support a lie. This commandment forbids false oaths. To take an oath is to call on God as witness to the truth of what we say, to say we are as truthful as God (see *Catechism*, #2150).

One speaks a friend's name with love. Our admiration shows through when we speak the word. The name of God is God. Jesus tells us we are reborn in baptism in the name of the Father and of the Son and of the Holy Spirit. We are reborn in God. We are friends at the table of the Trinity. It should never enter our mind to dishonor God, who is the divine name.

THIRD COMMANDMENT. *"Remember to keep holy the sabbath day" (Exodus 20:8).*

Jesus restored the Third Commandment to its purity. It had been strangled in all kinds of rules that became more important than its real purpose: entering into God's "rest." Jesus cut through the red tape with, "The sabbath was made for man, not man for the sabbath" (Mark 2:27b). He did not mean it wasn't made for honoring his Father, but that external acts of worship could wait for an hour or a day if one's neighbor had some urgent need.

Jesus fulfills the Third Commandment by giving us the perfect gift with which to worship the Father—himself. The Eucharist is at the heart of the Christian life, and the Sunday liturgy is where the Body of Christ is most clearly visible on earth today.

Sunday is the Christian sabbath. It is the Lord's day because Jesus rose on that day; therefore it is the day we celebrate his passion, death and resurrection. Catholics have a serious obligation to take part in Sunday Eucharist unless they have a serious reason (illness, care of an infant) or are dispensed by their pastor or parish priest (see *Catechism*, #2181).

It is a *happy* obligation for friends and lovers who are always "much obliged." (If I cannot make a planned visit to my friend, I call him or her and say I am sorry. And I really am.) It is a *burdensome* obligation only if it is not part of wanting to follow Jesus in his friendship to his Father.

We also rest from any work or activity that inhibits worship of God, the joy of the day, and relaxation of mind and body. Sunday traditionally belongs to good works, to the service of the sick, infirm and elderly, to attending to families and neighbors. It is a time for reflection, silence, culture and meditation (see *Catechism*, #2185–2186).

THE FIRST THREE VIRTUES

The total commitment of friendship also tells us what the first three virtues are: faith, hope and love. The absolute friendship is *faith*. It is both entering into a personal relationship with God and freely accepting what God has revealed. It is giving ourselves to God through Jesus in a way we cannot give ourselves to any human being. It is total trust—in the dark, if necessary. It is a risk gladly taken—"Whatever you say." It is burning all the bridges behind us. It is believing God's word as we can believe no human being's word. More than that, it is entering into a dynamic relationship which grows and deepens as experiences multiply (see *Catechism*, #151).

Faithful friendship merges into a confidence that is unshakable—hope. I trust my friend. I trust an absolute Friend absolutely. It is not wishful thinking—like hoping I win the Powerball Lottery or hoping I don't have to give a speech. It is, rather, expectation of what I do not yet see: I expect God to be the perfect Friend and to give me the power to be a worthy friend in return. I am absolutely certain of forgiveness, patience, generosity, faithfulness. I can expect these. I can base my life on Christ's promises, so sure am I of their fulfillment. Hope protects me from discouragement, keeps me going when the way is dark and assures me of eternal happiness (see *Catechism*, #1817).

I may have a terrible temptation to abuse this hope by simply presuming on God's friendship without reciprocation. But it does not seem possible for anyone who has known God in Jesus ever to despair of his forgiveness.

As for *love*, what else is friendship but love? What else is absolute friendship but absolute love? It is "naturally" so on God's part, and the purpose of human life is the attempt to let God make our love absolute in return.

JESUS' FIRST RECORDED "COMMANDMENT"

After John had been arrested, Jesus came to Galilee, proclaiming the gospel [Good News] of God. "This is the time of fulfillment. The kingdom of God is at hand. Repent, and believe in the gospel." (Mark 1:14–15)

Thus Mark (Matthew, too) summarizes the beginning of Jesus' public ministry. Jesus gave people ample reason to understand, however dimly, that in him the Kingdom had indeed come. They could sense, from his whole personal presence, that he brought good news, indeed *the* Good News. Only when we sense this can we repent.

In fact, the word *repent* has been weakened by joking use in imitation of countless preachers. We must go back to what the word literally means: "Change your outlook, change your way of life!"

Change *from* what? Change *to* what?

Many "converts" have never turned from God. Their whole lives have been nourished by God's word, at least as it comes to them through a sincere conscience. They have never had to "turn" from a seriously sinful way of life. But they did have to be changed from mere human beings, members of a race alienated from God, to a "new creation," living God's own life. Gradually, or all at once, they understood the love of God, the evil of sin, the privilege of grace, and their lives became a process of constant change for the better.

For those who really have turned away from God with full consciousness and freedom, these words are indeed the first commandment: "Repent, and believe the gospel." They are life-or-death words. When Jesus was asked whether the Galileans whom Pilate murdered were being punished as sinners, he said, "By no means! But I tell you, if you do not repent, you will all perish as they did!" (Luke 13:5).

This is jolting, and Jesus meant it to be. A good doctor does not shield a patient from essential danger. It is useless for us to pile up all sorts of supposedly meritorious practices—going to Mass every Sunday, scrupulously avoiding adultery, murder and robbery—without even seeing our fundamental selfishness, superficiality and self-sufficiency. It is useless to "go through" sacramental ritual—baptism, Eucharist—unless we let God thoroughly change our heart, our whole outlook and way of life. Or rather, unless we let God fill us with the determination to enter seriously upon this lifelong process.

But notice the positive and reassuring love of God which surrounds the strong words of Jesus about repentance: "the good news of God"; "the time of fulfillment" (of God's promise of salvation); "the reign of God is at hand." God can only be a loving parent; Jesus can only be one who heals. And the church—you and I—must be the witness of this.

HOW CAN ANYBODY KEEP THESE COMMANDMENTS? Since we are considering the first and fundamental commandments, we should also consider the first heresy: "If you try hard enough, you can save your soul. If you work at it, you can be holy. You can put God in your debt."

It is hard for us to believe that our virtue is not our own—though we find it easy to let our sin be somebody else's fault. After all, we say, nobody helped me stay honest and pure and sober. I was the one who got up in the dark and went to Mass or said my prayers. I deserve the credit.

God does give us credit for freely doing what our Creator asks us to do. But the most basic fact of life is that without God, we can do nothing. I cannot do a single good act without power flowing into me from God. It doesn't come from "outside," like current through a wire, but from the heart of my being, where God lives. It is not just a psychological "inspiration"—though it should be that, too. It is God offering and giving us the power to make courageous and generous decisions and to do the good thing.

If I "die" to my intense desire for revenge, the power of Jesus (whether I am conscious of it or not) joins that "death" to his and gives me another little share in his Resurrection. The *Sacramentary* says it best: "Our desire to please you is itself your gift" (Preface #40). Or, as Scripture has it:

It was not you who chose me, but I who chose you and appointed you to go and bear fruit that will remain. (John 15:16)

REFLECTION/DISCUSSION STARTERS

1) Reflect on the statement: "Jesus is our Law. And following that Law will take us miles beyond the Ten Commandments, which are only the minimum, the guard-rails of morality." What does Jesus' directive, "Follow me," mean to you?

2) Consider the first three commandments in light of Jesus. How does he transform and fulfill them, bring them to perfection?

3) Give some examples of how faith, hope and love mark a true friendship. How do these virtues exist in our total commitment of friendship with God?

4) Jesus' call to us to "repent" basically means: "Change your outlook, your way of life." What kind of change is this, especially if a person's whole life has not been turned away from God? Have you experienced such a change?

5) What is mistaken about the attitude that I can be holy by my own efforts?

SCRIPTURE READINGS
Exodus 20:2–11; Deuteronomy 5:6–15.

SUPPLEMENTARY MATERIAL
Catholic Updates: "Do Catholics Worship Images?" by Teresita Scully; "Sunday Mass: Easter All Year Long" (John Paul II's *Celebrating the Lord's Day [Dies Domini]* in shortened form); "The Ten Command-ments: Sounds of Love From Sinai," by Alfred McBride, O. PRAEM.

. | CHAPTER 25 | .

JESUS' LIGHT ON COMMANDMENTS FOUR THROUGH TEN

COMMANDMENTS FOUR THROUGH TEN CONCERN THE WAY WE TREAT OTHER people. All but the Fourth are negatively stated, drawing lines over which we may not step. Considering them only as negative, we cannot say they represent the extreme boundary even of natural morality. A person is not good merely because he or she does not kill or commit adultery or steal.

But God did not leave the Jews with only a list of negatives. In two separate places in the Old Testament he made clear the attitude with which they should keep all commandments: "You shall love the Lord, your God, with all your heart" (Deuteronomy 6:5) and "You shall love your neighbor as yourself" (Leviticus 19:18). Bringing all commandments to unity, Jesus combined these two commandments with his own specific command:

This is my commandment: love one another as I love you. (John 15:12)

Whatever may be said as to whether or not Jesus taught a "new morality," this simple sentence lifted Christian morality beyond the most idealistic dreams of all the Platos of the world. Christians may still find it very difficult to form their conscience about a particular situation, as we have seen. But Christians have absolutely no doubt about the spirit, the attitude, the disposition, the heart of whatever they decide.

The standard of Christian conduct is not a law but a person. Not "What would Jesus do?" but "What would Jesus' feelings be in this kind of situation, and how would he handle them? What would be his reasons for acting, his manner?"

Can we know how Jesus felt? Certainly, because we know how we feel. He had the same basic human feelings that we have because he was a true and normal human being. Ours are mixed with sinfulness and bad memories, perhaps, but there is a basic similarity in all human emotion.

One of the results of prayer has to be a deeper appreciation of Jesus the man. He cannot be telling us merely to imitate him externally (like the brother who coughed whenever Saint Francis coughed) but in our innermost decisions.

WHAT IS LOVE? Love has had many definitions, most of them ending with words like moon and June. Jesus summed it up simply: "Treat others the way you would like to have them treat you" (see Matthew 7:12).

Jesus calls us to look into the depths of our hearts, where we find great incompleteness, loneliness and insecurity. We need other human beings who take us seriously, respect us, give us their trust and their affirmation, their bread and their forgiveness when we need it, and their willing and glad acceptance always.

This very unromantic definition of love will never make the hit parade but will suffice for all seasons: To love others is to give them what they need insofar as we are able.

Need is a deceptively simple word. What do you need? That's what others need. How far can you fulfill that deep human need which splits into a thousand needs in the prism of everyday life? My human resources—physical, emotional, spiritual—are limited, but the limits do not have to be further narrowed by my selfishness. Without craftiness or evasion, I can conscientiously let the light of Jesus shine on every circumstance and decide with *his* spirit.

Sounds complicated? So is life. But would I want anyone to do less for me? Can I claim to have the spirit of Jesus and do less for others?

PASSING ON GOD'S LOVE. Saint John was still a "son of thunder" when he bluntly stated:

> If anyone says, "I love God," yet hates his brother, he is a liar; for whoever does not love the brother whom he has seen cannot love God whom he has not seen. (1 John 4:20)

Love of God, as we have said, is the response of total trust and self-giving to the utter generosity of God. It is unthinkable that I could experience God's unfathomable love without feeling an urgent need to pass on that love to others. And this means treating people not only as I would like to be treated but as Jesus would treat them. I know what I hope for from God—and I am sure it will be forthcoming. My neighbor must be as sure of me as I am of God.

A beautiful story in the Gospels reveals an unexpected depth in love extended to a neighbor in such a simple act as sharing food. Jesus says, "I was hungry and you gave *me* food" (Matthew 25:35a; emphasis added). These words are addressed to us individually as we struggle to love our neighbors just as surely as "I am Jesus, whom you are persecuting" (Acts 9:5c) was addressed to Paul.

The second half of the story (Matthew 25:35–46) does indeed relate the condemnation of those who refused the neighbor—that is, Jesus—food and drink, clothing and shelter, comfort and presence. But we should not let this obscure the tremendous glory Jesus declares is ours, even when we act without awareness of what we do: "… [W]hatever you did for one of these least brothers of mine, you did for me" (Matthew 25:40b).

Loving our neighbor as Jesus did means *serving* our neighbor in all the areas superficially defined in negative terms by the Fourth through Tenth Commandments: marriage and family life, sexuality, physical and spiritual goods, justice, truth, respect. At the Last Supper, to show the meaning of his death and the purpose of the eucharistic bread, Jesus washed the disciples' feet in the manner and spirit of a faithful servant. Then he said, "I have given you a model to follow, so that as I have done for you, you should also do" (John 13:15).

It is not enough to refrain from adultery with someone else's spouse; I must serve them as persons, as husbands and wives, as people called to love. It is not enough to refrain from stealing: I must serve all people in their right to be treated justly.

A NONEXCLUSIVE LOVE. We simply cannot imagine Jesus saying, "You owe me one." He had some uniquely intimate relationships with friends, as we all do, but it is unthinkable that he measured his relationships with others according to what they might do for him. He did what he asks us to do: "When you hold a lunch or a dinner, do not invite your friends or your brothers or your relatives or your wealthy neighbors, in case they may invite you back and thus you have repayment. Rather, when you hold a banquet, invite the poor, the crippled, the lame, the blind; blessed indeed will you be because of their inability to repay you. For you will be repaid at the resurrection of the righteous" (Luke 14:12–14). Obviously Jesus would not have us exclude our friends; he just wants to be sure we don't exclude the others.

Love is concern for another's happiness. We want to please the people we love, to see the smiles on their faces, or their relief from pain or worry. To love as Jesus did is to let this instinct open us up to the needs and feelings of those who are not our intimates as much as we reasonably can. "Reasonably" here is not an avenue of escape, but a call to embrace the full truth of a situation.

As always, charity is its own reward. To break through our selfish shell is to enter upon maturity and full human life. Jean-Paul Sartre once said, "Hell is other people." The exact opposite is true. Hell is not-loving-others set like cement for eternity. I am essentially incomplete: I need God absolutely—but, just as absolutely, I need you to show me God's care and concern.

All very beautiful. But what of the unfairness, the selfishness, the meanness and just plain "orneriness" of these people presumably sent to show me God's love?

DO AS JESUS DOES. Jesus' commandments here are very specific. They identify several aspects of the problem and may be summarized thus: Don't judge others in your mind. Don't take revenge in your anger. Forgive those who hurt you. Love your enemies. And always the presupposition: *as I have done.*

Do Not Judge. When Jesus says, "Stop judging, that you may not be judged" (Matthew 7:1), he means the judgment of *condemnation.* I simply cannot help making an intellectual judgment about what is obvious. Everybody in town knows that this man is ambitious; even little children notice that this woman is determined to get revenge on the husband who deserted her.

What I may not do—in fact, *cannot* do—is judge the internal morality of anyone's actions but my own. I simply do not know how much awareness of sin other persons have. I simply do not know how free they are, what pressures of emotion and passion are upon them. I don't know their full emotional history, the love or lack of love with which they were raised, the ignorance or emotional disorder that may plague them. I don't know. I cannot make a moral judgment. I can only deal with externals.

Do Not Take Revenge. "...[W]hoever is angry with his brother will be liable to judgment" (Matthew 5:22b).

Anger is what I *feel*—it's like hunger, sadness, joy. It's there as a fact before it becomes moral. So I can call the Better Business Bureau and lodge a complaint against the company that cheated me; I can scold the dog for not asking to go out. So far so good. Or I can go after the salesperson with a gun and beat the dog to a bloody pulp. Not so good.

Jesus is addressing himself to my *response*, my choice as to how to use my anger. Will I be a crazy firefighter and turn the hose on the crowd or the other firefighters instead of on the fire? (The gushing water, like my anger, is neither good nor bad.)

Jesus says I may not retaliate; I may not seek revenge. "...[O]ffer no resistance to one who is evil. When someone strikes you on [your] right cheek, turn the other one to him as well" (Matthew 5:39b). I may not inflict hurt just to be inflicting hurt—unlike a parent who must, in real love for a child, teach the child that we must take the consequences of our actions and therefore "grounds" the youngster for a week.

"Turning the other cheek" means, *at least*, no revenge. Then Jesus pushes us a little further: We have to seek reconciliation. With the dog it's easy; she is loving and lovable and will make the first move, putting her head in my lap and wagging her tail until I tell her she's forgiven. That crooked salesperson will be a little harder. I'm really going to have to put a lot of effort into a friendly hello next time I pass that person on the street. Which leads us to forgiveness.

Forgive. Peter once asked Jesus, "Lord, if my brother sins against me, how often must I forgive him? As many as seven times?" Jesus answered, "I say to you, not seven times but seventy-seven times" (Matthew 18:21b–22).

According to the Jewish system of numerical symbolism, "seven" means some *definite* number of times. There must be a limit, Peter reasoned. But Jesus uses the same symbolic system ("seventy-seven" means an infinite amount) to make it indefinite: No definite number of forgiving acts makes our forgiveness perfect. It must go on, endlessly, like God's.

To forgive is to deal with a person, not an offense. It means that I still accept you and love you; your past makes no difference in that. I will not make you pay, vindictively, for your sin (though I have every right to ask the return of my money). You are worthy of my love, in Christ. Your action does not alter that.

Love Your Enemies. "But to you who hear, I say, love your enemies, do good to those who hate you, bless those who curse you, pray for those who mistreat you.... For if you love those who love you, what credit is that to you? Even sinners love those who love them" (Luke 6:27–28, 32).

One can absorb such "hard sayings" only in the light of Jesus' example of perfect human maturity. Jesus simply turns the world's values and standards upside down (though psychiatrists are coming close to realizing that to be "normal" is ultimately to be the image of God).

Jesus gives only one reason for loving the hard to love people: "that you may be children of your heavenly Father, for he makes his sun rise on the bad and the good, and causes rain to fall on the just and the unjust" (Matthew 5:45). To be like God—that is enough.

APPLYING JESUS' COMMANDMENTS TO COMMANDMENTS FOUR THROUGH TEN

THE FOURTH COMMANDMENT. *"Honor your father and your mother" (Exodus 20:12).*

The more a child knows about Jesus in his full humanity—including therefore his normal childhood and youth—the more will he or she see the Fourth Commandment as a natural and welcome part of life. The Fourth Commandment involves four things: reverence, obedience, love and gratitude.

Reverence recognizes parents as representatives of God, and therefore possessed of a special dignity as cocreators with God. Beyond the dignity of every human being, a child senses that particular worth of the persons who are the living source of his or her human life. Since religion is "caught, not taught," parents, of course, must live their own lives in a spirit of reverence and humility before God. No fathers and mothers are without faults; still, there is a special sinfulness in the scorn or bitterness, ridicule or contempt which children may visit on their parents.

Obedience accepts the fact that there is order in creation. Ultimately it is the acceptance of the authority of God, who did not put everyone equally on the same level. There is equality in dignity, but also a necessary subordination.

God does not speak directly to us, but through persons and—unless we are willing to welcome chaos—through persons in authority. Conscience must ultimately be our guide, and all children must grow up to make their own moral decisions. But conscience is only gradually formed and informed through the guidance of others.

Children (young and old) want to know "Why?" And since they must come to the place where their adult decisions have a solid moral "why" basis, parents must gradually direct the normal questioning and critical spirit of children toward understanding the reasons for their commands and rules—and the reasons why, perhaps, a day may come when they will have to say, "We must obey God rather than men" (Acts 5:29).

Having children is only a beginning; parents must also see to their growth—physical, intellectual, moral and spiritual. Theirs is the primary responsibility for educating children; they are the first teachers. They fulfill this responsibility first by creating a home filled with loving kindness, forgiveness, respect and unselfish service (see *Catechism,* #2221, 2223).

Children in their formative years can sin seriously by directly rejecting the just authority of parents, by insolence and refusal to cooperate in the home, by causing parents great sorrow or financial hardship.

Grown children can sin, too, of course. Scholars speculate that the Fourth Commandment originally applied to *grown children* primarily. There was a temptation, evidently, to simply abandon parents when they became "unproductive" and a financial burden, feeble or senile—a temptation simply to leave them behind in the desert when the caravan moved on. The modern equivalent is the refusal of adult children to help their parents financially and humanly according to their means and ability. A nursing home may be a godsend and a pleasant haven for a mother's or father's latter years. It may also be a convenient desert in which to abandon them. Adult children are to support their parents in times of illness, loneliness and sorrow, and when old age saps their strength (see *Catechism,* #2218).

Love and gratitude bring us back to the fundamental commandments of Jesus discussed above. Outside of one's spouse and children, who is more worthy (and in need) than parents of being loved "as I have loved you"? More likely to be the Jesus who says, "As often as you do it to these, you do it to me"? More worthy of patience, forgiveness and the withholding of judgment? More deserving of being loved as we love ourselves?

The Fourth Commandment speaks of the family, the domestic church. God calls the family to be a community of faith, hope and love, a communion of persons that reflects the communion of the Trinity (see *Catechism,* #2204–2205).

It also speaks of civil authority. It asks us to extend to lawful authority the same respect, obedience, gratitude and love we owe our parents (remembering again that sometimes we must obey God, not humans). And, in turn, it demands of civil authority what it demands of parents: justice, respect for the rights of individuals, support for families and those who are in need. Civil authority, like authority in the church, is there to serve (see *Catechism,* #2209, 2234–2237).

THE FIFTH COMMANDMENT. *"You shall not kill" (Exodus 20:13).*

Implicit in the love and forgiveness spoken of above is a basic reverence for life itself, human life above all.

A Christian sees the world, and especially all human beings, as made for Christ, the eternal God and our brother. Human life is God's greatest creation: the mysterious, graced body-spirit made to be a conscious and free manifestation of God's own life and love, made to be possessed by God in a face-to-face ecstasy forever.

Human beings are precious—just as they are. They are not valuable because of what they can do or what they have; not because of talent, beauty, strength or money. Just as they are. Bodies may be crippled for this relatively brief lifetime and minds clouded by physical or emotional damage. Life may burn low in the sick and the old, or violently in the criminal, or exasperatingly in our "enemies." But every person is loved into existence by a kindly God.

ABORTION. If one believes in the dignity of the human person, indeed believes that all human beings are body-spirit persons in God's care; if one believes that only God can—and does—create the light of reason and the freedom of spirit that characterize each new human being; and if one observes, with the exactitude of science itself, that nothing is "added" to this newly conceived person except warmth and nourishment, then there is no possibility of treating a not-yet-born person as a piece of unwelcome tissue, to be extruded and destroyed like a tumor or foreign substance in the body. One must conclude that this is a human being from the beginning, and has a right to be treated as such—cared for, defended (see *Catechism*, #2274). Catholics and many others simply respect life in this case.

What about the case in which a mother is certain to die, not because of the presence of an unborn baby, but because of reasons with which the baby is only indirectly connected: tubal pregnancy or uterine cancer?

To achieve a good result, one may do something (good or neutral in itself) which may also have a bad result, provided that the good intended outweighs the evil and there is no alternative. The evil is not intended, and it is not the means of achieving the good result. It is only permitted. (This is known as the principle of double effect.)

For instance, if the *only* way you can avoid an oncoming car and certain death is to jump off a bridge, it is obvious that breaking your legs by falling to the street below is not the *means* of saving your life. You jumped (a good thing, or at least neutral) to save your life (a very good reason). Indirectly, you caused damage to your body, but this was not your intention. It was an inevitable result which was obviously a lesser evil than losing your life.

So, in the case of a pregnant woman who has a cancerous uterus, removal of the damaged organ is necessary to save the mother's life. In neither case is the death of the baby the *means* of saving the mother's life. Cruel as this may sound, it is at least the lesser of two evils. At least two persons do not die. It is as much as truly loving and caring persons can do.

The principle of double effect has constant application in our lives.

EUTHANASIA. Directly ending a life, Kevorkian-style, because a person is debilitated by sickness or injury, is a serious failure to respect the God-given spark of life. It is, to put it bluntly, murder (see *Catechism*, #2277).

On the other hand, we are not obliged to use all the wonders of modern medical technology to keep a person alive when machines or procedures offer no hope of healing or relief. At such times, we admit our creaturely helplessness before death. Sometimes we can only pray, comfort and ease pain as we wait for God to call a loved one home (see *Catechism*, #2278–2279).

RESPECTING THE LIFE OF OUR BODY. Those who oppose abortion are sometimes accused of one-sided worry about life before birth, but not after; that is, of not being actively concerned that so many people live without proper nourishment, subject to disease, deprived of decent living conditions.

But there are other people who are in trouble as far as nourishment, sickness and "fitting" living conditions are concerned: *ourselves.* We have nutrition books by the scores, as our affluent society realizes the toll that junk food and overeating are taking. Americans are said to average ten pounds overweight. Alcohol and drugs have become symbols of a national tragedy. The Fifth Commandment, seen through the eyes of one who believes the body to be the temple of the Holy Spirit, forbids not only the vivid violence of murder, but also the slow, silent violence of self-indulgence (see *Catechism*, #2290–2291).

SELF-DEFENSE. I may choose to lay down my life for my brother or sister, but I may also defend my life—and others'—from anyone who wishes to harm or destroy that life. Catholic tradition has evolved these principles (whether for individuals or nations):

1) One may do what is necessary—but no more—to stop an aggressor. (If calling the police suffices, I have no reason to inflict injury; if escape is possible, I have no reason to use a gun.)

2) All non-injurious means must first be tried, if possible.

May one ever shoot another in self-defense? It may be difficult, considering the idealism of Christian love, to imagine a Christian deliberately killing another human being. But, applying the principles just cited, one can imagine a situation in which nothing short of the aggressor's death will save the life of the innocent party.

Let us suppose, for instance, that a man has already killed three hostages and is certainly about to kill the rest. The only weapon you have is a gun. You shoot to stop him from killing others (the good effect referred to in the double-effect discussion above). If there were any other way, you would choose it. You do not will his death, though it is probably inevitable. Vindictiveness is not your motive. You simply have no other way to save the lives of the hostages.

WAR. The church has a long tradition of teaching about war, and Vatican II reiterated these principles. In May 1983, after thorough discussion and lengthy dialogue with civil leaders, the U.S. bishops published *The Challenge of Peace: God's Promise and Our Response*.

"How we treat our enemy is the test of whether we love our neighbor," the bishops wrote, "and the possibility of taking even one human life is a prospect we should consider in fear and trembling. How is it possible to move from these presumptions to the idea of a justifiable use of lethal force?"

The bishops list the traditionally taught conditions for a just war (see *Catechism*, #2309):

1) *Just purpose.* "War is permissible only to confront a 'real and certain danger'; that is, to protect innocent life, to preserve conditions necessary for decent human existence, and to secure basic human rights."

2) *Competent authority.* "War must be declared by those with responsibility for public order, not by private groups or individuals." And, "While the legitimacy of revolution in some circumstances cannot be denied," just-war teaching must be rigorously applied.

3) *Comparative justice.* Which side is sufficiently "right"? Are the values at stake critical enough to override the presumption against war?

4) *Right intention,* that is, for the reasons listed under "just purpose." Right intention means pursuing peace and reconciliation, avoiding unnecessarily destructive acts or unreasonable conditions (that is, unconditional surrender).

5) *Probability of success*—to prevent irrational resort to force or hopeless resistance. But sometimes "defense of key issues, even against great odds, may be 'proportionate witness.'"

6) *Proportionality.* This is one of two extremely important principles (the other is discrimination) which must be applied both in deciding to wage war and in conducting war. This principle demands that the damage to be inflicted and the costs (spiritual and human, not just material) incurred by war must not be out of proportion to the good expected by taking arms. This principle applies in all self-defense (see above). To take the obvious example: Wiping out a nation (or the world!) is out of proportion to anything a nation may have done.

7) *Discrimination,* by its very name, means that a nation may not attack without discriminating between innocent civilians and military personnel and targets. Vatican II said, "Any act of war aimed indiscriminately at destruction of entire cities, or of extensive areas along with their population is a crime against God and man" (*Pastoral Constitution on the Church in the Modern World,* 80; see *Catechism,* #2314).

Both the principles of proportionality and of discrimination apply to the condemnation of total war. To destroy civilization by total war as it could be waged today would be a monstrously disproportionate response to aggression. Also, "Just response to aggression must be discriminate: It must be directed against unjust aggressors, not against innocent people caught up in a war not of their making."

These principles apply to *any* disproportionate or indiscriminate use of weapons, including non-nuclear—for example, the firebombing of entire cities to make the enemy surrender. One may not directly kill innocent people for any reason. One may not do evil to achieve good. (It might happen that a relatively small number of civilians may be killed, for instance, when an offensive is launched against a massed tank concentration. But their death is not the means of stopping the enemy, it is not directly intended and a far greater evil is prevented.)

NUCLEAR WAR. Speaking from these principles, the U.S. bishops say, "Under no circumstances may nuclear weapons or other instruments of mass slaughter be used for the purpose of destroying population centers or other predominantly civilian targets." This repeats the condemnation issued by Vatican II (above). The bishops apply this principle "even to the retaliatory use of weapons striking enemy cities after our own have already been struck. No Christian can rightfully carry out orders or policies deliberately aimed at killing noncombatants."

The bishops carefully word their statement on the initiation of nuclear war: "We do not perceive any situation in which the deliberate initiation of nuclear war, on however restricted a scale, can be morally justified. Non-nuclear attacks by another state must be resisted by other than nuclear weapons."

What about "limited" nuclear war? The bishops admit the *theoretical* possibility of a limited nuclear exchange, but advance many reasons why they think it is not a real possibility.

The bishops define deterrence as "the dissuasion of a potential adversary from initiating an attack or conflict, often by the threat of unacceptable retaliatory damage." In his 1982 message to the United Nations, Pope John Paul II said, "In current conditions, 'deterrence' based on balance is certainly not an end in itself but, as a step on the way toward a progressive disarmament, may still be judged morally acceptable.... Yet it is indispensable not to be satisfied with this minimum."

After wrestling with the problem of deterrence, the U.S. bishops made these statements: (1) If nuclear deterrence exists only to prevent the use of nuclear weapons, then it is not acceptable that we go beyond this (planning for repeated nuclear strikes, planning to "win" a nuclear war). (2) If nuclear deterrence is our goal, then "sufficiency" in arms is enough—we do not need "superiority." (3) Nuclear deterrence must be a step toward progressive disarmament. (4) Some weapons seem to be useful primarily for a first strike, and this goes beyond mere deterrence.

The bishops express the fear that even this conditional acceptance of nuclear deterrence (for example, presuming steps are taken toward meaningful and continuing reductions in nuclear stockpiles and eventually the phasing-out of nuclear arms altogether) "might be inappropriately used by some to reinforce the policy of arms buildup."

Military Service and Conscientious Objection. The bishops recognize in principle the right of a government to require military service, provided the government shows it is necessary—"legitimate defense." They repeat their support for conscientious objection in general and for selective conscientious objection to a particular war, either because of the ends being pursued or the means being used (see also *Catechism,* #2311).

The Sixth and Ninth Commandments. *"You shall not commit adultery....* *You shall not covet your neighbor's wife"* (Deuteronomy 5:18, 21).

As in the other negative commandments, this represents an extreme boundary. Implied in "keeping" the commandments is human love and, for Christians, a love that mirrors that of Christ and his church.

How far from merely avoiding sin is the free and joyful consecration of two Christians who are already totally committed to Christ! They see each other as complement one to the other.

Love is the glad fulfilling of another's needs, and sexuality is an obvious sign of human incompleteness. Human life does not begin or continue through one person. Life, and the beginning of life, demands communion.

We are always sexual, male or female. We live our sexuality all the time—not necessarily with genital activity but as beings whose very bodies are God's sign that all human beings need each other for life, for spirit, for faith, for survival. This plan of creation set forth in male and female bodies is the greatest argument against selfishness. No one can fulfill God's creation plan alone. And on the broad scale of life, the primary sin is *not needing* God; the second is like it: *not needing others,* living in a self-oriented, self-sufficient life.

Sexuality, then, is not something that has to do merely with our bodies, but with our whole persons. A human being is not just a body or just a spirit, but a body-spirit. In loving others in Christ, Christians respect their own body-persons and the body-persons of others (see *Catechism,* #2332–2335).

Chastity. Chastity may be called the virtue of using our sexuality within Christian love in a way that is appropriate to our state of life (see *Catechism,* #2349).

For the married, it means loving reverence for one's spouse both in the full-bodied exercise of genital sex and in all the other situations of life. It prompts the loving physical-spiritual expression of love and is disciplined against all tendency to abuse and selfishness.

Married love enfleshes God's own generosity and life-giving love. Married love is by its nature life-giving—not only to the couple, but also to their children. The ability to make love and the ability to make life are inseparable. Married chastity therefore includes openness to conception (see *Catechism*, #2366–2367).

Even couples who choose to postpone adding to their families for good reasons (as opposed to selfish reasons) must respect the link between love and life in their choice of means. "Natural" family planning, which relies on tracking the fertility cycle, does not disrupt the natural unity between intercourse and fruitfulness. Artificial contraception does rend the two and is therefore a serious offense against chastity (see *Catechism*, #2370).

For the unmarried, chastity means reserving genital activity for the life-long covenant of marriage—or renouncing it for the sake of religious life (see *Catechism*, #2349). In the face of a pagan culture, chastity says that total physical expression was intended by God to express the total commitment of a whole person to lifelong faithfulness, trust and service.

Some people, by no choice of their own, are sexually attracted only to persons of the same sex. As human beings, they are entitled to respect, compassion and sensitivity; no one has a right to discriminate against them. Nevertheless, the church holds homosexual acts to be seriously sinful and calls such people to the chastity of the unmarried (see *Catechism*, #2357–2359).

Chastity knows what even the pagans find out: Without the commitment of marriage, genital sexuality is ultimately empty and unsatisfying, prey to insecurity, immaturity and selfishness (see *Catechism*, #2339).

ABUSE. Like all sin, failures in chastity are abuses of God's good gifts. Adultery is the abuse of a sacred covenant, an injustice. Like fornication (the intercourse of unmarried persons), adultery is stealing the physical and emotional pleasures of marriage without being willing to put lives on the line in a promise of faithfulness. Unchastity is the abuse of persons—even if both persons can rationalize the abuse.

Masturbation denies the relationship between sexuality and relationship and wrongfully seeks solitary pleasure. We can say it is objectively wrong, but we also have to acknowledge that maturity, habit, stress and other factors affect a person's inner guilt (see *Catechism*, #2352–2353).

The Sixth Commandment also precludes physical actions whose nature is such that they cannot but propel any normal human beings to intercourse. The expression of love between unmarried persons is just that— an expression of Christian love. It is not naïve, but fully recognizes the accelerating nature of physical expression. Neither is it prudish, preoccupied only with danger. It begins and is able to end in a love grounded in love for Christ himself.

It is possible, especially if we consider the passionate nature of sexuality, that one's mind or freedom can be so clouded by emotion that full guilt, or even partial guilt, is not incurred for particular acts. All depends on what the fact of the matter is. On the other hand, it is possible to incur guilt by a conscious permitting of factors which gradually dull the conscience. Both holiness and sin (hence chastity and unchastity) are acquired by slow degrees, by accumulating decisions.

The Ninth Commandment addresses our inner attitudes, what we choose to store in our hearts. It precludes reducing people to playthings in our minds by entertaining lustful thoughts or enjoying pornography (see *Catechism*, #2354). The Internet makes accessing pornography much easier and more addictive. This commandment nurtures the virtues of modesty and purity.

Statistics indicate a great loss of respect for chastity today. Modern pagans probably view virginity in the unmarried as unusual as did their Roman counterparts. Christians are called to stand before the world with a courage that simply takes for granted that virginity of heart and body is part of the normal preparation for marriage (see *Catechism*, #2522–2525).

The development of chastity—self-control—is, like all human growth, a lifelong process.

THE SEVENTH AND TENTH COMMANDMENTS. These two laws command respect for the rights of all human beings to material goods. Taken literally, the Seventh Commandment refers to external actions. It forbids taking, keeping or damaging what belongs to another. Yet it also demands *justice*, a sense that the earth and its goods were given to all people, and that my right to this property is tempered by the common good (see *Catechism*, #2401–2403).

As with the other commandments, Jesus offered very little specific teaching on justice. His concern was the basic attitude that must precede and enliven the observance of all commandments.

He was concerned with the total well-being of people—with their dignity, with mutual love and support, with total trust in God through all life's circumstances. He also turned his attention to food and to healing and to freeing the little people from the hypocrisy and injustice of their leaders.

He did not propose tax relief or welfare or Social Security. He proposed no economic or political theories because there was—and still is—a terrible urgency to convert hearts to a spirit of concern for other human beings. Human structures built by loving hearts will consider others' needs in every age and system.

JUSTICE OR CHARITY? Justice is said to concern what people have a right to; charity is said to go *beyond* rights. The trouble with these definitions is that they seem to make charity *optional.*

Christians know that charity is the heartbeat of life. With Jesus they look at all human beings, but especially to those close at hand, and say to themselves, "What do they need? What can I reasonably do for them, in the spirit of Jesus?"

Who ever heard of people who love each other making up lists of each other's rights and ignoring what is optional?

FULLY HUMAN LIFE. Vatican II is clear on what Catholics are called to do: "There must be made available to all people everything necessary for leading a life truly human, such as food, clothing and shelter; the right to choose a state of life freely and to found a family, the right to education, to employment, to a good reputation, to respect, to appropriate information, to activity in accord with the upright norm of one's own conscience, to protection of privacy, and to rightful freedom, even in matters religious" (*Dogmatic Constitution on the Church*, #26).

PRIVATE PROPERTY. Every human being has a right to have a share of material goods sufficient for subsistence. This is *prior* to anyone's natural right to own private property. We are to regard our lawful possessions not merely as our own, but also as common property in the sense that they can be of benefit also to others. All the children of God are obliged to come to the relief of the poor (see *Catechism,* #2443), "and to do so not merely out of their superfluous goods" (*The Pastoral Constitution on the Church in the Modern World,* 69).

Economic activity and production is meant to serve human needs. The purpose of any economic system (yes, including the "freedom" of capitalism) is not just to increase the GDP, but first to serve people (see *Catechism,* #2426).

The work people do is part of God's creating action. Work is not only something we "ought" to do; it also affirms our dignity as creatures made in God's image. The work we do should enable us to provide for our basic human needs and those of our dependents (see *Catechism,* #2427–2428).

I AM MY BROTHER'S KEEPER. The Christian's maturely formed conscience looks with the eyes of Jesus on all fellow human beings. There must be a Christian bias in favor of the weak, the poor, the little people. It is more than a matter of strict justice that we *care for* (not merely take *care of*) the emotionally disturbed and the handicapped, especially those who must live in institutions.

Above all, a Christian feels pain at the specter of hunger in the world and anger at the political and economic systems which cause it. One of the most blasphemous ways to pervert the Bible is to use Jesus' words, "The poor you will always have with you" (Matthew 26:11), as an excuse for writing off slums and all the human degradation they involve as "a normal function of society." Those who think Jesus scorned "welfare" would do well to read the parable of the rich man and Lazarus (Luke 16:19–31).

Societies can be just as sinful as the individuals who make it up. We are accomplices to violence and injustice when we allow our social structures to demean and oppress some people (see *Catechism,* #1869). The very purpose of human social structures—governments, economies—is to affirm and protect the dignity of each and every person (see *Catechism,* #1929–1931).

A Christian is on the side of those who have no power in society, or very little; those who suffer the inheritance of decades or centuries of subhuman experience, the lack of normal relationships, the erasure of human dignity. One thinks immediately, in our country, of blacks, Native Americans, Spanish-speaking Americans, Appalachians—all "those people" about whom it is so easy to compose a sour gospel of welfare abuses, shiftlessness and waste.

CATHOLIC SOCIAL TEACHING AND THE U.S. ECONOMY. In November 1984 the U.S. bishops issued the first draft of a pastoral letter on Catholic social teaching as compared with the U.S. economy. The first half of the letter deals with general principles; the second half, with particular opinions and suggestions.

Central emphasis is placed on human dignity. The bishops remind their people that every judgment about economic life must ask two questions: What does this do *for* people and *to* people, especially the poor and deprived members of the community, who have a special claim to our concern?

Whether or not a community acts justly is measured by its treatment of those whose side Jesus took—the powerless and the poor. The teaching of the Bible is the basis for a "preferential option for the poor," which challenges the church—Christians—to speak for those who are defenseless and poor. The church is called to be the community of disciples of Jesus in solidarity with those who suffer, and in confrontation with the sinful structures that institutionalize injustice (see *Catechism*, #1869).

Human beings should be able to find self-realization in their work and to fulfill their material needs by a just wage. The United States has indeed made great strides, but we still need a new national consensus that all persons have economic rights, and that society has the moral obligation to ensure that no one is hungry, homeless, unemployed or otherwise denied what is needed to live with dignity. Unequal distribution of income, wealth, education or job opportunities on the basis of race, sex or any other arbitrary standards can never be justified.

There are three principles which should be given priority in our economy: (1) The fulfillment of the basic needs of the poor must have the highest priority. (2) Increased participation by the marginalized takes precedence over the preservation of privileged concentrations of power, wealth and income. (3) Meeting human needs and increasing participation must be priority targets in the investment of wealth, talent and human energy.

All people have a right to employment, to just wages, to collective bargaining. People also have the duty to work. Workers and unions have responsibilities to society as a whole. Managers, investors and businesses must remember that no one can ever own economic resources absolutely or use them without regard for others. Catholic teaching defends the right to private property, but this is not an unconditional and absolute right. No one can keep for exclusive use what is not needed when others lack the necessities of life.

Government has a positive moral function—protecting basic rights, ensuring economic justice for all, enabling citizens to coordinate their actions toward these ends. As for the scope of government, the principle of "subsidiarity" is primary: What can be accomplished on a lower level should not be transferred to a higher (see also *Catechism*, #1883).

The human race is one moral community. We must work for the good of the whole human race. Our Christian faith and the norms of human justice impose distinct limits on how we view material goods and what we consume. Such limits are needed if we are to avoid what Pope Paul VI called "the most evident form of moral underdevelopment, avarice and greed."

The church itself is bound by all the moral principles that govern the just operation of any economic endeavor—and that includes all the schools, hospitals, retirement homes, social service agencies or other institutions under its auspices.

SINS? It would seem that the greatest sins are committed against the Seventh Commandment by omission. Everyone is convinced that outright stealing is wrong, and that one must pay back whatever was stolen. Nothing is so sacred to some people as property.

But what of the sinfulness of paying unjust (though legal) wages that do not permit a decent family life, or perhaps any at all? What of deception in merchandising, defective work on cars or clothing? What of the cruelty of a society in which inflation must be fought by hurting the poor and the elderly more than anyone else?

SOCIAL SIN. A good sign of the times, though we haven't done much about it yet, is the awareness of social sin, sin built right into the culture and its political and social institutions.

In an apostolic exhortation Pope John Paul II addressed this issue of social sin. To speak of social sin, he says, is to recognize that there is a mysterious human solidarity whereby each individual's sin affects others in some way. There is a solidarity on the religious level also—the deep and magnificent mystery of the Communion of Saints, whereby we can say that "every soul that rises above itself raises up the world." By the same token, anyone who lowers oneself through sin also drags down the whole church and, in some way, the world.

Social sin is every sin against justice—whether by the individual against the community, or vice versa. It is every sin against the rights of the human person, beginning with the right to life, including the life of the unborn. It is every sin against others' freedom, especially the freedom to believe in and adore God.

Social sin is every sin against the common good. The term can be applied to the sins of leaders (political, economic, union) who, though they have the power, do not work for the improvement of society.

Having said all this, however, the pope carefully pointed out that one meaning of "social sin" is not acceptable: that which contrasts social and personal sin and leads to the watering down—or abolishing—of personal sinfulness, as if one had only a social responsibility. In this case blame is placed on some vague entity like "the situation," "society" or "structures." But real responsibility always lies with individuals. Society, or a situation, does not perform moral acts. A situation is not morally good or bad—only individuals are. Thus, social sin is the accumulation of many persons' sins.

The Tenth Commandment probes our mind and heart, where all sin begins, and forbids injustice in willful desire and intention. It forbids coveting what belongs to another, and rules out greed and avarice arising from an excessive desire for wealth and power (see *Catechism*, #2536).

Jesus said, "... [E]veryone of you who does not renounce all his possessions cannot be my disciple" (Luke 14:33b). Our detachment from material goods is necessary if we are to enter the Kingdom (see *Catechism,* #2544).

THE EIGHTH COMMANDMENT. *"You shall not bear dishonest witness against your neighbor" (Deuteronomy 5:20).*

In the narrowest sense this commandment forbids perjured testimony. For Christians, it opens up the aspect of Jesus as the *Truth* to be followed.

Pilate asked cynically—or perhaps sadly—the meaning of truth as if it could not really be captured by the human mind and heart (see John 18:38).

What is truth?

To be true, a word or a symbol must correspond with reality, with the way things really are. Now, the Spirit of truth leads us to make our hearts and our actions correspond to the deepest reality seen and experienced by faith: God's love surrounding the world, healing and transforming it. We must act in accordance with this fullest reality. Christians, following Jesus, do not wish to cloud or distort the truth of his saving presence in their lives (see *Catechism,* #2464).

Jesus is, as he said, the Truth (see John 14:6). He is the perfect, accurate expression of God. He is "true God," the full reality of God. He is "true man," what humans were intended to be. His Father is the Truthful One who sent Jesus, assuring us we can trust him absolutely. The Spirit of Truth Jesus promised awakens us to the really real, the full view of life, the vision of faith.

Hence, truthfulness rests on love. It is not enough not to tell lies. Nor is it, on the other hand, always wise to tell everything. Truthfulness balances what ought to be expressed—what another has a right to know—with what ought to be kept secret. It includes not only honesty but also discretion (see *Catechism,* #2469). Truthfulness sometimes makes us hold our tongues when an honest but critical word would only wound.

Speech and symbol, silence and gesture, "body language"—all are to communicate with others in the expression of Christian love. The community gathered around the altar is nourished with the true bread that comes from heaven, and sincerely tries to show this communion by speaking what others need to hear, be it sympathy or forgiveness, frankness or warning.

Loving communication considers not just whether or not words are literally true but the whole context: who hears them, what is implied, what will probably be understood. (Sometimes, of course, others do not have a right to know certain facts, or one has a professional obligation not to reveal them.)

Lying most clearly offends against the truth (see *Catechism*, #2483). And lying is an unjust refusal to let reality be perceived by others.

It is not unjust to conceal the truth, or let others be deceived, when a higher good is thereby preserved. It is certainly *truth*—correspondence with the fullest reality—to say anything necessary to save the life of a hostage unjustly kept, or to conceal the identity of someone who is in imminent danger of being murdered. It is Christian charity to keep a secret whose revelation would unjustly damage the reputation or social status of a person.

The determining principle is love's *reality*. What, in the most sincere openness to God, is the true communication of God's will here and now?

SPECIFIC SINS. To make false charges or misrepresentations which defame or damage someone's reputation is *slander*. *Calumny* stresses the malice of such spoken or written words. *Detraction* is hurting someone's reputation by revealing unknown faults or defects without sufficient reason. *Rash judgment* is to assume without good cause that someone has committed a moral offense (see *Catechism*, #2477). All these sins require a sincere effort at restitution. I must do whatever I can to restore the reputation I have damaged (see *Catechism*, #2487).

Secrets are of three kinds: (1) *natural* secrets (those in which the revealing of the facts would, by their very nature, cause pain or damage); (2) *promised* secrets (those where the obligation of secrecy comes from a definite promise, though the secret may already be a natural secret); (3) *committed* secrets (those about which an explicit or implicit agreement is made before the secret is entrusted to someone). Committed secrets include all knowledge to which one has access as a professional (confessor, doctor, lawyer, counselor).

The obligation to keep something secret depends on the understanding between the parties when the secret is entrusted, and on the damage that would result from its revelation. A secret may be revealed for loving reasons—when keeping it risks greater damage to the common good, to an innocent third party, to the one to whom the secret was committed or to the owner of the secret.

These distinctions are cold and legal, however necessary. They are made warm and life-giving by the spirit of genuine respect and love for all human beings and a real compassion for their sufferings, whether these sufferings stem from actual sin or the accidents of life.

Love and truth—the truth that sees *all* reality—rest on each other. Faith is grounded in the security that God's word is absolutely dependable, divine love absolutely faithful. All our secrets are absolutely safe with God.

REFLECTION/DISCUSSION STARTERS

1) What does it mean to you that the standard of Christian conduct is not a law, but a person—the person of Jesus? Is it easier or more difficult to follow a person rather than a law or set of laws?

2) Consider Jesus' commandment of love. What kind of love are we to give to one another? How are we called to pass on to others our love of God?

3) Reflect on Jesus' commands: Do not judge; do not take revenge; forgive; love your enemies. In what situations did he issue these directives? Do these seem to be difficult commands to you? Why?

4) Discuss the Fourth through Tenth Commandments in light of Jesus' commandment to love as he loved. You may wish to consider these points: (a) Fourth—the reverence, obedience, love, gratitude we owe our parents; (b) Fifth—abortion, the principle of double effect, self-defense, just war and the use of nuclear weapons, respecting the body; (c) Sixth and Ninth—sexuality as marking the whole person, chastity in different states of life, the need for others; (d) Seventh and Tenth— justice versus charity, private property versus the right to subsistence, social sin; (e) Eighth—acting in accordance with truth, our hearts and actions corresponding to the deepest reality.

SCRIPTURE READINGS

Exodus 20:12–17; Deuteronomy 5:16–21; Matthew 25:35–46.

SUPPLEMENTARY MATERIAL

Catholic Updates: "Abortion: What the Church Teaches," by Helen Alvare; "End-of-Life Ethics," by Kenneth Overberg, S.J.; "The How and Why of Natural Family Planning," by Mary Shivanandan; "How Should We Think About the Poor? A Bishop Reflects," by Kenneth E. Untener; "Human Sexuality: 'Wonderful Gift' and 'Awesome Responsibility,'" by Richard Sparks, C.S.P.; "100 Years of Catholic Social Teachings," "The Death Penalty: Why the Church Speaks a Countercultural Message" and "A Consistent Ethic of Life," all by Kenneth R. Overberg, S.J.; "What Is 'Just War' Today?" by Thomas Shannon; "Why Catholics Care for Creation," by Joan Brown, O.S.F.; "Why the Church Opposes Assisted Suicide," by Wilton D. Gregory, S.L.D.

Scripture From Scratch: "Choosing Life: The Bible and Euthanasia," by Kenneth R. Overberg, S.J.; "Do We Love Our Enemies? The Bible and the Just War Tradition," by Lisa Sowle Cahill.

Books: Apocalypse: A Catholic Perspective on the Book of Revelation, by Stephen Doyle, O.F.M.; *Life Issues, Medical Choices: Questions and Answers for Catholics,* by Janet Smith and Christopher Kaczor.

Encyclicals: The Progress of Peoples (1987); *On Social Concerns* (1991); *100th Year* (1991, centennial of *Rerum Novarum,* addressing various social questions); *God Is Love* (2006); *In Hope We Are Saved* (2007).

PART SIX

VISIONS OF OUR FUTURE

. | CHAPTER 26 | .

JESUS' MOTHER AND OURS: MARY

OTHER THAN JESUS, ONLY ONE HUMAN BEING HAS ENTERED INTO THE FULLNESS of life he promises: Mary. After Jesus, there is no person so beloved by Catholics of all ages as Mary, the mother of Jesus, the mother of God (see *Catechism*, #963). Without our knowledge of her, Jesus would not be understandable—a mystic figure coming from nowhere. The Gospel pictures of a real baby in her arms are an essential part of our faith. Calvary and Easter are the heart of our faith, but Christmas must first touch our human hearts.

Luke gives us the most detailed picture of the infancy of Jesus and Mary's role in the divine mystery there. Let us look at the highlights of Mary's story as Luke tells it in the first two chapters of his Gospel.

THE ANNOUNCEMENT TO MARY. Luke 1:26–45 introduces us to Mary as "a virgin betrothed to a man named Joseph, of the house of David"—already a hint of an heir to David's throne. The angel Gabriel greets Mary: "Hail, favored one!" (or, as in the familiar prayer, "Hail, full of grace!"). Mary is the special object of God's favor.

"The Lord is with you." Mary is the flowering of all the faith that waited through the centuries for the coming of the Messiah. She is the greatest and humblest of the *anawim*, the poor in spirit. She senses the magnitude of the moment and is "greatly troubled." The angel reassures her: "Do not be afraid, Mary, for you have found favor with God. Behold, you will conceive in your womb and bear a son, and you shall name him Jesus. He will be great and will be called Son of the Most High, and the Lord God will give him the throne of David his father, and he will rule over the house of Jacob forever, and of his kingdom there will be no end."

Mary's Virginal Conception. Mary makes a forthright statement: "How can this be, since I have no [sexual] relations with a man?" She is betrothed but not married. Then Luke delicately describes the act of God whereby the Son will become human: "The holy Spirit will come upon you, and the power of the Most High will overshadow you. Therefore the child to be born will be called holy, the Son of God." Then, with magnificent simplicity, Mary says, "Behold, I am the handmaid of the Lord. May it be done to me according to your word."

She hurries to visit her cousin Elizabeth, and the unborn John the Baptist leaps with joy in his mother's womb, as David danced before the Ark of the Covenant (see 2 Samuel 6:14). "Blessed are you who believed," Elizabeth says, "that what was spoken to you by the Lord would be fulfilled."

Mary is, above all, the woman of faith. She trusted, even before Joseph was called to share her trust. Her perpetual virginity was her total openness and unreserved love of God. She had to suffer, for a time, the pain of Joseph's bewilderment, until he was told that "it is through the holy Spirit that this child has been conceived in her" (Matthew 1:20).

THE VIRGIN BIRTH. Caesar must count his people, and Mary must leave her home to give birth to her son in a strange town, in poverty. But Bethlehem is the town of David, and her son is a king. The first subjects to pay him honor are simple shepherds who become the first bearers of the Good News.

Mary and Joseph take the child to be presented in the temple and consecrated to God, according to Jewish custom. They make the offering of the poor—a pair of turtledoves or two young pigeons. A holy man assures Mary that this baby is "a light for revelation to the Gentiles, / and glory for your people Israel," but also that "you yourself a sword will pierce" (Luke 2:32, 35).

THE FINDING IN THE TEMPLE. Mary's faith was challenged as no one else's: to know the divine origin of this child and at the same time to see him as a helpless baby needing her motherly care, then a child with exploring eyes and wild feet, with sudden fears and laughter, with skinned knees and mud-streaked tunic. She pondered and waited.

A milestone along the way occurred at the first separation of mother and child. Remaining behind in Jerusalem in total adolescent absorption in the temple rabbis' wisdom, Jesus caused Mary and Joseph three days of anguished searching. When they found him, he revealed a depth they had not suspected: "'Why were you looking for me? Did you not know that I must be in my Father's house?' But they did not understand what he said to them" (Luke 2:49b–50).

Mary did not grasp, but she trusted, and waited, and may have suspected what the sword thrust would be. Then eighteen years of Gospel silence, of which all we know is that Jesus "advanced [in] wisdom and age and favor before God and man" (Luke 2:52)—and Mary with him.

"WOMAN." Like all mothers, Mary realized she would sooner or later suffer the pain and the pride of seeing her son take his place in the world. But even when Jesus began his public life, their separation was not complete. John tells of them together at a wedding in Cana and of her implicit request that he relieve the host's embarrassment when the wine ran out. His reply sounds cold: "Woman, how does your concern affect me? My hour has not yet come" (John 2:4b). The "hour" of Jesus is that of his glorification—the passion, death and resurrection by which our salvation is achieved. Only in view of that can Mary's request, even though she is his own mother, have any force.

Mary's greatest dignity is that she is a believer, one graced by God (even though that was never separated from her willingness to be Jesus' mother). The church has come to see her as the woman of Genesis, and to regard Genesis 3:15 as the "first Gospel":

I will put enmity between you and the woman,
  and between your offspring and hers;
He will strike at your head,
  while you strike at his heel.

The first woman was called Eve, because she was "mother of all the living" (see Genesis 3:20). Mary is the mother of him who is Life itself and thus of all those who are reborn with his life (see *Catechism*, #489). She is the mother of the church, the eucharistic community nourished by the Word made flesh in her. In Revelation 12:1 John is probably referring to God's people when he speaks of "a woman clothed with the sun," but the application to Mary is instinctive for all who read the passage.

Finally, it should be noted, Jesus did do something about the wine at Cana. He made some one hundred twenty gallons of it, and thus let a bit of his glory shine through. His disciples believed in him (see John 2:11). Perhaps only later they saw this as a fulfillment of an ancient prophecy. Not only would the Messiah bring bread in abundance, but the mountains would flow with wine (see Isaiah 25:6).

THE WOMAN AT THE CROSS. The sword pierced Mary's heart when a Roman soldier's sword pierced the side of her son, already stilled in death. She who had the greatest reason to expect a glorious messianic victory was for that very reason most tortured emotionally by his death as a criminal dispatched in disgrace and abandonment outside the city walls.

Perhaps she understood, in her deepest heart of faith, that this was her share of the new Adam's victory over the serpent. This was the crushing of the serpent's power, but it was also the wounding of the Savior's heel.

John's Gospel seems to present Mary as the woman of Genesis when Jesus says, from the cross, "Woman, behold, your son" (19:26c), referring to the beloved disciple—and, as Christian faith soon realized, to all the sons and daughters of God and of the "mother" church. When Jesus added, speaking to John, "Behold, your mother" (19:27b) he spoke to all who would be born of his death and resurrection.

PENTECOST. According to Acts 1:14, Mary was one of those who waited in prayer for the coming of the promised Spirit. One of the seven mysteries of the Franciscan rosary is "The Risen Jesus Meets His Mother." The Gospels have no record of this, of course, but who would deny that it happened? Then there would be no more "pondering" necessary, no more difficulty in grasping. Her faith—though she still had years on earth—was close to vision.

If Mary Magdalene wanted to continue to cling to the risen Lord, imagine the tender and ecstatic joy that must have filled Mary as she held him finally in her arms and understood. She could then be the calm and prayerful mother of the little church as it waited for the Spirit of Pentecost (see Acts 1:14).

Her mind and heart had long since been the dwelling place of the Holy Spirit. Now she moved quietly closer to the face-to-face vision.

THE ASSUMPTION. The faith of the church believes that Mary has received this face-to-face vision (see *Catechism*, #966). She has been taken body and soul—full humanity—to the eternal vision of God. She is "in" heaven already. It is not said that she did not die, only that she has already received, according to her faith and holiness, what we will receive in fitting degree when we are finally brought to the Father. We cannot "prove" this; we believe it.

THE IMMACULATE CONCEPTION. Considering the dignity God gave Mary, it was fitting that God made her the holiest possible ground in which the Vine could grow. Therefore, Catholics believe, Mary was conceived without original sin. This means that, just as she has received her eternal happiness ahead of us, so she was redeemed by the blood of her son at the very moment of her conception in her mother's womb—as we are at the moment of baptism (see *Catechism*, #491–492). Again, this cannot be proved, and it is useless to argue about it. It is the happily held faith of the church.

Catholics' conviction of the holiness of Mary is beautifully described by Pope Pius IX: God's grace was given her "in such a wonderful manner that she would always be free from absolutely every stain of sin, and that, all beautiful and perfect, she might display such fullness of innocence and holiness that under God none greater would be known" (*Ineffabilis Deus*).

MOTHER OF GOD. In the early centuries of Christian history the church responded to doctrinal problems with slow and painful deliberation. After the great Christological definitions, the Council of Ephesus in 431 summed up the faith of the church that Mary is truly the *Mother of God* because she is truly the mother of the one Jesus who is truly God and truly human in one Person (see *Catechism*, #495). This declaration of the Council was in response to the heresy that denied that there was a real union of the human and the divine in Jesus. Mary was not just the mother of a man morally united to God, but of the one Person who is God and a man. She is the mother of God.

HONORING MARY. Catholics honor Mary because they love her (see *Catechism*, #971). She is one of them, not a goddess or a superhuman being. She, too, had to be redeemed; she, too, had to make the decision to trust God absolutely and, in a fascinating mystery, to find that God in the fruit of her womb. She is the first of Christians, praying with the church and for the church (see *Catechism*, #965).

The prayer that has come to be a natural accompaniment to the Our Father for Catholics is the Hail Mary, which combines the words of the angel and of Elizabeth with the prayer of the church: "Hail Mary, full of grace, the Lord is with you; blessed are you among women, and blessed is the fruit of your womb, Jesus. Holy Mary, Mother of God, pray for us sinners now and at the hour of our death."

The rosary is a prayer of meditation on the great mysteries of the faith as experienced by Mary. A decade (one Our Father and ten Hail Marys) is recited during each meditation. The five Luminous Mysteries added by Pope John Paul II in 2002 emphasize Mary's role in Jesus' public ministry.

Devotion to Mary has received great inspiration from her appearance to children at Lourdes in France and at Fatima in Portugal. The message in each case was essentially the same: prayer and penance. Strictly speaking, these are "private" revelations made to individuals, unlike the public revelation of God in Jesus. A Catholic does not have to believe in these private revelations, though millions have happily chosen to do so.

PROTESTANT REACTION. Some Protestants have found Catholic devotion to Mary excessive, overshadowing the place of Christ. No doubt there have been instances of well-meaning overemphasis on Mary, and Vatican II warned against this. But it also gave Mary the honor of a special chapter in its greatest document, in which it said, "In the bodily and spiritual glory which she possesses in heaven, the Mother of Jesus continues in this present world as the image and first flowering of the church as she is to be perfected in the world to come. Likewise, Mary shines forth on earth, until the day of the Lord shall come, as a sign of sure hope and solace for the pilgrim people of God" (*Dogmatic Constitution on the Church*, 68).

REFLECTION/DISCUSSION STARTERS

1) Discuss the role of Mary in the church. What does recognition of Mary bring to the church community?

2) Reflect on the accounts of Mary in Scripture. What picture do they give to you of the woman she was?

3) Has your religious background included recognition of or devotion to Mary? What has Mary meant for you?

SCRIPTURE READING

Luke 1:26—2:52

SUPPLEMENTARY MATERIAL

Catholic Updates: "The Annunciation: The Angel's Message to Mary," by Edward Sri; "The Feasts of Mary," by Robert M. Hamma; "In Search of the Real Mary," by Elizabeth A. Johnson, C.S.J.; "Luminous Mysteries: Exploring Five Major Events in Jesus' Public Ministry," by Jack Wintz, O.F.M.; "Mary of History," by Robert Maloney, C.M.; "Mary of Nazareth: Jesus' Mother, Our Mother," by Alfred McBride, O. PRAEM.; "The Rosary: A Prayer for All Seasons," by Gloria Hutchinson; "The Rosary of the Virgin Mary," Pope John Paul II's Apostolic Letter *Rosarium Virginis Mariae* in condensed form.

Scripture From Scratch: "Mary: First and Most Perfect Disciple in the New Testament," by Raymond E. Brown, S.S.; "Mary's Magnificat," by Daniel Casey.

Books: Discovering Mary: Answers to Questions About the Mother of God, by David Mills; *Mary and Me: Catholic Women Reflect on the Mother of God,* by Ginny Kubitz Moyer; *Mary in Her Own Words: The Mother of God in Scripture,* by Father Gary Caster; *Mary's Flowers: Gardens, Legends and Meditations,* by Vincenzina Krymow; *The Miracle of Lourdes: A Message of Healing and Hope,* by John Lochran; *101 Inspirational Stories of the Rosary,* by Patricia Proctor, O.S.C.; *Praying the Rosary: New Reflections on the Mysteries,* by Gloria Hutchinson.

CD: Mysteries of the Rosary (revised to include the Luminous Mysteries), one disc.

. | CHAPTER 27 | .

JESUS WILL COME AGAIN!

WHAT THEOLOGY BOOKS TRADITIONALLY TREATED AS THE "LAST THINGS" ARE death, judgment, purgatory, heaven and hell. At first glance, four of these five are painful prospects. Can the vision of faith brighten the negative image?

DEATH. If we could take a strictly objective view (which we can't), we would say that our death is not the most important thing to consider. Rather, at the center of my life and all life, of time and eternity, is the death and resurrection of Jesus. That event makes sense of everything else. Jesus joins my death to his and makes it beautiful. His Resurrection prepares the way for mine (see *Catechism,* #1681).

Jesus shrank from death, at least from the horrible death that awaited him, so we need not feel guilty about our own fears. Death is not natural. It is a tragic tearing apart (no matter how slowly) of God's beautiful creation.

But suppose our death could be a gentle and instantaneous passage through the veil between time and eternity. Would that remove our fear? Probably not, but the fantasy at least brings us closer to the attitude faith produces in us, deep down, below our natural revulsion.

A fully Christian attitude looks first to the death and resurrection of Jesus for light and strength. It sees the possibility of suffering as Jesus did and shrinks away in human weakness. But it also sees Jesus, in his overall life-commitment, straining toward this "baptism" (see Luke 12:50) and longing to eat *the* Passover meal "before I suffer" (Luke 22:15b). The shadow of Jesus' cross fell across his life from the beginning, and he fully and freely accepted it.

Jesus made a deliberate decision to die. Or, rather, his death was the final completely voluntary act of total self-giving to his Father. That attitude was there all the time, his "fundamental option" which was not swayed one inch by the terror that came upon him in Gethsemane.

So Christians, taking their life as a whole, place it in God's hands. "Into your hands I commend my spirit" (Luke 23:46b) is the prayer of their lives, not something tacked on at the end. Even in fear and trembling, Christians can be confident in their heart of hearts that death is the greatest moment of life, a summing up, a concrete act that says, "My whole life is yours, and I freely give it to you" (see *Catechism*, #1020).

Obviously we are making this decision all our life. We leave it to a merciful God to give us strength at the actual moment of death to face courageously the natural fears of the moment. But now, in the calmness of prayer, we can see the light of eternity shining on that final moment. Is anything more likely to give us a healthy and peaceful appreciation of our present moment?

The problem, of course, is that I can unmake what I have made myself. Since this is a long slow process, human wisdom (we never dare hobble the grace of God) says that deathbed conversions as well as deathbed relapses are hardly probable.

JUDGMENT. The dictionary definition of judgment says nothing about condemnation. When God said, all through the Old Testament, that he would come to bring judgment for his people, God promised precisely judgment for them—like a judge vindicating the rights of the innocent, restoring what had been taken and awarding recompense. It was only when individuals deliberately refused to live by the covenant that God's judgment would turn against them.

In the New Testament the meaning of judgment is tempered by two emphases which run throughout like two vines intertwined: "already now" and "not yet." We are now saved, but we are not yet saved. We shall die, but we have already risen in Christ. Christ has come, Christ is with us all days, but Christ will come again. Christ is victorious, all things have been subjected to him. But, as Hebrews sadly says, "Yet at present we do not see all things subject to him" (2:8).

So there are two ways of looking at judgment: something that happens already now and something that has *not yet* happened.

Jesus situates judgment in the midst of daily life when he says that giving food to the hungry, welcoming strangers, clothing the naked, comforting the sick and visiting the imprisoned—a way of life—is the door to heaven. These things are done for him, even if one does not think of him explicitly (see Matthew 25:31–40).

The Particular Judgment. Judgment is *now.* My "particular judgment" at the moment of death will simply be the fact of what I have chosen to be, my "fundamental option" which we discussed above in chapter twenty-three (see *Catechism*, #1021). But now I am what I have made myself and now do deliberately affirm. It is like the image on film not yet developed.

True, God must "find guilty" all those who inflicted injustice and pain on the innocent. But, primarily, God saves—that is, God's judgment is for God's friends. Hence Jesus says:

> Amen, amen, I say to you, whoever hears my word and believes in the one who sent me has eternal life and will not come to condemnation, but has passed from death to life. (John 5:24)

God's loving judgment is an endless attempt—grace surrounding and filling us—to free us from all evil and possess us with divine life and love. God is not a detective hoping to trap us in evil, even though God cannot but demand truth and love.

THE GENERAL JUDGMENT. "He will come to judge the living and the dead," we pray in the Apostles' Creed.

Formerly, in Masses for the dead, there was a long and chilling sequence called the *Dies Irae*—"Day of Wrath":

> Day of Wrath! O day of mourning!
> See fulfilled the prophets' warning,
> Heav'n and earth in ashes burning!

A similar tone can be found in the "apocalyptic" passages of the Gospels—Mark 13, Matthew 24, Luke 21. How are we to understand these fearful passages?

First of all, scholars agree that two things are tangled together in these passages: the destruction of Jerusalem in 70 C.E. and the actual end of the world. It is impossible to sort out which verses refer to which event. Second, we must remember that the biblical way of thinking is largely foreign to modern ways. The people of biblical faith saw concrete historical events as the judgment of God—for instance, the Jewish people being taken into exile.

It is the reality of the final judgment that Jesus emphasized, not its date. He gave clear warnings against trying to calculate the date. The human race lives under the reality of a final judgment. When particular things happen (for instance, the fall of Jerusalem), this final judgment seems to break into history—a sort of preview. When it does, it reminds us that the books will be closed someday. This is a kindly warning to meet that judgment every day: "I am hungry now, and you give me to eat." The last judgment is always "near." Eternity is always hidden within time.

Christians, then, do not look forward to a final catastrophe, the terrible Day of the Lord described in parts of Scripture. Their "ministry of reconciliation" is to attempt to keep it from being a day of catastrophe for anyone.

For the Christian, the Last Judgment is the final and definitive establishment of the heavenly community, the kingdom in its full eternal glory. Then God will bring all to completion. Then there will be perfect happiness, eternal joy and peace (see *Catechism*, #1040–1043).

But the "General Judgment" cannot change the judgment with which we find we have judged ourselves when our lives end (see *Catechism*, #1038). And as we have seen, that judgment is made now: "Come, you who are blessed by my Father! Inherit the kingdom prepared for you from the foundation of the world. For I was hungry and you gave me food...." (Matthew 25:34–35).

RESURRECTION. We have already seen (Part III) that Jesus' Resurrection means our resurrection (see *Catechism*, #988). Jesus said, "I am the resurrection and the life; whoever believes in me, even if he dies, will live" (John 11:25b).

And Paul adds, "... [T]he one who raised the Lord Jesus will raise us also with Jesus and place us with you in his presence" (2 Corinthians 4:14b). We will come to the full blossoming of human life, in face-to-face communion with God.

For the trumpet will sound, the dead will be raised incorruptible, and we shall be changed. For that which is corruptible must clothe itself with incorruptibility, and that which is mortal must clothe itself with immortality. (1 Corinthians 15:52b–53)

Saint Paul anticipates our question:

But someone may say, "How are the dead raised? With what kind of body will they come back?"

You fool! What you sow is not brought to life unless it dies. And what you sow is not the body that is to be but a bare kernel of wheat, perhaps, or of some other kind.... So also is the resurrection of the dead. It is sown corruptible; it is raised incorruptible. It is sown dishonorable; it is raised glorious. It is sown a natural body; it is raised a spiritual body. (1 Corinthians 15:35–37, 42–44a)

It is useless to speculate. More exciting is the realization that when God has finally worked a way through human freedom, when evil and darkness no longer hold us, God will "let himself go." And if human beings can give such happiness to each other, what happiness will God give! (See *Catechism*, #997–1004.)

HEAVEN. We fear that heaven will get boring. We are prisoners of time, and one of our sad occupations is to "kill" it. We cannot imagine having enough to do to fill an infinite amount of time. But there will be no "time."

And that is our problem: trying to imagine what it means not to fear the loss of this present peace or pleasure or safety. Watch a wild bird or animal constantly alert, incessantly turning its head, on guard against danger.

We cannot imagine what the words mean: to be possessed eternally by fathomless happiness; to be *filled* with God's life, love, beauty, goodness. We can only try to hold these ideas in poor little boxes of human words, and the boxes collapse (see *Catechism*, #1027).

Best, again, to trust. What would I do for those I love without limit? Then, Jesus argues, "If you then, who are wicked, know how to give good gifts to your children, how much more will your heavenly Father give good things to those who ask him" (Matthew 7:11).

John describes the impossibility of imagining perfect happiness as well as our trust that it will come:

> Beloved, we are God's children now; what we shall be has not yet been revealed. We do know that when it is revealed we shall be like him, for we shall see him as he is. Everyone who has this hope based on him makes himself pure, as he is pure. (1 John 3:2–3)

THE COMMUNION OF SAINTS. In the Apostles' Creed we state one of the fundamental beliefs of the church: "I believe in the communion of saints."

Communion here means a sharing of the blessings of salvation, especially that of personal communion with all the "saints." And *saints* here means not just those who have been canonized by the church, but *all God's holy people* (see *Catechism*, #946). All who are in Christ have been made holy with the holiness of God. Thus Paul writes to the "saints" of Ephesus, Corinth, Achaia, Philippi, Colossus. Today he would write to the "holy ones" of Chicago or Brownsville or Ottawa—the ones gathered around the altar.

This communion/community has its basis in the community of God, the Holy Trinity. God gave us the Son to be our companion. He sits at our table, and he gives us the bread that fills us with the life of God. His Spirit is in us, and our communion with the Holy Spirit is communion with Christ and with his Father, because the Holy Spirit is that communion. All the members of Christ who share this life of God also share it with each other.

So, when the church as such prays for its members, or when one individual member prays for the whole church, or when one individual prays for another, this prayer takes place in the one Spirit. The Spirit takes the cry of the Bride of Christ and makes it resound before God along with the voice of Christ. The prayer may be expressed in active service, in Christlike suffering or the relief of suffering in others. In any case, "If [one] part suffers, all the parts suffer with it; if one part is honored, all the parts share its joy" (1 Corinthians 12:26). If our network of good friends on earth is so powerful a support, what must the support of all God's friends be! (See *Catechism*, #954–956.)

This intercommunion of love extends throughout the whole church—the members of Christ who are with him in heaven, his members in the purification of purgatory, and the faithful on earth. One for all, and all for one.

THE SAVING OF GOD'S BEAUTIFUL CREATION. Saint Paul says that "creation awaits with eager expectation the revelation of the children of God." Material creation, he says, was frustrated in achieving the end for which it was made because human sin disrupted the order in the world. But, Paul continues, "creation itself would be set free from slavery to corruption and share in the glorious freedom of the children of God." Meanwhile, "all creation is groaning in labor pains" as it strains toward its fulfillment (see Romans 8:8–22).

What will happen to our world?

"We await new heavens and a new earth," says the author of 2 Peter 3:13. Saint Jerome comments: "He did not say that we will see different heavens and a different earth, but the old and ancient ones transformed into something better." And Saint Thomas Aquinas adds, "God has formed all things that they might have being, and not that they might revert to nothingness" (see *Catechism*, #1042–1047).

We are realizing these days that we have abused God's beautiful creation instead of using it as God instructed Adam (see Genesis 1:28–31). Energy, sky and water, forests and fields, city and country are gifts of God to be treasured and cared for. Our world is being saved along with us; it deserves our reverent care.

HELL. In the end there can be only two groups of people (and let us hope one group is very small, or perhaps nonexistent; see *Catechism*, #1821): those who have accepted the responsibility of living according to truth and love as they experienced it, and those who have with full consciousness and full freedom rejected truth and love in their lives. The latter at death are *frozen* (an odd word to use in connection with hell) in their own life choice.

Hell is the state of being turned away from God by one's own free and deliberate option—a life-option shaped by many decisions freely made (see *Catechism*, #1033).

Even God cannot *force* love. Love must be freely given, or it is not love. God can surround us with a sacramental creation, send messengers of forgiveness, come in human flesh to die on a cross—but we must respond. Trust and love are the normal response; our whole being moves us to them. We are made for truth and love.

But it is possible to reject the light, to still the normal impulses of the heart, to *become* a habitual decision of selfishness.

There must come an end, after a million moments of offered mercy. Death is meant to be the fullest moment of decision for God. For one who has died in spirit long before, it is the summing up of the fundamental decision. Hell is living with that decision forever.

God does not "send" people to hell. God did not create hell. Hell, along with sin, suffering and death, was created by creatures. Our hell is *our* idea. The "hell" of hell is being unable to blame anyone, especially God, who did everything but take away freedom to save everyone from eternal misery (see *Catechism,* #1037).

PURGATORY. The word *purgatory* is not found in the Bible. The doctrine has been one of the sore points of disagreement between Catholics and Protestants, so it behooves us to know exactly what the Catholic church teaches.

The only officially declared teaching of the church is that there is a purgatory, and that the souls detained therein are aided by the prayers of the faithful, chiefly by the Eucharist. There is nothing about fire or length of time or agony.

We must not make purgatory into a flaming concentration camp on the brink of hell—or even a "hell for a short time." It is blasphemous to think of it as a place where a petty God exacts final punishment.

Purgatory was originally a Latin adjective meaning "cleansing," "purgative." The doctrine of the church does not depend on the word, but on the reality (or rather the probability) that almost all persons have some last, lingering reluctance in their service of God. We grow in the holiness God offers us through many developing stages, painfully, slowly. It is another instance of the divine patience that God loves us gently even though we shrink back in partial mistrust or selfishness.

Purgatory simply means this: If my death does not represent a total giving of myself to God's love in full faith, hope and charity; if there is any sinfulness in me, no matter how slight, it must be removed before I come face-to-face with God. God must purify me not only from gross sin in life, but from all defilement (see *Catechism*, #1030). This is not some arbitrary arrangement, but the nature of God.

How does God do this? We don't know. God's love brings me to full response. How long does it take? We don't know. How do the prayers of my friends on earth help me? The same way they helped me on earth.

The suffering of purgatory is not vindictive punishment. Saint Catherine of Genoa, a mystic of the fifteenth century, wrote that the "fire" of purgatory is God's love "burning" the soul so that, at last, the soul is wholly aflame. It is the pain of wanting to be made totally worthy of One who is seen as infinitely lovable, the pain of desire for union that is now absolutely assured but not yet fully tasted.

REFLECTION/DISCUSSION STARTERS

1) Reflect on your feelings about death. How did you feel when someone close to you died? How does being a Christian affect your view of death?
2) Though we speak of a Particular and a General Judgment, in what sense can we say that judgment is happening now?
3) Discuss the concepts of heaven, hell and purgatory. How do you understand them?
4) In the Creed we state our belief in the communion of saints. Whom do we mean by the "saints"? Of what does that "communion" consist?
5) Reflect on the idea that the present is, in a sense, a purgatory for us, a purification. What does this mean to you? Have you experienced that process of purification taking place in your life?

SCRIPTURE READINGS
Matthew 25:31–40; Mark 13; Matthew 24; Luke 21; Romans 8:18–22.

SUPPLEMENTARY MATERIAL
Catholic Updates: "The Communion of Saints: 'People Who Need People,'" by Leonard Foley, O.F.M.; "The 'Last Things': Death, Judgment,

Heaven and Hell," by Carol Luebering; "Raptured or Not? A Catholic Understanding," by Michael Guinan, O.F.M.; "Seven Disciplines of Successful Catholics," by Matthew Hayes; "Spirituality: What's Your Style?," by Kathy Coffey.

Walking With the Saints: This twelve-issue newsletter by various authors is available as reprints. Saints are grouped thematically.

Books: *Be Holy: A Catholic's Guide to the Spiritual Life,* by Father Thomas G. Morrow; *Beatitudes: Eight Steps to Happiness,* by Raniero Cantalamessa, O.F.M. CAP.; *Choosing Beauty: A 30-Day Spiritual Makeover for Women,* by Gina Loehr; *Purity 365: Daily Reflections on True Love,* by Jason Evert; *Saint of the Day: Lives, Lessons, Feasts,* 6th ed., edited by Leonard Foley, O.F.M., revised by Pat McCloskey, O.F.M.; *What Does the Bible Say About the End Times? A Catholic View,* by William Kurz, S.J.

Called to Holiness: This multimedia series from St. Anthony Messenger Press includes a CD *(Companion Songs for Called to Holiness: Spirituality for Catholic Women,* selected by David Hass) and the following books: *Awakening to Prayer: A Woman's Perspective,* by Clare Wagner; *Creating New Life, Nurturing Families: A Woman's Perspective,* by Sidney Callahan; *Embracing Latina Spirituality: A Woman's Perspective,* by Michelle Gonzalez; *Finding My Voice: A Young Woman's Perspective,* by Beth Knobbe; *Grieving With Grace: A Woman's Perspective,* by Dolores Leckey; *Living a Spirituality of Action: A Woman's Perspective,* by Joan Mueller; *Making Sense of God: A Woman's Perspective,* by Elizabeth Dreyer. Elizabeth Dreyer is the general editor of the series, which is on the Web at www.CalledtoHoliness.org.

. | POSTSCRIPT | .

A DISCUSSION OF PURGATORY MAY SEEM A WRY WAY TO END A BOOK ON OUR LIFE in Christ. But, as we saw, purgatory rests on a big *if*. There must be a period or process of purification if we need to be purified. It is possible that some persons are completely purified in this life.

So the present is purgatory too—adjective and noun. Being saved is being cleansed, liberated, raised up to the life of Jesus daily. Purification is the daily dying to whatever is selfish, untrue, un-Christlike, and daily being raised by him to a deeper sharing in his own life.

We are called to be like persons in purgatory in one crucial way: We are trying to learn to say the last words of the Bible as they say them, with bursting desire. To say them with no lingering strains of selfishness, with no lack of trust, with our whole heart and soul, mind and strength:

Come, Lord Jesus! (Revelation 22:20)

Believing in Jesus and the RCIA

"The only possible way of approaching the Christian life: total, lifelong, deepening 'conversion.'" Those words from chapter seventeen of this book provide both a key to the book and a guide to its use for the Rite of Christian Initiation of Adults (RCIA).

It is appropriate that author Leonard Foley, O.F.M., uses these words to speak of the restored catechumenate itself. For "lifelong conversion" is the quite overwhelming truth about Christianity which the RCIA has rediscovered for us.

Acknowledging the dynamic of God at work in the life of the catechumen, the RCIA moves through a process of search and growth, through encounters with Jesus, his death and resurrection, and the Spirit—all within the faith community. The RCIA reverberates with the experience of early Christians coming to the life-changing realization that Jesus is Lord.

No book can bring about that realization for us. Words—someone else's faith experience—cannot substitute for one's own experience. Even Scripture can serve only as an opening to the divine mystery, not as a replacement for personal belief.

Given that limitation, what place does *Believing in Jesus* have in the RCIA process? Clearly, it is not a book of lesson plans for each session. It is not structured around an existing RCIA schedule of topics. It has none of the actual rites that mark the stages of the catechumenate. It contains no descriptions of what the author calls the "countless details of Catholic life," the externals of the Catholic tradition.

What the book offers instead is a foundation, a focus and an attitude.

A Foundation, a Focus, an Attitude

Knowledge of Scripture, doctrine, the sacraments and morality establishes a *foundation* for Christianity and Catholicism. Thus, the information this book provides is quite rightly an indispensable element in the catechumen's journey toward membership in the community.

But this knowledge is not equivalent to the spiritual journey. One cannot reach mystery by piling fact upon fact and standing upon the results.

Believing in Jesus therefore goes beyond a fact-oriented, question-and-answer approach. Its focus is clearly and strongly on Jesus, as the title implies. There is a natural flow to its structure, moving from a grounding in the religious heritage, the belief in the one God, that was Jesus' own, to his life, death and rising, to the Spirit and the church, to the sacraments and Christian morality.

And the *attitude* touching every aspect of the book is that of "lifelong conversion."

That conversion is personal. It must arise from our hearts and souls, the centers of our being. It does not come about by studying a list of doctrines put before us and intellectually affirming them. It originates not in the mind but in the Spirit.

That conversion is also endless. Each Christian is engaged in an ongoing formation process that continues beyond childhood religion classes, beyond adult baptism. Ours is a lifetime journey, always a "becoming," as we reflect, pray, learn, search and grow, ever recognizing Jesus anew, ever deepening our insights. These are, after all, the "eternal questions."

Integrating This Book Into the RCIA Process

Believing in Jesus has been successfully used in the RCIA process by many parishes and in different ways: as the only text central to a program of study, as a supplement to group presentations, as one of a number of resource books. Some RCIA teams use it regularly, some suggest individual chapters, some simply make it available to those who choose to use it on their own.

The Reflection/Discussion Starters at the end of each chapter are designed to help RCIA teams easily and effectively integrate the book into their established programs. They presume that session formats already exist, with time allotted for prayer, presentation, discussion and, perhaps, readings, song, breaks.

Most RCIA teams have a schedule of topics with which they are comfortable. A look at the Contents of *Believing in Jesus* indicates that the chapters cover commonly used subject areas. Several possibilities for structuring a program or supplementing one already in use suggest themselves.

A NONSEQUENTIAL APPROACH. Chapters can be treated out of sequence; some may not be discussed at all. One possible approach is:

Pre-Catechumenate
Scripture: Chapters 1, 2
Trinity: Chapter 11
Prayer: Chapter 12
Church: Chapter 13
Liturgy/Eucharist: Chapter 15
Sacraments: Chapter 16

Catechumenate
Jesus' Life and Teachings: Chapters 3, 4, 5
Jesus' Death and Rising: Chapters 6, 7
Jesus: God and Man: Chapter 8
Visible Church/Orders: Chapters 14, 22
Baptism: Chapter 17
Confirmation: Chapter 18
Reconciliation: Chapter 19
Anointing of the Sick: Chapter 20
Marriage: Chapter 21
Mary: Chapter 26

Period of Enlightenment
Jesus in Paul's Writings: Chapter 9
Spirit: Chapter 10
Christian Morality: Chapter 23
Commandments One to Three: Chapter 24
Commandments Four to Ten: Chapter 25

Mystagogia
Death, Judgment, Heaven, Hell: Chapter 27

A SEQUENTIAL APPROACH. There is also something to be said for following the sequence of chapters in the book. The structure has a certain integrity, with one chapter building upon another. A suggested division is:

Pre-Catechumenate: Chapters 1 through 6
Catechumenate: Chapters 7 through 22
Period of Enlightenment: Chapters 23 through 25
Mystagogia: Chapters 26, 27

Of course, no one chapter-by-chapter schedule will correspond to the interior process experienced by each person. But having the text offers the catechumen the chance to move freely about the book—going back to certain sections, reflecting, being provoked and inspired, moving on through the deep, rich spiritual complexity of believing in Jesus.

Using *Believing in Jesus* With Catechumens

REFLECTION/DISCUSSION STARTERS. It is recommended that participants read the appropriate chapters and reflect on the questions before they meet together. Catechists should avoid lecturing from the book and let the significant points of each chapter emerge in a natural and unforced way from discussion.

This is a time for sharing one's insights and unique perspective, one's own faith experience and encounters with God. An atmosphere of encouragement and respectful openness is vital, for the exchange of what is deepest in us is taking place.

The Reflection/Discussion Starters are meant to move back and forth between factual orientation and personal reflection; both are important. Some will demand intense personal questioning and cannot be answered quickly. Some may take an entire lifetime of experience and reflection, for they are eternal questions, open-ended in the ultimate sense.

Catechists should be wary of conveying an attitude that these questions have certain "right" responses or can be closed off in any way. And catechumens should know that their own questions are an integral part of the process. The goal is an easy and comfortable give-and-take between catechumens and their sponsors and catechists, moving from experience to fact and back to experience.

SCRIPTURE READINGS. The readings suggested at the end of most chapters are not the only biblical passages of importance for that chapter, nor are they always even the most important. Catechists can guide catechumens in exploring other relevant Scripture passages. The New Testament is, after all, not just a basis for our belief in Jesus but, with Tradition, *the* basis. And the Old Testament provides the origins, the tradition out of which Jesus taught.

In the RCIA process catechumens move with the entire church community through the celebrations of the liturgical year. Fittingly, many programs use the lectionary as a guideline for session topics. Every program should strive to deepen participation in the liturgical year with the Liturgy of the Word.

Whether found in the weekly readings or in the chapter contents, Scripture is a rich source to be plumbed and very much a part of ongoing conversion.

SUPPLEMENTARY MATERIAL. Supplementary materials are of six types.

1) *Catholic Update* is published by St. Anthony Messenger Press. Its four-page length and adult-education approach makes it particularly suited for use in RCIA programs. (*The Catholic Update Sourcebook,* published annually, contains preview copies of every *Update* in print and includes a topical index.)

2) *Scripture From Scratch,* another St. Anthony Messenger Press publication, is similar in format to *Catholic Update* and available as reprints. Each four-page issue contains an article on a Scripture-related topic, questions for reflection, suggestions for further reading and ideas for praying with Scripture. Both publications are available at group rates. *Scripture From Scratch* ceased publication in December 2005, but all back issues are still available. *The Ultimate Scripture From Scratch Sourcebook* contains preview copies of every issue in print, plus a topical index.

3) St. Anthony Messenger Press is responsible for almost all the books suggested for further reading. In October 2003 it purchased the Charis imprint from Servant Publications. These and subsequent books under this imprint are now known as Servant Books.

4) Several documents from Vatican II and encyclicals are also included. Unlike *Catholic Update, Scripture From Scratch* or CDs, the books, documents and encyclicals are truly supplemental to the program, probably not usable within the group process. They can, however, provide beneficial resources for an individual to pursue.

5) The CDs listed are also produced by St. Anthony Messenger Press. Where only one tape or talk in a series is appropriate, that one is indicated; it can be purchased separately.

6) Unless otherwise indicated, the DVDs recommended in Appendix B are produced by St. Anthony Messenger Press. The *Catholic Update* videos are approximately thirty minutes each and have four components: Story, Witness, Teaching and Music. They also have study guides.

Additional Activities

The exchange of individual faith expressions is essential to the RCIA and can be prompted and enhanced in ways other than Reflection/Discussion Starters and supplementary material. For instance, methods like these can serve as the core of some presentations:

Chapter one (Old Testament) and fifteen (Eucharist): a Passover meal;

Chapter four (Parables): writing one's own parable based on one's life and experience of God;

Chapter ten (Spirit) and eighteen (Confirmation): inviting someone from the charismatic renewal to speak;

Chapter eleven (Trinity): exploring personal concepts of God and their evolution;

Chapter eleven (Trinity) and twenty-seven (Death, Judgment, Heaven, Hell): examining the question of suffering and death with someone who ministers to the dying or the bereaved;

Chapter fourteen (Visible church) and twenty-one (Marriage): discussing divorce, contraception, Humanae Vitae and dissent;

Chapter fourteen (Visible church) and twenty-two (Orders): a panel presentation on roles of the laity, priests and religious, and ways to serve in the church;

Chapter fourteen (Visible church) and twenty-two (Orders): examining the place of women in the church with speakers active in enhancing women's roles;

Chapter sixteen (Sacraments): creating individual time lines of one's life, indicating significant moments of change and growth;

Chapter fifteen (Eucharist), seventeen (Baptism), eighteen (Confirmation), nineteen (Reconciliation), twenty (Anointing), twenty-one (Marriage) and twenty-two (Orders): examining the rites of the sacraments, using role-playing when appropriate (especially helpful for reconciliation);

Chapter twenty-one (Marriage) and twenty-two (Orders): a panel presentation with married, single, religious and ordained persons speaking on different vocations or states of life;

Chapter twelve (Prayer): demonstrating methods of prayer and prayer experiences. (This can actually be an ongoing process if session agendas regularly expose the catechumens to different prayer forms using Scripture, group prayer, silent prayer, meditation, song and so on. Common Catholic prayers and practices such as the rosary or the Stations of the Cross can also be used.)

For Individual Catechumens and "Born" Catholics

So far our focus has been on using *Believing in Jesus* in a group situation. But individual catechumens may also find the book helpful for highlighting significant points and for triggering personal reflection. The section entitled "Special Resources for Candidates for Full Communion With the Roman Catholic Church" on pages 312–313 may be especially useful.

Many "born" Catholics will want to use *Believing in Jesus* for the same purpose. As the restored catechumenate has reminded us, we are called continually to deepen our love of God, repeatedly to say yes to Jesus, to encounter the Spirit over and over in every aspect of our lives. We members of the Christian community are called to accompany the catechumens on their journey because it is our journey, too.

Indeed, for some—perhaps many—of us that journey may scarcely have begun. *Believing in Jesus* cannot "make" one believe in Jesus. But if readers —whether catechumens or "born" Catholics—let themselves be challenged by its words and shared faith experience, they may find it a genuine opening to God through Jesus in the Spirit, an opening they never quite knew before.

. | APPENDIX B | .

General Resources (various publishers):

Catechism of the Catholic Church: Revised in Accordance With the Official Latin Text Promulgated by Pope John Paul II, second edition (Our Sunday Visitor, 2000, 928 pages).

Catholicism (rev. ed.), by Richard McBrien. (HarperSanFrancisco, 1994, 1286 pages). Covers the whole field with clarity and scholarship.

Collegeville Bible Commentary: Based on New American Bible with Revised New Testament, ed. by Robert Karris, O.F.M., and Diane Bergant, C.S.A. (Liturgical Press, 1989, 1301 pages). This compilation of thirty-six popular-level pamphlets includes all the books of the Bible. Has a map section; also available in separate paperback volumes for Old Testament and New Testament.

Compendium of the Catechism of the Catholic Church (United States Conference of Catholic Bishops, 2006, 204 pages). This is a "faithful and sure synthesis" of the *Catechism of the Catholic Church.*

Dictionary of the Bible, by John L. McKenzie, S.J. (Simon and Schuster, 1995, 954 pages). Two thousand entries with over two hundred charts and illustrations. A classic reference work, first published in 1965.

An Introduction to the New Testament, by Raymond E. Brown, S.S. (Doubleday, 1997, 878 pages). A masterpiece, directed to the general reader.

New Jerome Biblical Commentary, edited by Raymond E. Brown, S.S., Joseph Fitzmyer, S.J., and Roland Murphy, O. CARM. (Prentice Hall, 1990, 1475 pages). The best of Catholic biblical scholarship.

United States Catechism for Adults, by the United States Catholic Conference of Bishops (USCCB, 2006, 637 pages). Provides the cultural adaptation that the *Catechism of the Catholic Church* invites. (Available in print from Catholic bookstores. The audio version from St. Anthony Messenger Press has sixteen compact discs with study guides.)

Vatican Council II Constitutions, Decrees, Declarations: A Completely Revised Translation in Inclusive Language, edited by Austin Flannery, O.P. (Costello, 1996).

All the other resources in this appendix are available directly from:
St. Anthony Messenger Press
28 W. Liberty St.
Cincinnati, OH 45202
(513) 241-5615
Toll-free: 1-800-488-0488 (8:00 AM to 4:00 PM Eastern time)
Web site: http://www.AmericanCatholic.org or http://catalog. AmericanCatholic.org

General Resources (St. Anthony Messenger Press)
Catholic Update Sourcebook. A new edition is published each summer, giving indexes of topics, authors, a twelve-month calendar coordinated with the liturgical cycle and a copy of every *Catholic Update* in print. The St. Anthony Messenger Press Web site offers prices for all its publications.

The Ultimate Scripture From Scratch Sourcebook. This edition gives indexes of titles, authors, all *Scripture From Scratch* issues, a calendar coordinated with the liturgical year and a leader's guide to help design mini-courses. This newsletter has ceased publication, but all issues published remain available.

Part I. Getting to Know the Bible
Catholic Updates:

"Choosing and Using a Bible: What Catholics Should Know," by Donald Witherup, S.S.

"Finding Your Way Through the Old Testament," by Virginia Smith

"How to Understand the Bible: Examining the Tools of Today's Scripture Scholars," by Norman Langenbrunner

"A Popular Guide to Reading the Bible," by Macrina Scott, O.S.F.

"The Whole Bible at a Glance: Its 'Golden Thread' of Meaning," by Virginia Smith

Scripture From Scratch:

"Bread and Board: Daily Life in the Time of Jesus," by Virginia Smith

"Exodus and Exile: Shaping God's People," by Virginia Smith

"From Jesus of Nazareth to Lord of All," by Eugene LaVerdiere, S.S.S.

"From Mount Sinai to the Sermon on the Mount: The Laws of Moses and Jesus," by Alfred McBride, O. PRAEM.

"Gnosticism and the Creation of the Canon," by Elizabeth McNamer

"The Holy Spirit as Paraclete: The Gift of John's Gospel," by Raymond E. Brown, S.S.

"'In Praise of Wisdom': The Wisdom Writings in the Bible," by Margaret Nutting Ralph

"Inspiration: God's Word in Human Words," by George Martin

"Interpreting the Bible: The Right and the Responsibility," by Sandra Schneiders, I.H.M.

"John's Jesus Story: 'Come and See,'" by Virginia Smith

"A Kaleidoscope of Biblical Women," by Macrina Scott, O.S.F.

"Luke's Gospel: Like Entering a Painting," by Eugene LaVerdiere, S.S.S.

"Mapping the Biblical Journey," by Virginia Smith

"Mark's Urgent Message," by Sean Freyne

"Matthew's Gospel: A Community Effort," by John Wijngaards

"Optimists and Pessimists Read the Book of Revelation," by Leslie Hoppe, O.F.M.

"Reading the Good Book," by Carol Luebering

"The Vocabulary of Faith: Religious Concepts in the Bible," by Elizabeth McNamer

"What Scripture Says...and Doesn't Say: Reading the Bible in Context," by Margaret Nutting Ralph

"Where Did We Get our Bible? (The Canon of Scripture)," by Elizabeth McNamer

"The Wow and Woe of the Psalms," by Daniel Durken, O.S.B.

Books:

Bible Stories Revisited: Discover Your Story in the Old Testament, by Macrina Scott, O.S.F.

The Catholic Bible Study Handbook: A Popular Introduction to Studying Scripture, second revised edition, by Jerome Kodell, O.S.B.

Finding Your Bible: A Catholic's Guide, by Timothy Schehr

The Great Themes of Scripture: Old Testament and New Testament, both volumes by Richard Rohr, O.F.M., and Joseph Martos

Journeys series: Luke, Mark, Matthew, all by Raymond Apicella; John, by Carolyn Thomas, S.C.N.

150 Bible Verses Every Catholic Should Know, by Patrick Madrid

Things Hidden: Scripture as Spirituality, by Richard Rohr, O.F.M.

CD:

Great Themes of Paul: Life as Participation, by Richard Rohr, O.F.M., eleven discs with study guide.

New Great Themes of Scripture, by Richard Rohr, O.F.M., ten discs.

Richard Rohr on Scripture: Collected Talks (volume two). Four discs for talks (Faith in Exile: Biblical Spirituality for Our Times; Hearing the Wisdom of Jesus; The Parables: Letting Jesus Teach Us and Love Your Enemy: The Gospel Call to Nonviolence).

Sermon on the Mount, by Richard Rohr, O.F.M., six discs.

DVD:

Scripture From Scratch I: A Basic Bible Study Program, by Virginia Smith and Elizabeth McNamer. Eight discs, sixteen talks taped before a live audience. One copy each of the Participant's and Facilitator's Manuals. (Preview disc available separately.)

Scripture From Scratch II: The World of the Bible, by Virginia Smith and Elizabeth McNamer. Four discs, sixteen talks taped before a live audience, utilizing maps, charts, graphical text and footage from the Holy Land.

Understanding the Bible, with Stephen Doyle, O.F.M. Two discs, junior high to adult audiences

Part II: Jesus' Journey to Death and Life

Catholic Updates:

"How the Gospels Were Written," by Leonard Foley, O.F.M.

"What Is 'The Kingdom of God'?" by Richard P. McBrien

"Who Is Jesus?" by Leonard Foley, O.F.M.

Scripture From Scratch:

"The Christmas Stories: Exploring the Gospel Infancy," by Raymond E. Brown, S.S.

"The Galilee Where Jesus Walked," by Bargil Pixner, O.S.B.

"The Healing Jesus: Interpreting the Miracle Stories," by Helen Doohan

"Jesus: The Man From Nazareth," by Elizabeth McNamer

"The Passion Narratives: The Cross Takes Center Stage," by Carol Luebering

"The Tantalizing Parables Jesus Told," by Virginia Smith

"Who Killed Jesus?" by Daniel J. Harrington, S.J.

Books:

Jesus' Plan for a New World: The Sermon on the Mount, by Richard Rohr, O.F.M., with John Feister

John the Baptist: Prophet and Disciple, by Alexander J. Burke, Jr.

A Retreat With John the Evangelist: That You May Have Life, by Raymond E. Brown, S.S.

A Retreat with Luke: Stepping Out on the Word of God, by Barbara E. Reid, O.P.

A Retreat with Matthew: Going Beyond the Law, by Leslie Hoppe, O.F.M.

DVD:

The Vision of the Gospels, by Rev. Michael Himes, four presentations on one disc with study guide

Part III: The World Starts Over

Catholic Updates:

"How to Read the Resurrection Narratives," by Raymond E. Brown, S.S.

"An Invitation to Prayer: A Guide for Deepening Our Prayer Life," by Father Edward Hays

"Lenten Stories From John's Gospel: Baptismal Dramas of Water, Light and Life," by Raymond E. Brown, S.S.

"Pathways of Prayer," by Jack Wintz, O.F.M.

"The Trinity: The Mystery at the Heart of Life," by Leonard Foley, O.F.M.

"We Believe in the Resurrection," by Thomas Groome

"Who Is the Holy Spirit?" by Elizabeth A. Johnson, C.S.J.

Scripture From Scratch:

"The Bible: Our Wellspring of Prayer" and "The Lord's Prayer," both by Leonard Doohan

"A Contemplative Prayer Journey With Jesus," by Armand Nigro, S.J.

"The Cross Makes a Christian," by Jerome Murphy-O'Connor, O.P.

"Ephesians," by Ronald Witherup, S.S.

"How Jesus Prayed," by Michael Patella, O.S.B.

"Paul: Letters From a Traveling Theologian," by Elizabeth McNamer

"Resurrection Stories: Catching the Light of God's Love," by Hilarion Kistner, O.F.M.

"Why Me? Suffering and Meaning," by Daniel J. Harrington, S.J.

Books:

Catholic Prayers for Every Day and All Day, edited by Leonard Foley, O.F.M., revised by Patti Normile

Paths to Prayer, by Robert F. Morneau

Saint Paul, Called to Conversion: A Seven-day Retreat, by Ronald Witherup, S.S.

Things Hidden: Scripture as Spirituality, by Richard Rohr, O.F.M.

CD:

Centering Prayer: Renewing an Ancient Christian Prayer Form, by M. Basil Pennington, O.C.S.O. (audiobook read by David Abbott), seven discs.

DVD:

Paul, Apostle to the Church Today, with Stephen Doyle, O.F.M., two discs, junior high to adult audiences

Seeking Jesus in His Own Land, with Stephen Doyle, O.F.M., one disc, junior high to adult audiences

Part IV: The Saving Work of Jesus in the World Today

Catholic Updates:

"Baptism: Our Lifelong Call," by Nicholas Lohkamp, O.F.M.

"Confirmation: A Deepening of Christian Identity," by Carol Luebering

"Creating a Culture of Vocation," by Janet Gildea, S.C.

"Eucharist: A Short History," by Alfred McBride, O. PRAEM.

"God Is Love" (Pope Benedict XVI's first encyclical in condensed form)

"How 'All of Us' Celebrate the Mass," by Sandra DeGidio, O.S.M.

"How Catholics Understand Grace," by John Feister

"Infallibility and Church Authority: The Spirit's Gift to the Church," by Kenneth R. Overberg, S.J.

"Interchurch Marriages: How to Help Them Succeed," by Elizabeth Bookser Barkley

"Lay Ministry: Not Just for a Chosen Few," by Thomas Richstatter, O.F.M.

"Nine Things That Make Us Catholic," by Thomas Groome

"The RCIA: The Art of Making New Catholics," by Sandra DeGidio, O.S.M.

"Sacrament of Baptism: Celebrating the Embrace of God," by Sandra DeGidio, O.S.M.

"Sacrament of Holy Orders: Priesthood in Transition," by Thomas Richstatter, O.F.M.

"The Sacrament of Reconciliation: Celebrating God's Forgiveness," by Sandra DeGidio, O.S.M.

"Sacraments: It All Starts With Jesus," by Thomas Richstatter, O.F.M.

"Seven Secrets of Successful Stewards," by Paul Wilkes

"Spirituality of Marriage: Becoming Signs of God's Love," by Carol Luebering

"Ten 'Peak Moments' of Church History: From Pentecost to Vatican II," by Alfred McBride, O. PRAEM.

"Ten Reasons for Going to Mass," by Leonard Foley, O.F.M.

"Ten Tips for Better Confessions," by Thomas Richstatter, O.F.M.

"A Tour of a Catholic Church," by Thomas Richstatter, O.F.M.

"A Walk Through the Mass: A Step-by-Step Explanation," by Thomas Richstatter, O.F.M.

"What Are Sacraments?" by Joseph Martos

"What Does It Mean to 'Be Church'?" by Greg Friedman, O.F.M.

"Why Confess My Sins?" by Leonard Foley, O.F.M.

"Why the Church Is Granting More Annulments," by Jeffrey Keefe, O.F.M. CONV.

Scripture From Scratch:

"Eucharist," by Thomas Bokenkotter

"First Among Disciples: Peter's Primacy in the New Testament," by Pheme Perkins

"The Lectionary and the Liturgical Year: How Catholics Read Scripture," by Thomas Richstatter, O.F.M

Books:

The Compact History of the Catholic Church, by Alan Schreck

The Mass: A Guided Tour, by Thomas Richstatter, O.F.M.

Experience the Reconciling God (This is the program planner for the *Catholic Update* video of the same title, see below.)

The Story of the Church (rev. ed.), by Alfred McBride, O. PRAEM.

Why Go to Confession: Questions and Answers About Sacramental Reconciliation, by Rev. Joseph M. Champlin

From the *Handing on the Faith* series:

Your Child's Baptism, by Carol Luebering

Your Child's Confirmation (rev. ed.), by Carol Luebering

Your Child's First Communion, by Carol Luebering

Your Child's First Penance, by Carol Luebering

Documents:

Dogmatic Constitution on the Church (Chapters I, II, IV)
Constitution on the Sacred Liturgy (Chapters I, XI)
Pastoral Constitution on the Church in the Modern World
Decree on the Ministry and Life of Priests

Encyclical:

Church of the Eucharist

CD:

Rebuild the Church: Challenge for the New Millennium, by Richard Rohr, O.F.M., five discs
United States Catholic Catechism for Adults, by the United States Catholic Conference of Bishops, sixteen discs with study guides

Catholic Update DVD:

(Approximately 30 minutes total, with four segments: Story, Witness, Teaching and Music. Study guides available.)
Adult Baptism: Exploring Its Meaning
Becoming Catholic: An Adult's Faith Journey
The Church Celebrates the Reconciling God
Eucharist: Celebrating Christ Present
First Communion: Taking a Place at the Table
Forming Adult Disciples (On Fire With Faith series)
Forming RCIA Sponsors
The God Who Reconciles
Infant Baptism: A Gift to the Community
Preparing Your Child for First Reconciliation
Sacrament of Anointing
Understanding the Sacraments
A Walk Through the Mass
What Makes Us Catholic? Discovering Our Catholic Identity

DVD:

A Lenten Journey With Father Michael Himes, one disc with study guide and four programs (What Is Temptation Really?; Danger and Desire; God Sees Into the Heart; Endless Possibilities)

Ikonographics DVD (St. Anthony Messenger Press):
The Mass for Children and Young People, written by Gaynell Cronin. One disc with three programs and study guides: *The Mass for Younger Children* (grades 1 to 3), *The Mass for Older Children* (grades 4 to 8) and *Why Do We Go to Mass on Sunday?*

Special Resources for Candidates for Full Communion with the Roman Catholic Church

Catholic Updates:
"Bringing Your Marriage Into the Church: Convalidation of Civil Marriages," by Joseph Champlin
"The Creed: Faith Essentials for Catholics," by Thomas Bokenkotter
"Nine Things That Make Us Catholic," by Thomas Groome
"The Roman Curia: How the Church Is Run," by Pat McCloskey, O.F.M.
"Sacramentals: Embracing God Through Creation," by Joanne Turpin
"Seven Disciplines of Successful Catholics," by Matthew Hayes
"Seven Secrets of Successful Stewards," by Paul Wilkes
"Ten Questions About Annulment," by Joseph Champlin
"Tradition in the Catholic Church—Why It's Still Important," by Monika Hellwig
"Vatican II: The Vision Lives On!" by Leonard Foley, O.F.M.
"What Catholics Believe: A Popular Overview of Catholic Teaching," by Leonard Foley, O.F.M.
"Why Be Catholic?" by William J. O'Malley, S.J.

Books:
Lost and Found Catholics: Voices of Vatican II, by Christopher M. Bellitto
When a Catholic Marries a Non-Catholic, by Robert Hater
Why Be Catholic? Understanding Our Experience and Tradition, by Richard Rohr, O.F.M., and Joseph Martos

CD:
The Mystery of Faith: An Introduction to Catholicism, by Michael Himes, three discs with study guide

DVD:

Foundations of Christianity: Mystery, Conversion, Faith, Hope and Love, by Michael Himes, two discs with study guide

The Mystery of Faith: An Introduction to Catholicism, by Michael Himes, three discs with study guide

Part V: Our Grace-full Response to the Commandments of Jesus

Catholic Updates:

"100 Years of Catholic Social Teaching," by Kenneth R. Overberg, S.J.

"Abortion: What the Catholic Church Teaches," by Helen M. Alvare

"The How and Why of Natural Family Planning," by Mary Shivanandan

"How Should We Think About the Poor? A Bishop Reflects," by Kenneth E. Untener

"Human Sexuality: 'Wonderful Gift' and 'Awesome Responsibility,'" by Richard Sparks, C.S.P.

"The Ten Commandments: Sounds of Love From Sinai," by Alfred McBride, O. PRAEM.

"Understanding Sin Today," by Richard Gula, S.S.

"Your Conscience and Church Teaching: How Do They Fit Together?" by Nicholas Lohkamp, O.F.M.

Scripture From Scratch:

"Choosing Life: The Bible and Euthanasia," by Kenneth R. Overberg, S.J.

"Do We Love Our Enemies? The Bible and the Just War Tradition," by Lisa Sowle Cahill

"Sin in the Bible," by Ronald D. Witherup, S.S.

Books:

Being Catholic: What We Believe, Practice and Think, by Archbishop Daniel E. Pilarczyk

Care for Creation: A Franciscan Spirituality of the Earth, by Ilia Delio, O.S.F., Keith Douglass Warner, O.F.M. and Pamela Wood

Catholics and the Death Penalty: Six Things You Can Do to End Capital Punishment, by Robert Hopcke

Conscience in Conflict: How to Make Moral Choices (rev. ed.), by Kenneth R. Overberg, S.J.

From Wild Man to Wise Man: Reflections on Male Spirituality, by Richard
Rohr. O.F.M.

God, I Have Issues: 50 Ways to Pray No Matter How You Feel, by Mark E.
Thibodeaux, S.J.

*Lessons From the School of Suffering: A Young Priest With Cancer Teaches us
How to Live,* by Jim Willig, with Tammy Bundy

Meet Dorothy Day: Champion of the Poor, by Woodenne Koenig-Bricker

Meet Fulton Sheen: Beloved Preacher and Teacher of the Word, by Janel
Rodriguez

Meet Padre Pio: Beloved Mystic, Miracle Worker and Spiritual Guide, by
Patricia Treece

Mornings With Henri J.M. Nouwen: Readings and Reflections, compiled by
Evelyn Bence

The Mystery of Faith: An Introduction to Catholicism, by Michael Himes

Mystics: 10 Who Show Us the Ways of God, by Murray Bodo, O.F.M.

The New Rosary in Scripture: Biblical Insights for Praying the 20 Mysteries, by
Edward Sri

Reaching Jesus: Five Steps for a Fuller Life, by David Knight

Twelve Tough Issues and More: What the Church Teaches and Why, by
Archbishop Daniel E. Pilarczyk

What It Means to be Catholic, by Joseph M. Champlin

From Wild Man to Wise Man: Reflections on Male Spirituality (rev. ed.), by
Richard Rohr, O.F.M., and Joseph Martos

What Jesus Said and Why It Matters Now, by Timothy D. Fallon

Would You Like to Be a Catholic?, by Eugene Kennedy

Encyclicals:

The Progress of Peoples (1987); *On Social Concerns* (1991); *God Is Love*
(2006); *In Hope We Are Saved* (2007)

CD:

The Autobiography of St. Thérèse of Lisieux: The Story of a Soul, translated by
John Beevers, performed by Sherry Kennedy Brownigg

Breathing Under Water: Spirituality and the 12 Steps, by Richard Rohr, O.F.M.,
two discs

Fire From Heaven: A Retreat for Man, by Richard Rohr, O.F.M., seven discs

The Great Mysteries: Experiencing Catholic Faith from the Inside Out, by Andrew Greeley, foreword by Rev. Robert Barron, read by Paul Smith, five discs

Letting Go: A Spirituality of Subtraction, by Richard Rohr, O.F.M., six discs

Mother Teresa: Come Be My Light, edited by Brian Kolodiejchus, M.C., ten discs

The Restless Heart: Finding Our Spiritual Home in Times of Loneliness, by Ronald Rolheiser, five discs

Rebuild the Church: Richard Rohr's Challenge for the New Millennium, five discs

Richard Rohr on Transformation, four discs containing these talks (Jesus: Forgiving Victim, Transforming Savior; The Spirituality of Imperfection: The Maternal Face of God; Dying: We Need It for Life)

A Spirituality for the Two Halves of Life, by Richard Rohr, O.F.M. and Paula D'Arcy, six discs

True Self, False Self, by Richard Rohr, O.F.M., six discs with study guide

DVD:

Assisi Pilgrimage: Walking in Faith with Francis and Clare, written and directed by Greg Friedman, O.F.M., one disc with study guide. (Original two-hour edition is D1222; one-hour broadcast edition is D2222)

Befriending God in Prayer, one disc

The Mystery of Faith: An Introduction to Catholicism, by Michael Himes, three discs with study guides

Praying Our Questions, one disc

Praying the Rosary, one disc

The Vision of Vatican II for Today, by Michael Himes, two discs with a study guide

The Way of the Cross: Stations on Our Journey of Faith, one disc with leader guide

Part VI: Visions of Our Future

Catholic Updates:

"Communion of Saints: Key to the Eucharist," by William Shannon

"The Communion of Saints: 'People Who Need People,'" by Leonard Foley, O.F.M.

"The Feasts of Mary," by Robert M. Hamma

"The 'Last Things': Death, Judgment, Heaven and Hell," by Carol Luebering

"Mary of Nazareth: Jesus' Mother, Our Mother," by Alfred McBride, O.PRAEM.

"Saints: Holy and Human," by Michael D. Guinan, O.F.M.

"What Catholics Believe About the End of the World," by Kenneth E. Untener

"What It Means to Be 'Saved,'" by Mitch Finley

Scripture From Scratch:

"The Communion of Saints," by Elizabeth McNamer

"Mary: First and Most Perfect Disciple in the New Testament," by Raymond E. Brown, S.S.

"Mary's Magnificat," by Daniel Casey

"Where Do We Go From Here? An Overview of the Afterlife," by Virginia Smith

Books:

Angels of God: The Bible, the Church and the Heavenly Host, by Mike Aquilina

Francis: The Journey and the Dream (rev. ed.), by Murray Bodo, O.F.M.

Franciscan Prayer, by Ilia Delio, O.S.F.

Here on the Way to There: A Catholic Perspective on Dying and What Follows, by William H. Shannon

I Choose God: Stories From Young Catholics, by Chris Cuddy and Peter Ericksen

Praying the Rosary: New Reflections on the Mysteries, by Gloria Hutchinson

Radical Grace: Daily Meditations, by Richard Rohr, O.F.M., edited by John Feister

Saint of the Day: Lives, Lessons, and Feasts, 6th revised edition, edited by
Leonard Foley, O.F.M., revised by Pat McCloskey, O.F.M.

To Live as Francis Lived, by Patti Normile

Thresholds to Prayer, by Kathy Coffey

What Does the Bible Say About the End Times? A Catholic View, by William
Kurz, S.J.

CD:

A Spirituality for the Two Halves of Life, by Richard Rohr, O.F.M., and Paula
D'Arcy, six discs

DVD:

Francis of Assisi. The story of Francis is retold in lively animation. One disc
(primary-adult)

Our Lady of Guadalupe. The famous story about the Virgin of Guadalupe
shows God's special concern for the power and powerless of every
age. One disc (junior high to adult), available in English and Spanish

Praying the Rosary (Teach Us to Pray series)

The Way of the Cross: Stations on Our Journey of Faith. One disc with study
guide

. | INDEX | .

CPSIA information can be obtained
at www.ICGtesting.com
Printed in the USA
LVOW03s1216070817
544102LV00001B/8/P